Educational Opportunity

in an Urban American

High School

the students.
didn't know what questions
to ask the teachers,

EDUCATIONAL OPPORTUNITY IN AN URBAN AMERICAN HIGH SCHOOL

A Cultural Analysis

PATRICK JAMES MCQUILLAN

State University of New York Press

Published by
State University of New York Press, Albany

For information, address the State University of New York Press,
State University Plaza, Albany, NY 12246

Production design by David Ford
Marketing by Nancy Farrell

Library of Congress Cataloging-in-Publication Data

McQuillan, Patrick J.
    Educational opportunity in an urban American high school : a
cultural analysis / by Patrick James McQuillan.
        p.   cm.
    Includes bibliographical references (p.   ) and index.
    ISBN 0-7914-3499-0 (hc : alk. paper). — ISBN 0-7914-3500-8 (pb :
alk. paper)
        1. Education, Secondary—Social aspects—United States—Case
studies.   2. Education, Urban—United States—Case studies.
3. Educational anthropology—United States—Case studies.
4. Educational equalization—United States—Case studies.
5. Educational change—United States—Case studies.   I. Title.
LC191.4.M39   1997
373.73'09173'2—dc21   96-52324
                                                        CIP

10 9 8 7 6 5 4 3 2 1

This book is dedicated to Katherine Murray, Bill McLoughlin, and Martha Rodenhaver McQuillan, three exceptional people with fire in their hearts, light in their eyes, and kindness in their souls.

CONTENTS

ACKNOWLEDGMENTS

In conducting this research, I came to view many of those who contributed to my work at Russell High—students, teachers, and administrators—as friends. Although my research guidelines preclude me from thanking them directly, I want to express my appreciation to these persons for welcoming me into their school, classrooms, and lives.

I am also tremendously grateful for the support and insights provided by those who helped me conceptualize and write this book over the past ten years: Mary Apodaca, Adeline Becker, Bill Beeman, Ruben Donato, Margaret Eisenhart, Shirley Brice Heath, Marida Hollos, Ernie House, Ken Howe, Tom James, Alice Kaiser-Drobney, David Kertzer, David Kobrin, Margaret LeCompte, Phil Leis, Dan Liston, Mitch Nathan, Lucile Newman, Reba Page, Seymour Sarason, Jrene Rahm, Brenda Rudman, and Hervé Varenne.

I also want to acknowledge the Exxon Education Foundation for its support as well as the students I have taught at the University of Colorado and Rhode Island College who read and responded to portions of this manuscript. Their reactions and ideas helped me think differently about my writing and shaped the final product. In addition, I thank those anonymous reviewers who provided feedback on earlier drafts of this work. In many cases, they pushed me to rethink my ideas in ways I found quite productive. I am also grateful to Priscilla Ross, Jennie Doling, David Ford, and the staff at State University of New York Press for guiding me through this long process.

Of course, I must thank Ries and Casey for their editorial and spiritual support. As for Jody, words seem inadequate . . . but thanks, a lot.

PREFACE

Prior to conducting research at Eastown's Russell High, the focus of this ethnographic study, I viewed formal education in a very positive light. From my perspective, schools were avenues to social mobility and self-fulfillment. They were also fun, engaging, and rewarding places. None of my classmates from elementary and secondary school, nor those of my four siblings, were disadvantaged by their schooling, at least not that I noticed. My undergraduate years reinforced this conception of formal education, as the overwhelming majority of my classmates seem to live rich and fulfilling lives. My own teaching experiences were mostly in upper-income schools that consistently produced "successful" graduates. And prior to my research at Russell High, I studied the development of hypertext-based computer materials in courses at Brown University. As far as I could tell education was not disadvantaging any of those students.

Even my experiences with low-income students of color supported this optimistic view of educational opportunity. During my first year as a high school teacher I was a live-in tutor for six African American students who attended the suburban school where I taught as part of the A Better Chance (ABC) program. Although the students faced many dilemmas in leaving their homes and friends to attend an otherwise all-white school, they did quite well, at least by middle-class white standards. All went to respected colleges (Colgate, Dartmouth, George Washington, and Rennselaer Polytech being the four I recall). All received financial aid. After graduating, three of the six (that I knew of) secured well-paying jobs in professional fields.

The one aberration in my experience was a year I spent teaching and writing my master's thesis at a state school for boys. The thesis was essentially a critique of the behavior modification system that structured so much of what happened at the school. However, since I knew little about students' previous educational experiences and because I focused on the behavior modification program, I saw the school as an aberration, not part of a systemic process. As a result of these experiences, for me, schools were pretty good places. And many other Americans see educational opportunity in much the same way. But educational opportunity in Eastown was very different.

I began my research at Russell High as part of a larger study of the Coalition of Essential Schools, a national secondary school reform initiative. Since this study was designed to examine school reform in-depth, I focused at first on what happened within Russell's "Coalition" program, known as the "Essential School." However, because we had secured long-term funding for this work, I had time to learn not only about the Essential School, but Russell High, the community of Eastown, and the city's other public schools.

During this five-year period I was completing a Ph.D. in cultural anthropology. In preparing for my doctoral qualifying exams as well as spending a great deal of time at Russell High, my views of education shifted. I read Jean Anyon, Samuel Bowles and Herbert Gintis, Henry Giroux, Lois Weis, Paul Willis, and Peter Woods. I gradually realized that what they described—in terms of who defined "valid" knowledge, who set the conditions for learning, and so on— was being enacted at Russell High as well as in negotiating the conditions of my doctoral exams. I was now both observing and living what these and related authors had written about formal education. As a consequence, I began to see education in a more political light. Opportunity was neither as simple nor as straightforward as I once assumed.

Russell High was very different from my previous experiences in the field of education. The school was often a confusing and depressing place. Few people were excited or enthusiastic about going there—students, teachers, or administrators. The building was old and run-down. The hallways were regularly filled with student litter. A sense of school spirit, of people being there for their mutual benefit, was terribly lacking. Disrespect and mistrust were rampant. Dropout and failure rates were high. Many teachers seemed truly battle-weary. Administrators were mainly concerned with preserving order. In my view, many persons associated with Russell High were being exploited (and oftentimes exploiting others) and their actions (and inaction) played a part in creating their condition. On many occasions, I left the school bewildered and disappointed.

Given the nature of my experience at Russell High, I approached this writing with ambivalence. Sorting through the wide-ranging emotions and experiences that I associate with the school was not easy. Nonetheless, I hope to walk the difficult line alluded to by Michelle Fine: "To write about an institution that routinely and traditionally has reproduced social injustice, despite even the best intentions of its educators . . . to tell a social secret that many have committed to silence" (1991: vii). My intent is not to blame; it is to expose the pervasiveness of cultural predispositions that condition American society to interpret ongoing and pervasive student failure as individual failure, and therefore to ignore systemic factors that are intimately connected with this far-too-common injustice. It is a call for collaborative action, to question the taken-for-granted and continue the slow process of rethinking and restructuring America's urban schools.

intent

defining opportunity

1

(handwritten: equity and quality)

(handwritten: ethnography = desc. of culture)

Educational Opportunity
Through the Lens of
American Culture

(handwritten in left margin: desegregation / integration)

> We see things not as they are, but as we are.
> —The Talmud

American society generally treats educational opportunity as a serious matter, one deserving thoughtful consideration. This is not surprising. Politicians, sports heroes, Hollywood actors, and everyday, ordinary people commonly portray educational opportunity as a critical feature to American life: a fundamental democratic right, a means to personal fulfillment, the cornerstone to a healthy society.

(handwritten right margin: all have a right to go to school)

In the late sixties and early seventies, school desegregation was a highly visible, public concern in Eastown,[1] the east coast city where I conducted this five-year ethnographic study. At the time, a sizable percentage of Eastown schools were out of compliance with federal desegregation regulations. To avoid having a federal court mandate a desegregation policy, the school system initiated its own school integration plan. The "Initial Proposal for City-Wide Integrated Education," drafted by a cross-section of the community, spoke directly to issues of educational opportunity:

> The major problem confronting Eastown Schools is that of providing quality education for all public school children. Research shows and experience in urban schools supports the fact that quality education requires that children of the different races, nationalities, and economic and social backgrounds receive the same educational opportunities, regardless of accident of birth and location of home. (August 1967)

As concerns linked to school desegregation continued to surface, the State Board of Education issued a policy statement "reaffirming its position on equality of educational opportunity":

[F]or all to achieve their maximum potential, both the State and local educational system must strive for equity in education. Only through such a commitment can equality of educational opportunity be achieved. The State Board of Education firmly believes that social, or economic circumstances should never be allowed to interfere with an individual's achieving his full potential through the educational process. These opportunities should be made available to all persons in our society according to their educational needs, and regardless of social or economic circumstances. (June 1970)

Three-and-a-half years after drawing up its initial plan for "city-wide integrated education," the Eastown School System presented its "Plan for the Desegregation of Senior High Schools." Once again, educational opportunity was a paramount concern:

[M]eaningful desegregation can occur only if all high schools in the system are raised to the highest standards so that the quality of education does not vary according to income or the social status of a given neighborhood . . . [W]ith thoughtful planning, bold policies, and vigorous actions, there are sound reasons to believe that the speed of segregation can be slowed, its severity reduced, and the effectiveness of school programs substantially improved. (February 1971)

Despite such public commitment to equality of educational opportunity, twenty-five years later (1996) Eastown schools remained effectively segregated and issues of race/ethnicity and socioeconomic status continued to pervade the city school system. This ethnography offers a way to understand why this has occurred—why certain systemic injustices have endured—and why these developments have been met with general indifference. Focusing on issues of equity and opportunity, the following chapters reveal how American conceptions of educational opportunity—what students, teachers, and administrators at Russell High, the site of this study, considered reasonable, appropriate, and normal—undermined the education students experienced. This is a cultural analysis that examines what people believed and valued, and how these beliefs and values influenced educational opportunity. To appreciate this analysis, it will help to understand how I employ the concept of culture.

UNDERSTANDING CULTURE

Throughout this ethnography educational opportunity is examined through the lens of American culture. Drawing on the ideas of Clifford Geertz, I define culture as "the framework of beliefs, expressive symbols, and values in terms of which individuals define their world, express their feelings, and make their judgments" (1973: 144–45). In this view, culture offers insight into how people interpret or "make sense" of what occurs in their lives and the lives of others; and these understandings shape subsequent actions and interpretations. Culture is therefore something of a paradox: People create culture, but their cultural values predispose them to perceive the world in particular ways.[2] Culture does not determine social action, nor is it predictive; but it defines the possible, the logical. It is this aspect of culture—its potential to delimit, but not determine, how we perceive the world, and thereby to influence how we act—that is central to this study (Geertz, 1973; Keesing, 1980).[3]

Although our cultural values are intertwined with many aspects of our lives, people are often unaware of their influence. As Margaret Mead is alleged to have said, "If humans were fish, the last thing they'd discover would be water"—the point being that our most intimate and fundamental values can be so taken-for-granted that they are least apparent, and consequently seldom questioned. Mead's concern is critical because culture is never neutral: "[All] cultural models carry within them values and perspectives on people and on reality" (Gee, 1990: 90). As culture shapes our preferences, often in subtle ways, it promotes valuing one thing over another—light skin over dark, strict child-rearing practices over permissive ones, innovation over continuity (Spindler and Spindler, 1987). Further, because cultural values encourage people to interpret their worlds in particular ways, they can also "hide from us other ways of thinking . . . [such that certain cultural models] come to seem 'inevitable,' 'natural,' 'normal,' 'practical,' 'common sense'" (Gee, 1990: 91–92). Accordingly, Ray McDermott and Hervé Varenne discussed the "disabling" potential of culture:

> *Culture* is generally taken to be a positive term. . . . [B]ut every culture, we must acknowledge, also gives. . . a blind side, a deaf ear, a learning problem. . . . For every skill that people gain, there is another that is not developed; for every focus of attention, something is passed by; for every specialty, a corresponding lack. People use established cultural forms to define what they should work on, work for, in what way, and with what consequences. . . . Being in a culture

may be the only road to enhancement; it is also very dangerous. (1995: 331–32)

While cultural values, by definition, represent what society has deemed valid and legitimate, these values can serve the interests of some but not others (Bellah, et al., 1985). At Russell High, what students, teachers, and administrators accepted as "natural . . . normal . . . common sense" often times disadvantaged students and undermined the professional efficacy of teachers and administrators. Frankly stated, watching the routine unfold could be disturbing. Underprivileged students regularly battled their teachers for the right not to learn. For many teachers, 'reform' meant devising more effective ways to punish students. During the five years of my research, I knew of no instance when an administrator visited a teacher's classroom. Such practices were commonplace, the expected and accepted.

To gain some sense for how and why this occurred, I analyze the "symbolic forms—words, images, institutions, behaviors" (Geertz, 1983: 58) through which people constructed and enacted their conceptions of educational opportunity. In this introductory chapter I first present a cross-section of American society—an educational historian, a movie star, a newspaper editor, a Russell High student, a motivational speaker, and the National Commission on Excellence in Education—enacting culture; that is, in various contexts, expressing their views on education and educational opportunity. Generalizing from their remarks, I outline four prominent ways in which Americans understand and represent educational opportunity, four cultural views of educational opportunity that are central to this ethnography.

PREVAILING AMERICAN CONCEPTIONS OF EDUCATIONAL OPPORTUNITY

Because American conceptions of educational opportunity are informed by our cultural beliefs, there is an order to how we portray and enact educational opportunity. We value some forms of knowledge and not others. Some educational practices are considered normal, others atypical. To appreciate the patterning of American values and beliefs that are central to this analysis, I first present a sampling of Americans as they discuss their views on education and educational opportunity. I later frame their remarks in terms of American culture.

In *The Schools We Deserve*, Diane Ravitch, assistant secretary of education to the Bush administration, presented educational opportunity as key to forming a free, united, and democratic nation from a populace of diverse backgrounds and languages:

> For most of our history, penniless immigrants have streamed through our port cities; their transition from poverty and illiteracy into the vast American middle class owes much to the public schools. . . . Sometimes crudely, but almost invariably with remarkable success, the public schools made them Americans and taught them the language and ideas with which they could later demand equality and justice. (1985: 8–9)

The recent Hollywood movie, *Dangerous Minds*, featured Michelle Pfeiffer, an ex-Marine turned high school English teacher, defending the integrity of educational opportunity in urban America. When students questioned whether educational opportunity was real for them, the star of this film was unequivocal about the opportunity available to students who made the right choice:

> AFRICAN AMERICAN GIRL: Man, you don't understand nothin'. I mean, you're not bussed here.
>
> MICHELLE PFEIFFER: Do you have a choice to get on that bus?
>
> AFRICAN AMERICAN GIRL: Man, you come and live in my neighbor-hood for one week and then you tell me if you got a choice.
>
> MICHELLE PFEIFFER: There are a lot of people in your neighbor-hood who chose not to get on that bus. What do they choose to do? They choose to go out and sell drugs. They choose to go out and kill people. They choose to do a lot of other things. But they choose not to get on that bus. The people who choose to get on that bus, which are you, are the people who are saying, "I will not carry myself down to die. When I go to my grave, my head will be high" [quoting Dylan Thomas]. THAT IS A CHOICE! THERE ARE NO VICTIMS IN THIS CLASSROOM![4]

choice

Like Michelle Pfeiffer's students, in December 1994, a sizable number of Hispanic students in the Denver public schools challenged the assumption of educational opportunity—staging a walkout to protest what they saw as a lack of attention to their needs and interests by city schools. In response, *The Rocky Mountain News* included the following remarks in a feature editorial:

1994 student protest in Denver

> I'd like to say a few words to the Hispanic students who staged a school walkout the other day. . . . I haven't forgotten that plenty of

people of my generation marched on school days during the civil rights era and the Vietnam years. But it's also time you began to draw distinctions: There's a big difference between marching to protest discriminatory laws or an unpopular war and marching to protest the fact that you're not learning enough. A government can pass better laws or bring its soldiers home. But a government can't learn for you.

Sure, it's helpful if you have a great curriculum and teachers who make every subject fascinating and parents who have read to you since your were in diapers and who keep plenty of books and newspapers around the house. But even if you have none of these advantages, you still need to learn. And it's still your responsibility—your job.

You hear all kinds of fancy talk about education these days but the simple truth is that building up your brain is just like building up your body. Neither your parents nor your gym teachers can do exercises to make you strong. No one can learn how to throw a basketball or swing a tennis racquet or do a back flip for you. It's the same where your mind is concerned: No one can learn for you how to read well or write clearly or do arithmetic accurately; no one can understand for you how to analyze a problem or think logically. . . .

I'm now going to tell you something I wish someone had told me when I was your age: The most important thing you can learn is how to learn. That's the skill you absolutely must develop. . . . Now, much more than in the past, most people have to keep on learning throughout their lives and they have to do most of that learning on their own. Instead of ducking that reality or protesting it, why not grapple with it while you're still young? It won't get easier later. . . .
(Rocky Mountain News, 1994:37A)

Educational opportunity was also a topic discussed by an ex-Russell High student and me. After completing my research at Russell I stayed in touch with a number of persons, one being a student: Elena Santa Rosa. Elena left Russell after her sophomore year to attend a highly respected private school on scholarship, and later went to an Ivy League university. She is presently enrolled in a prominent medical school. For a period, we corresponded about her experiences in Russell's "Essential School," a school-within-a-school program linked to the national school reform movement, the Coalition of Essential Schools. I initiated our interaction by sending her a copy of Chapter 2 from this book and asking for her reactions. (The chapter analyzes student resistance to reforms attempted in a history class.) In recalling how the Essential School "individualized"

Coalition of Essential Schools.

its policies and practices for students, Elena expressed concern about
the education *she did not receive*:

[Y]ou describe one objective of the Essential School as to "[allow]
students to master course material at their own rate," which was
always my impression. However, you add "without penalizing them
for the time this might require" (emphasis mine). My observation is
one I have been making since my days at the Essential School: "their
own rate" does NOT necessarily mean "slower." Therefore, working
at one's own rate should not necessarily involve penalization of any
kind, even in a "regular school" context. It is natural that you have
stated this as such, especially because Essential School faculty and
staff used similar terminology. But it was this attitude that drove
me away from the school. While resources were available to those
whose "own rate" was slower than most, those whose rates were
faster were largely ignored. . . . (October 8, 1994)

Elena and I also discussed her sense for why students in the
history class completed little work and why they seemed to care little
about their education:

I wonder whether these students' main obstacle was their confusion
or unwillingness to exert themselves. I don't think most of us were
that confused. If [the teachers] had kept the syllabus intact, as
well as their expectations, you would have seen students get their
butts in gear. Granted, the novelty and difficulty [of the course]
exacerbated the degree of laziness exhibited by most. . . . I think
most of us just didn't want to bother. . . . I say this having the
benefit of hindsight and having gone through two years at [a private
school] and three at [an Ivy League university]. That the syllabus
may have looked somewhat insurmountable is an assessment with
which I agree. But I also think that to simply accept a curriculum
without exposing our teachers to a good measure of bitching and
moaning would have been rare at Russell. It happened in every
other class. . . . (October 8, 1994)

In most classes I took, things started very slowly in terms of student
participation. This was especially true with student teachers, as
students tested to see how little work they could get away with. . . . I
and everyone else was trying to go through high school without doing
anything. . . . I was doing nothing. I would get home in the afternoon
and do absolutely nothing but watch TV and hang out with friends.
We had plenty of time; we didn't want to waste it doing homework.

. . . The fact was, we were lazy, we hated high school, class was boring. No one ever conveyed to me that it was too challenging. They might have said it was "too much work" but that was very different from "it's too hard"; too much work just implies not enough time to watch TV or hang with friends. I don't know. I just think when a high school kid says, "I don't get it," he might be saying it's just too much trouble to try to get it. I say that totally from personal experience; to this day I do this. It's not like we're going to admit to being lazy. Picture two scenarios:

(1) "But [teacher], I tried to get started on the timeline but I don't get it. What events do you want us to talk about?. . . I don't know how to pick my own events or how they fall under one theme. Couldn't you at least tell us what themes to work with? I'm so confused. . . ."

(2) "Actually, I didn't have time to start the timeline last night because the MTV video awards were on and my two best friends came over. Maybe I could've gotten started if you told us what to do because I find spitting facts back at you a lot easier than actually analyzing them. That's what I tell all the other teachers too."

I think scenario 1 is the more likely. I've used it myself at Russell, at [my private school], and at [the Ivy League university]. (November 12, 1994)

The work I did was that required for [a course I took that year at a local university] and only if I had some time to kill and nothing better to do would I do Russell homework. I would much sooner just go to [a friend's] and talk for seven hours every evening. In the two years she and I were best friends and next-door neighbors, I don't remember studying with her even once!! You are probably thinking I am full of it, since I kept all my grades at the A level at Russell. This was not difficult. All it took was a little effort just before deadlines. I was still following the pattern of "getting by with doing as little work as possible." But "as little work as possible" still meant good grades in my case. This sounds boastful and I do not mean it to be. I just put in whatever minimal effort was required to do well. I never did completely buy into the "slack-off" ideology and liked to see As on my transcript. This is obviously different from many of my classmates who probably didn't give a rat's ass as far as As were concerned. Maybe they thought As were harder to get than they were. Or maybe they actually found it difficult to get As. . . . (February 12, 1995)

In October 1989, Russell High enlisted a "motivational expert," Anthony Carmello, to present a two-hour assembly entitled, "A

Lifestyle By Choice, Not Chance." Issues linked to educational opportunity consistently surfaced in his talk, one being the opportunity students had to attend college:

> HEY FOLKS, COME ON! You can go to college anywhere you choose. . . . You got to know how to play the game. You want to go to [an Ivy League university] and you're not accepted. What do you do about it? You go somewhere else, and you prove yourself. You ace your courses. . . . [If] you are an honors student. . . [y]ou will transfer into. . . almost any school you choose. . . . People tell me, "*Mr. Carmello, I can't go to college after high school, I've got to work*" [said in a pathetic voice]. . . . What do you do if you've got to work after Russell High and you want to go to college? YOU GO TO SCHOOL NIGHTS! THE [UNIVERSITY] EXTENSION! THE [COMMUNITY COLLEGE], TWO CAMPUSES! [THE STATE COLLEGE]! Do you know what it costs to go to [State College] nights? It costs about $120 a credit hour. One of the finest universities in the area. . . . You go to college any way you choose.

Personal responsibility, and its link to opportunity, was another prominent theme in Carmello's presentation. To highlight this interrelationship, Carmello involved a student from the audience:

> I want you [directing himself to a student], to answer this question: There are many contributing factors to your life—your family, your friends, this school. Who else is responsible for what you become? Tell me honestly, don't pay me lip service! Speak your mind. [Student says something.] Did everyone hear what he said [pointing to the student]? [Audience: "NO!"] He said, "I AM RESPONSIBLE FOR MYSELF!" . . . THAT'S THE DIFFERENCE BETWEEN WINNERS AND LOSERS! WINNERS TAKE RESPONSIBILITY FOR THEIR OWN LIVES! THEY MAKE THINGS HAPPEN! Losers, you know what losers tell me? . . . "Me, I'm not responsible. It's his fault." That's the "loser's lament." DON'T TAKE RESPONSIBILITY FOR YOUR OWN LIFE! BLAME THE OTHER GUY. . . . WINNERS MAKE THINGS HAPPEN. LOSERS LET THINGS HAPPEN. You said it all [motioning toward the student]. You are responsible. NO ONE CAN HOLD YOU DOWN! . . . THE ONLY LIMITATIONS ARE THOSE THAT ARE SELF-IMPOSED!

Perhaps the most widely-cited and most influential document to emerge of late in the educational arena has been *A Nation at Risk*

(1983), the "open letter to the American people" written by the National Commission on Excellence in Education. Educational opportunity was central to the Commission's message. Quoting then President Ronald Reagan, the report acknowledged that "few areas of American life [are] as important to our society, to our people, and to our families as our schools and colleges" (1983: 2). It continued:

> Our concern [with the quality of education in our country]. . . goes well beyond matters such as industry and commerce. It includes the intellectual, moral, and spiritual strengths of our people which knit together the very fabric of our society. . . . A high level of shared education is essential to a free, democratic society and to the fostering of a common culture, especially in a country that prides itself on pluralism and individual freedom. . . .
>
> Part of what is at risk is the promise first made on this continent: All, regardless of race or economic status, are entitled to a fair chance and to the tools for developing their individual powers of mind and spirit to the utmost. This promise means that all children by virtue of their own efforts, competently guided, can hope to attain the mature and informed judgment needed to secure gainful employment and to manage their own lives, thereby serving not only their own interests but also the progress of society itself. (1983: 3–4)

Citing a Gallup Poll (1982) of the "Public's Attitudes Toward the Public Schools," the authors continued to emphasize the importance and value of education:

> People are steadfast in their belief that education is the major foundation for the future strength of this country. They even considered education more important than developing the best industrial system or the strongest military force, perhaps because they understood education as the cornerstone of both. . . . It is, therefore, essential—especially in a period of long-term decline in educational achievement—for government at all levels to affirm its responsibility for nurturing the nation's intellectual capital. (1983: 12–14)

In its concluding remarks, the report focused on students. Speaking to the issue of their educational needs, the Commission observed:

> We must emphasize that the variety of student aspirations, abilities, and preparation requires that appropriate content be available to satisfy diverse needs. Attention must be directed to both the nature of the content available and to the needs of particular learners. The

most gifted students. . . . may need a curriculum enriched and accelerated. . . . Similarly, educationally disadvantaged students may require special curriculum materials, smaller classes, or individual tutoring. . . . (1983: 20)

The report's closing statements also included advice for students:

You forfeit your chance for life at its fullest when you withhold your best effort in learning. When you give only the minimum to learning, you receive only the minimum in return. Even with your parents' best example and your teacher's best efforts, in the end it is *your* work that determines how much and how well you learn. When you work to your full capacity, you can hope to attain the knowledge and skills that will enable you to create your future and control your destiny. If you do not, you will have your future thrust upon you by others. (1983: 29)

In these various statements, Americans presented their views on education and educational opportunity. In particular, four beliefs about educational opportunity under gird the preceding discussions and are central to this overall study. *First and most fundamentally, Americans portray educational opportunity as a valuable social resource, vital to the well-being of both individuals and society.* As Diane Ravitch wrote, "public schools made [penniless immigrants] Americans and taught them the language and ideas with which they could later demand equality and justice." For motivational expert Anthony Carmello education was key to personal success. So, too, for Elena Santa Rosa, whose actions said a great deal about her values. When given the choice, she attended the best school possible, from high school through medical school. And the National Commission on Excellence in Education stated flatly that quality education is "essential to a free, democratic society. . . . [It] is the major foundation for the future strength of this country. . . . more important than developing the best industrial system or the strongest military force."

A second cultural belief that runs throughout this ethnography is that educational opportunity is essentially an individual matter, a view that, in practice, often intertwines some related manifestations of individualism (Fine and Rosenberg, 1983; MacLeod, 1987). For one, learning is understood as an individual experience. As *The Rocky Mountain News* observed: "[A] government can't learn for you. . . . [B]uilding up your brain is just like building up your body. Neither your parents nor your gym teachers can do exercises to make you strong." Schools therefore need to serve the interests of individual students. Elena Santa Rosa criticized her school-within-a-school program because it did not serve her particular needs: "[W]hile resources were readily available to those whose 'own rate' was slower than most, those whose rates were faster were largely ignored." Making a comparable point, *A Nation at Risk* noted, "the variety of student aspirations, abilities, and preparation requires that appropriate content be available to satisfy diverse needs." And American schools consistently honor this sense of individualism. Since all students are individuals with particular needs and interests, schools have developed a "shopping mall" of offerings (Powell, et al., 1985) to meet their needs and interests. So all students can explore these opportunities, they are scheduled individually. Despite the increasing popularity of cooperative learning, students work and are graded primarily as individuals (Kohn, 1992).

Moreover, realizing educational opportunity is closely linked to individual effort. Americans typically explain educational success and failure in terms of individual attributes, a reflection of personal strengths or shortcomings, not broader social factors—the assumption being that each person "controls his [sic] own destiny, and. . . does not need help from others" (Hsu, 1983: 4). As Lamar Alexander, Secretary of Education under President Bush, explained, "This is the country that grew up reading *The Little Engine that Could*" (Klein, 1991: 5), the children's story about a train that overcame great obstacles through dogged perseverance. This conviction, commonly termed "rugged individualism," is embodied in the lives of Americans as diverse as Abraham Lincoln and Rocky Balboa, Harriet Tubman and Madonna. Michelle Pfeiffer drew on this assumption when she told students, "THERE ARE NO VICTIMS IN THIS CLASSROOM!"—implying that students would be disadvantaged only if they allowed this to happen. In a related vein, Elena Santa Rosa saw failure as reflecting students' "unwillingness to exert themselves." Anthony Carmello put it succinctly, "I AM RESPONSIBLE FOR MYSELF!" The closing remarks from *A Nation at Risk* epitomized this point of view. Despite its rhetoric of institutional and systemic failings, the report concluded with a note to students: "[I]n the end it is *your* work that determines how much and how well you learn" (emphasis in original). Thus, in terms of education's most basic features—what is studied, how it is studied, how it is evaluated, who succeeds, and why—Americans view formal schooling as primarily an individual experience.

The third perspective on educational opportunity that informs this study concerns the taken-for-granted nature of this democratic right.

In American society, few question whether public schools offer educational opportunity; they assume they do. Although the two previous beliefs represent historically enduring views of educational opportunity, this particular belief points to a shift in American values. During the post-*Brown* era, the American government, at least, felt that those who had been disadvantaged for generations through segregated schooling, inequitable funding, and being defined as socially and academically inferior needed assistance to establish a foothold in American society. Yet, increasingly, Americans no longer question the reality of educational opportunity. It exists. There is no need for affirmative action. Quotas are now defined as discriminatory, rather than ameliorative. The playing field is assumed to have been leveled, at least enough so that students of color and urban students warrant less concern.

As Jeannie Oakes found, "[even though] schools fail to serve all students equally well . . . [They] are seen as essentially neutral . . . as color-blind and affluence-blind. . . . All children are seen as entrants in an equal, fair, and neutral competition" (Oakes, 1986: 63). According to the 22nd Annual [1990] Gallup Poll of the "Public's Attitudes Toward the Public Schools," many Americans shared this view. To the question, "In your opinion, do black children and other minorities in this community have the same educational opportunities as white children?" 79 percent of the total sample answered, "Yes"; 15 percent said, "No" (Elam, 1990).[5]

That educational opportunity is not at issue is also implicit in the historical record. While myriad policy changes have followed *A Nation at Risk* and there is a clear lack of support for the status quo, most schools remain strikingly uniform institutions (Newmann and Clune, 1992. There are 180 days in a school year. Each day is divided into six, seven, or eight periods. The typical period lasts about fifty minutes. The school itself remains a hierarchical bureaucracy made up of independent, discipline-specific departments. The dominant pedagogy continues to be didactic instruction. If society felt something were drastically wrong with the American high school, its institutional structure and practices would not have remained so unchanged for the past 100 years.

In line with this understanding of educational opportunity as taken-for-granted, Diane Ravitch wrote, "Sometimes crudely, but almost invariably with remarkable success, the public schools made [penniless immigrants] Americans and taught them the language and ideas with which they could later demand equality and justice." Anthony Carmello told his audience, "HEY FOLKS, COME ON! You can go to college anywhere you choose." And Michelle Pfeiffer was adamant in this regard: "The people who choose to get on that bus, which are you, are the people who are saying, 'I will not carry myself down to die. When I go to my grave, my head will be high' [quoting Dylan Thomas]. THAT IS A CHOICE!" In other words, opportunity exists.

The final view of educational opportunity that under girds this cultural analysis is that what constitutes educational opportunity should be defined for, not by, students. Consequently, the intended beneficiaries of public education have little say in formally defining educational opportunity for themselves (Fine, 1991; Sarason, 1990, 1996). As not-yet-adults, schools treat students in ways "that largely deny their representational status as active citizens" (Giroux, 1996: 31), entrusting them with little power or responsibility. In this sense, Diane Ravitch's use of language is subtly revealing. She wrote, "the public schools made them [immigrants] Americans." That is, students did not do this to themselves; the schools did it to them. Throughout *Dangerous Minds*, Michelle Pfeiffer's actions embodied a similar assumption; she stood in the front of the class, dominating and directing all classroom talk. Likewise, Anthony Carmello mainly "talked at" students. The National Commission on Excellence in Education made its own symbolic statement: the Commission included no student members, nor were any students quoted in *A Nation at Risk*.

Studies of American schools and classrooms fully accord with this view, portraying students as subordinate, passive recipients of information, not as active and responsible participants in a school community (Everhart, 1983; Powell, et al., 1985). Most school reform efforts have adopted the same attitude. As Michael Fullan and Susan Stiegelbauer maintained, "When adults do think of students . . . they rarely think of [them] as participants in a process of change and organizational life. . . . [Rather,] they think of them as the potential beneficiaries of change" (1991: 170; quoted in Corbett and Wilson, 1995: 13).[6] In terms of formal power and responsibility, students are institutional nonentities.

But there is an ironic and counterproductive sense of empowerment to the student's predominantly passive role. Although having little formal power, because of their numbers, students simply overwhelm many schools and promote values that serve their perceived interests. In essence, they collectively determine much of what goes on. As Elena Santa Rosa said, "to simply accept a curriculum without exposing our teachers to a good measure of bitching and moaning would have been rare at Russell. It happened in every other class." As studies of U.S. schools and communities throughout the twentieth century reveal, students view school as a

not academic

social institution (as do many adults, including parents); they focus on the extracurricular, not academic; and they consistently seek to limit responsibility so they can realize their social interests (Henry, 1963; Holland and Eisenhart, 1990; Hollingshead, 1949; Lynd and Lynd, 1929; Steinberg, et al., 1996). Theodore Sizer put it bluntly, "School's . . . attraction for many kids is simple: it is where their friends are" (1992: 126).

The previous discussion outlined four prominent ways in which educational opportunity is understood in contemporary America. It is a critical asset and resource, a key to personal fulfillment and society's well-being. It is fundamentally an individual phenomenon; which, in turn, means that schools must meet the varied needs of diverse students, and that educational success, in great part, will reflect individual effort. Further, educational opportunity is commonly unquestioned and taken-for-granted by Americans. And finally, educational opportunity is something defined for, not by, students. Certainly, these particular perspectives are not the only way to interpret the words and actions of those previously cited. For this study, however, what is critical is that these points of view dominate. Not only did these conceptions of educational opportunity inform people's rhetoric, they shaped the practices, policies, and actions of school personnel and students, often to the detriment of the educational process.

In constructing a cultural analysis of Russell High this ethnography does not attempt an in-depth examination of race/ethnicity or socioeconomic status and educational opportunity, common foci of research on urban schooling.[7] This is not to deny the relationship between these factors and educational opportunity. It is to explore a related issue, the influence of American culture on urban schooling. That is, Russell High, as an institution, embodied a commitment to prevailing conceptions of educational opportunity; the school promoted these values as well. Assumptions derived from these beliefs surfaced in assemblies and media accounts of the school. When these taken-for-granted views were challenged in the late sixties by African American students, the institution was thrown into turmoil. Ultimately, Russell students experienced educational opportunity in similar ways, for similar reasons, and with many similar outcomes. Issues of race/ethnicity and socioeconomic status are explored as they intersect with these manifestations of culture.

Initially, my research at Russell High focused on a reform initiative at the school (Muncey and McQuillan, 1996). Over time it became apparent that this urban school played a role in reproducing the conditions and beliefs that allowed existing social and economic inequities in Eastown to endure. In making this critique, I therefore seek to blend theory and practice: to examine the taken-for-granted at Russell High from a cultural point of view; and then to consider the implications of such understanding for promoting educational opportunity more equitably (Anderson, 1989; Brodkey, 1987; Lather, 1986; Simon and Dippo, 1986). As Seymour Sarason has maintained for some time, those seeking to improve schools must first thoroughly understand the "assumptions and conceptions that are so over learned that one no longer questions or thinks about them . . ." (1971: 193). In line with Sarason's concern, this study reveals how prevailing American conceptions of educational opportunity permeated the school system and undermined students' education.

Given the critical nature of this ethnography, I stress an additional point: What I describe is not a malicious conspiracy. Far from it. It is normal, accepted behavior. It is the interaction of a value system, an institution, and ordinary people, often very well-intentioned, who have come to understand their world in specific ways—and therefore not to understand it in other ways—doing what they believe they should.

A CULTURAL BLIND SPOT

Understanding how Americans view educational opportunity is essential because it also exposes how we do not view educational opportunity. As readers are reminded throughout this work, culture can hide as well as highlight. Because we emphasize the individual, we often overlook the collective.[8] Because educational opportunity is so taken-for-granted, we seldom look at it critically. Because students are institutional nonentities, their views inform very little of what occurs in schools. As a consequence, our understandings of educational opportunity are incomplete and distorted. Urban dropout rates, suspension rates, and failure rates can soar while the country invests proportionately less in its most needy schools (Alexander and Salmon, 1995; Kozol, 1991). The American population can grow increasingly polarized, in terms of income and race/ethnicity, while schools not only promote these undemocratic outcomes but also the attitudes that allow society to accept these divisions as equitable.[9]

Moreover, issues of educational opportunity in urban America are intensifying. By the year 2000, over one-third of all school children will be from lower-income groups or will be ethnic, racial, or linguistic minorities—the vast majority segregated in urban neighborhoods.[10] Schools will be one of the few organizations with a chance to address their needs. If American society continues to be blinded by our own cultural predispositions, this country will continue to treat a dysfunctional system and widespread failure as problems only of individuals within the system, not failings of the system itself. And opportunity will remain little more than an illusion in too many urban schools.

METHODOLOGY

At its heart, this study is an ethnography, a research methodology that is well-suited for understanding educational opportunity. For instance, ethnographic research is long-term in nature. This study encompassed five school years, August 1986 through June 1991.[11] Consequently, I followed two classes of students ('90 and '91) from their first day of school to graduation. I watched an effort at school reform go from inception through development to its demise. I observed courses from September to June. I saw educational opportunity play out over time and gained an appreciation for the interrelationships among the multiple and interrelated factors that influenced students' education. In addition, this extended research design allowed me to shift my research foci as new developments emerged at the school.

A second feature of ethnographic research, its holistic orientation, was also useful for examining educational opportunity. What happens in a classroom on any particular day, for example, is likely shaped by the interaction of many factors—a teacher's view of her/his profession, the students' collective understanding of what "real school" should be, the structure of the school system, and the material being taught. Ethnographic research is designed to consider various features of any social system as they interact and influence one another, thereby more closely paralleling real life.

Finally, ethnographies attend to issues of culture, what people believe and how they interpret what they experience. In this study, it was critical to explore conceptions of educational opportunity because doing so revealed why the status quo at Russell High proved so enduring despite clearly unequal educational outcomes among Eastown students.[12]

At the school itself, I relied on three primary sources of data: formal and informal interviews, ethnographic observations, and archival research (e.g., school documents and records). I conducted formal interviews with standardized protocols on a regular basis with

Russell students, faculty, and administration. In total, I interviewed ninety-seven students (approximately one-quarter were interviewed more than once), fifty-one of sixty-six full-time teaching staff (roughly one-third were interviewed more than once), and the entire school administration—including the principal, two assistant principals, director of studies, department chairs, and guidance counselors. The principal and two assistant principals were interviewed multiple times. I also conducted informal interviews in various contexts—with a teacher over coffee, walking to class with a student, or while the principal monitored the cafeteria.

The ethnographic observations I conducted fall into four categories: (1) classroom observations; (2) school meetings (including entire school faculty meetings, department meetings, assemblies, school reform-related meetings, and meetings with parent groups); (3) day-in-the-life studies (when I spent an entire day with a particular student, teacher, or administrator); and (4) informal observations (e.g., eating lunch in the cafeteria or teachers' room, attending extracurricular activities, or walking the hallways). Archival documents available on Russell High included a faculty newsletter, the school newspaper, reports on the school authored by faculty and outside researchers, copies of student work, and school memos that detailed dropout and attendance rates and the number of course failures, for example. I used newspaper articles and a television news special to analyze how local media portrayed educational opportunity. To create a socioeconomic and demographic picture of Eastown, I drew on U.S. census data. Although this work represents a collaborative effort, my perspective dominates. I decided what the final product would be. Nonetheless, those who were directly involved with this research had an opportunity to respond to what I wrote. (The Appendix, Methodological Reflections, offers a more detailed discussion of research methods.)

ORGANIZATION OF THE BOOK

The following chapters are divided into four sections. The first, Educational Opportunity in Practice, examines the day-to-day life of the school. To challenge the prevailing characterization of educational opportunity as a largely individual phenomenon, Chapter 2 emphasizes the collective point of view to consider how the nature of the Russell student population influenced classroom learning—specifically, how student resistance to a curriculum that differed markedly from most Russell classes led a team of teachers to modify their goals, pedagogy, and curriculum in favor of less demanding and more rote conceptions of schoolwork. Once again challenging individualist assumptions about educational opportunity, Chapter 3 draws on the notions of cultural and social capital to reveal how the collective nature of the student population reverberated throughout the school, influencing the work of the administration, guidance counselors, and teachers—and ultimately students' education. While most Americans would say they value a high school education, Chapter 4 details a day-in-the-life of a lower-track Russell High senior that throws into question the basis to this popular belief.

The second section, The Resilience of the Status Quo, describes how prevailing conceptions of educational opportunity endured. Chapter 5 examines the efforts of Russell faculty to reassess educational practice, efforts which, over a three-year period, consistently aimed to improve discipline and order but never to change the nature of the education students received. Chapter 6 offers an historical perspective on the school, describing how Russell High evolved from being a respected school to being seen as a catch-all for the city's least able students—in particular, how a "riot"[13] in 1969 signaled the school's ultimate loss of respectability.

The third section, Promoting Faith in Educational Opportunity, offers insight into why educational opportunity was often unquestioned at Russell High and in Eastown. Chapter 7 presents an assembly in which the speaker assured students that educational opportunity was real and that success was largely a matter of individual effort. To understand how local news media conveyed similar messages, the chapter also examines a television special on Russell High. To situate this research in a community context, Chapter 8 looks at how during the eighties Eastown grew increasingly divided, in terms of race/ethnicity, income, education, and neighborhood—divisions which paralleled developments throughout U.S. cities. Further, these educational, socioeconomic, and neighborhood divisions are explored as a way to understand why educational opportunity remained largely unproblematic.

The concluding section and chapter, So What?, draws on findings from the previous chapters and considers their implications for educational practice. The ensuing proposals for urban school reform all derive from a single, overarching assumption: to be successful reform must be undertaken systematically. Moreover, to be systematic reform initiatives must attend to issues of culture, what people value and believe. In this regard I emphasize two areas for reform that are simple in focus but have wide-ranging implications: providing teachers with more time to do their work and giving students greater power and responsibility.

PART
I

EDUCATIONAL OPPORTUNITY
IN PRACTICE

2

WINNING THE BATTLE AND
LOSING THE WAR

A Look at One Russell High Classroom

> Negotiation is arguably the main strategy
> employed by teachers and pupils in interaction
> with each other. Indeed . . . it is the essential
> mode of interaction. . . . Before "teaching" and
> "learning" can occur, certain rules of procedure
> have to be established and maintained.
> —Peter Woods, *Sociology and the School*

During my research at Russell High[1] it was estimated that the school had a forty percent failure rate; two of every five courses students took, they failed. Over those five years, the dropout rate exceeded fifty percent.[2] Offering some understanding of the conditions underlying such extensive failure, this chapter examines how students reacted to an effort by a team of three teachers to implement a U.S. history curriculum that differed markedly from students' previous experiences; and, in turn, how the teachers responded to the students' actions. Specifically, over the course of the year students aggressively resisted the teachers' attempts to introduce change into the classroom; so much so that the teachers modified their original goals as well as their pedagogical and curricular strategies in favor of less authentic, less demanding, and more traditional conceptions of schoolwork (Ball, 1980; Becker, 1990; Moll and Diaz, 1987; Page, 1987b; Powell, et al., 1985).

*real
school*

In analyzing these developments I focus on the collective nature of the students' actions. That is, students consistently drew on their shared sense of "real school" (Metz, 1990) and reasonable teacher expectations to justify their resistance to change. And when they resisted their teachers, they often did so in a collective fashion, building on one another's ideas, taking turns challenging their teachers, and providing moral support for each other. In so doing, students enacted their informal power so as to implicate themselves in their own educational failure—in terms of the grades they received, the skills they never developed, and how their actions reinforced faculty perceptions of student indifference (Chandler, 1992; McDermott, 1987; Willis, 1977). As Joan Roberts observed, "In many classrooms, student-teacher transactions can be understood as processes of political conflict in which students win the battle and lose the war" (1971: 75; see also, Anyon, 1980: 272; Ogbu, 1987: 317).

Data for this chapter derive from research conducted from September 10, 1987, through June 9, 1988, the final exam for the course. During this time I observed thirty classes (slightly more than one-third of the total class meetings), each of which lasted an hour and forty-five minutes. I formally interviewed each teacher twice and fourteen of the seventeen students at least once. The interviews were complemented by regular, informal discussions with these persons before and after classes and during class breaks. Initially, I planned to end my research in February. The teachers, however, encouraged me to continue my work and I did so in May. Still, I attended no classes in March or April.

performance based curriculum vs. coverage

THE COURSE

The U.S. history course these teachers designed had many ambitious goals and differed in many ways from most Russell classes, one key difference being its performance-based curriculum. Rather than organizing the class in terms of "coverage," the typical structure at Russell as well as most American high schools, the course was predicated on students completing seven projects. In a jointly authored article, the teachers discussed their curriculum:

> A performance-based course requires that students demonstrate they have learned what the teacher feels is essential. The teacher must first determine what he or she wants students to know and be able to do; then, projects are designed which require those abilities. The teacher's job is helping students acquire what they need to

know in order to do their projects. . . . [B]y successfully doing the projects, the students will have demonstrated that they have mastered the course material.[3]

In the course syllabus, a novelty for Russell students in and of itself, the team outlined some assumptions that informed the curriculum:

> One of the basic ideas of [this course] is that what counts is not how much time you spend in class, but what you actually learn. Therefore, we are going to tell you now. . . exactly what it is we expect you to know and be able to do by the time you complete this course. How much time it takes you to master the material and to learn the new skills is not what's most important. What is most important is that by the time you finish U.S. history you will have new knowledge, understanding, and skills. . . . You will show your teachers that you have this new knowledge, understanding, and skills by successfully completing seven projects. . . . All the work that we do in class will be designed to teach you what you need to know in order to do a good job on each of the projects.

Following this introduction the syllabus outlined three main areas of study and described projects associated with each:

1) What history is:
An *Oral History Project* based on interviews and written sources. The choice of subject matter will be largely up to you—as long as you have your teacher's agreement that it is a workable subject. Some possible subjects are: your family, substance abuse, prejudice and discrimination against high school-age people, Russell High School, minority workers in Eastown, a labor union, teenage mothers/fathers, recent immigrants, lawyers and the court system, or popular music.

2) Chronology and periodization in U.S. history:
A *Time Line* which charts the major periods in U.S. history. You will define the major periods in U.S. history, but you will have to justify your choices and convince your teacher that your choices are valid.

A *Written Test* on chronology, periodization, and typically significant dates, events, and people in U.S. history.

An *Oral Test* in which the teacher asks you questions that you have to answer orally right then and there.

Russell High was a member of CES

3) Finding and facing your own place in U.S. history:
You have a lot of choice about the work you do in this area but each project must demonstrate three things: a) an in-depth understanding of your topic; b) a good sense of your own or your own group's place in U.S. history; and c) that you have drawn some intelligent conclusions from your study of the past about your own life choices. The projects include:

A *Formal Written History Research Paper*. This paper will include footnotes . . . and a bibliography.

Any *two projects* of your choice as long as they fulfill the three [previously cited] requirements. . . . These might be essays, art work, a short story, a play, an interview, another formal research paper, or a video. For the three projects in this area you will investigate any of the following themes:

1) Economic development: capitalism and the free enterprise system.

2) The Constitution, the expansion of democracy, and law and order.

3) Freedom, racism, and internal dissent.

4) Foreign policy: growth and expansion (Manifest Destiny and imperialism).

5) Everyday life: Women, children, and family life; ways of earning a living; fashions; or crafts.

Besides the performance-based curriculum, this course differed from most Russell classes in other ways. For one, homework, at least initially, was not required. In the teachers' view, both in-class work and suggested out-of-class work were required to complete projects successfully. Whether assigned or not, the team assumed students would do homework. The teachers also sought to create a democratic context in which to teach U.S. history, to accord students some formal power and implement a measure of shared governance in the classroom. In addition, this class was part of a school-within-a-school (SWAS) program that was created through Russell High's membership in the Coalition of Essential Schools—a national, university-secondary school reform program. As part of the Essential School, this class met for a double-period every other day. In this program, students received no failing grades. Since Essential School faculty felt that too many students received low Cs and Ds on the basis of "seat time" but without mastering critical skills and content, the program restricted its grading scale to A, B, C (no lower than 75), and "incomplete." Work receiving a grade below 75 was returned for students to redo.

These features of the Essential School had specific consequences for this class. For instance, nearly one-third of the students in the course had incompletes from their previous history class, Western civilization. The expectation was that when students finished "Western civ" they would begin U.S. history.[4] At first, the teachers worked with both groups of students in the same classroom but found this format difficult. Consequently, one teacher resolved to spend most of his time with the Western civ students in a different classroom while the other teachers worked with the remaining U.S. history students.

I conducted the research for this chapter during the second year of the Essential School, when the program had two teams of four teachers—representing the disciplines of English, social studies, science, and math—and a coordinator who administered the SWAS program and taught one class, the U.S. history course discussed in this chapter. To assist these teams as well as the school more generally in its restructuring efforts, a local university and the Eastown School System jointly funded three professors—with expertise in English, social studies, and biology—to work in various capacities throughout the school to promote reform. The social studies professor and a student teacher he supervised also taught this U.S. history course. The professor had a Ph.D. in history and considerable secondary school teaching experience. The student teacher had a B.A. in religious studies and was working toward a master's degree in teaching. The coordinator had a master's degree in history and had taught for over fifteen years in Eastown. Of the seventeen students who were part of the U.S. history class, eight were African American, eight white, and one Hispanic. There were ten female and seven male students.

Before examining a series of ethnographic vignettes from the class it is useful to consider one assumption that informed the team's efforts. As the teachers wrote:

Why does high school history so often seem dry and dull to students? As subject matter, it is intrinsically fascinating: it's about people and their lives, and what was important to them. . . . Part of the difficulty lies in how history is defined. Famous people just like everyone else had childhoods, made friends and enemies, fell in love, worried over their homes and families, grew old, and feared death. But that is not what textbooks try to capture. By and large, textbooks concentrate on the public lives of the powerful and rich. The thread of this country's history, as one historian has written, is "laws and wars. . . ." [E]ncouraging students to be student-historians and to make some of the real choices about history that professional historians make . . . should involve and motivate students from diverse backgrounds and with varied interests.

Although the teachers expected that allowing students to define history for themselves, to critically assess their own place in the expanse of American history, and to be democratic participants in the classroom would motivate them, most expressed little interest in these opportunities. Rather, students were often disruptive, ignored their teachers, and completed little work. To say the least, students appeared unengaged; from a more critical perspective, they seemed insulting, hostile, immature, and lazy. Indeed, the three teachers (to varying extents) as well as the students commonly attributed student resistance and failure to complete work to a lack of individual effort. Yet factors over which individual students had little control—in particular, the relative difficulty and novelty of the course, the behavior of one's classmates, and the prevailing student attitude toward education at Russell High—had a marked influence on the education students experienced.

SIX ETHNOGRAPHIC VIGNETTES

The following vignettes from six classes were selected on the basis of three criteria: they are "thick" enough (Geertz, 1973) to illuminate multiple aspects of classroom interactions; they are adequately separated from one another over time so as to reveal how classroom interactions evolved; and they are representative of what occurred in this class, they are not exceptional. The vignettes are assessed from an interactionist perspective that assumes schoolwork is, to some extent, a negotiated entity for which students "seeking basically the comfort of their own perspective and reality, will tend to react according to how the teacher's techniques mesh with that reality" (Woods, 1983: 134; see also, Ball, 1980; Sarason, 1990; Waller, 1932; Woods, 1978, 1980). Thus, much of what occurred in this course can be understood as a negotiation process in which teachers sought to implement a performance-based curriculum while students contested this innovation and clung to their own view of "real" school.

September 10, 1987

INTRODUCTORY NOTE. *In contrast to most Russell High classes, the team planned to teach its course within a democratic classroom structure. In this, the second class of the year, teachers and students collaboratively set guidelines for classroom behavior and agreed upon a process for resolving contentious issues. Outlining their rationale the teachers wrote, "The U.S. is a democratic country. The students are learning U.S. history. What could be a more appropriate context?"*

At the start of class the teachers handed out a questionnaire that listed eight questions students were to read, discuss, and reach consensus about regarding their applicability to the class. The questions were:

1. Who decides what the rules are for this classroom?
2. Do you have to raise your hand every time you want to speak?
3. Are there times when it is alright to interrupt another student or a teacher?
4. What should happen if you come late to class?
5. Are you allowed to cut a class? What should happen if you cut a class?
6. Is there any time when it is alright to hit another person in this classroom?
7. Should the break [for this double-period class] *always* be right between periods three and four?
8. At what times will you be able to go to the bathroom?

After students read the questions, the class divided into small groups to discuss them. The teachers roamed among the groups. After each group had discussed the questions, the university professor directed further discussion before students and teachers voted on each policy. In determining when students should use the bathroom, for example, the professor asked for comments. One student volunteered: "Some people who say they need to go to the bathroom might be lying. They are going to see friends. I think maybe the teacher should check to see if the student might just be going to see a friend." When no further comments were forthcoming, the class voted unanimously to use the bathroom only during the break between class periods, except in cases of emergency. In all, the following rules were established:

1. Rules for this classroom are decided by . . . students and teachers together. When there is no consensus, we follow majority rule in a democratic vote.

2. When there is discussion going on, a student should raise his or her hand and be called on before speaking.

3. In general, people should not interrupt each other.

4. Everyone should be in class on time.

5. Students are responsible to attend every class.

6. There is to be no hitting of another person.

7. The break will be taken between periods 3 and 4. Students will use the bathroom then.

It took roughly thirty minutes to create these rules. In the remaining time, the coordinator worked with Western civ students on a project related to the French Revolution and the professor met with U.S. history students to go over the seven projects for the year. When class ended, the professor told students:

> You have a chance to do well here, not just in this class but in school in general. But you need to work at home to do so. You should set up a timeline to follow so that you will know what work you will do in class when you get here.

SUMMARY. In the five years of my research at Russell, this was the only class I knew of where creating a democratic context was ever attempted. Although the teachers were enthusiastic about the possibilities of collaborative governance, the effort generated little excitement among students. In fact, never again did students or teachers attempt to resolve any classroom issue through the process identified this day. Further, even though the professor encouraged students to plan how they would complete the seven projects, as the year progressed many expressed confusion with such long-term planning as well as with having to work on multiple projects simultaneously.

October 22, 1987

INTRODUCTORY NOTE. *This mid-October class, when the first student projects for the year were due, provides a sense of how students and teachers negotiated aspects of the performance-based curriculum.*

As was common, a few students straggled into class a bit late. Others, talking with friends, never seemed to notice when the bell rang. Before beginning class, the university professor spent a few moments addressing his concern with student inattention: "Could I have your attention please? We need your help to figure out a way to start class when the bell rings without having to stand up in front of class and ask you to be quiet. What can we do?" No student said anything. He continued, "Is this reasonable: As soon as we stand up here and are obviously ready to start, we can? Can you tell your neighbor to be quiet if he or she doesn't realize it? Any objections?" There were none.

Subsequently, the U.S. history students left the room to watch a video and the Western civ students remained. The video, created by the student teacher, was to prepare students to conduct oral history interviews by providing examples of effective and ineffective interview techniques. After watching the video, students listed such mistakes from the ineffective example as "unprepared," "rude," "sloppy," "inappropriately dressed," and "forgot to take notes." For the second interview they noted how the person was "on time," "made eye contact," "had knowledge about her subject," "used the interviewee's answers to formulate new questions," and was "more polite." The class then took a five-minute break.

When the second half of class began, students raised various questions about the timelines, which were due the previous week but which only one student had completed: "Do I need to have a map with this timeline?" "What kind of map do I need?" "How many essays are we supposed to have with our timelines?" After addressing these and other questions, the student teacher began reviewing one girl's timeline. Shortly thereafter, she told the student, "This isn't appropriate. You've only listed events without explaining why you've included them with the timeline." The student, somewhat upset, insisted that no one had told her she had been doing anything wrong.

In working with other students the student teacher realized that many were frustrated and confused by the assignment. Most still had questions, and she considered their work inadequate. She then asked the professor to leave the room with her to discuss the matter. After meeting in the hallway they returned and the professor addressed the class:

> Sometimes things that are new and different need to be done over and over before they are fully understood—for example, a corner kick in soccer. If you did it wrong, it would be absurd for the coach to say, "I've already shown you. Why do it again?" For the timeline, you need to realize it covers an historical period. It's a way to organize things over time. If you made a timeline from your birth to now, you'd list key events in your life.

He then asked students to suggest how they might structure a timeline for their lives. The first three students he called on said they could think of no key events. The fourth said that a key event in his life was "when I got my braces." A girl who couldn't hear him said, "Why don't you speak up?" Apparently insulted, he retorted, "At least I wash my hair." Rising from her seat she fired back, "Your haircut makes you look like a fag and you know it!" The professor defused the argument but the analogy was pursued no further.

The student teacher then said that although the timelines were due that day, many students did not fully understand the essay component of the assignment—they had difficulty explaining why they defined their period as they had as well as how the events listed supported their theme for the period. Almost in unison students replied, "Yeah, it's wrong!" The student teacher rejoined, "It's not *wrong*. There are things you did that are *inadequate*." The professor added, "Historians can show the passage of time anyway that they want. What you need is not just a list of dates. What's important is that you look at those dates as an historian and label the periods in a way that makes sense to you." The student teacher then explained how the incomplete policy fit with the performance-based curriculum:

> The advantage to doing the project this way [i.e., where students can revise their work] is that you're not penalized if something is inadequate. You should look at each time period that you do as a trial run. The final project is not due until April 29th. That's what will be graded. . . . We don't expect you to get it 100 percent right the first time.

In response, the girl who had been told that she needed to redo her work remarked, "Why not tell us this at the beginning of the course because your paperwork is confusing? After we do it one way, you tell us it's wrong." The professor replied, "Honestly, it's so different from other things that you've done in history class that you need to try it before the teachers can explain it to you. You need to experiment and then get feedback. It doesn't make sense until you try it. It's like with sports or playing the piano." She retorted, "Well I'm saying that when you described the timeline, you said we could do it like this and then when we did it, we got confused." The professor answered, "I'm sorry to confuse you, but it's not a waste of time because you learned something." Visibly upset, the student responded, "But it makes us mad and we're so confused that we just might not do it." The professor then spoke to the entire class: "How many people think that being confused is part of learning?" Only he and the student teacher raised their hands.

After the professor described the timeline assignment once again, another girl noted, "You told me all I had to do was write an essay for the Age of Discovery and list ten events. That's all." The professor replied, "That's all for the Age of Discovery. Then you have to do one for each other period too." A second student then tried to explain the timeline assignment to this girl. Looking exasperated, she said, "Forget it, because I don't understand what you're saying." The professor then outlined the timeline project once more. When he finished the student teacher commented, "You're not doing work over. You just have to add to the core structure that you've already created. What you've done is not a waste." The professor followed up that remark saying, "In writing your essay, prove to us that the titles you have chosen are appropriate." The girl whose work had been returned then said, "But you called it wrong." The student teacher reiterated, "It's not *wrong*. It's *inadequate*." The student replied, "But it's not *right*." The student teacher continued, "All you need to do is expand upon what you did." Various students reacted: "That's a lot of work." "The teachers don't explain it enough." "I'm not doin' it." "How come it's not clear?" The student teacher replied, "In every class I've allowed time for you to ask questions." A student then asked, "So how many essays do we have to write?" She responded, "One for each timeline." Another student cut in, "I'm not doing it."

The student who said that she would not do the assignment then asked, "What if Paul [who had already completed a timeline] did it wrong? He made a tape. He played music with it. Is he going to have to do it over?" The question was not answered. The girl whose work was returned asked, "So how *will* we be graded?" The professor explained, "You will not receive an incomplete unless you don't work. As long as you make progress, you won't be penalized for learning, even if it takes a long time. But to finish U.S. history you have to finish all seven projects." The student then asked, "And we have to do an oral history too? We have to finish all of this?" The professor responded, "To do this, you need to do the [optional] homework and ask questions in class and work in class." The student replied, "But I do the homework and then I bring it in and you tell me it's wrong."

In response, the student teacher raised the issue of student effort, "People need to work in class, too, in order to get this work done. Sometimes you are not that productive in class because of the different student interactions that are going on." A boy commented, "But I think that when we asked questions today it was productive." She answered, "I'm trying to give in-class assignments to prepare people for larger assignments." The bell then rang to end class.

SUMMARY. This class revealed several developments that continued throughout much of the year: For one, students, often in concert, questioned the rationale behind many aspects of the course, thereby requiring the teachers to clarify their expectations and limiting the amount of work done during class. At one point, students took turns questioning the number of essays they were to do, the basis to the teachers' grading scheme, whether a student who included music with a project would have to redo the project, and whether students used time productively. And this collective resistance seemed effective. One contentious issue, for instance, concerned whether students were to do one or three essays per timeline. Although at first divided, the teachers eventually decided to require one essay rather than three, suggesting that student negotiation made it difficult for them to maintain their initial expectations. Further, negotiation and the consequent disorder obscured some student concerns. When a student attempted to describe a timeline for his life, the activity was halted by a shouting match.

Students also completed little work. Only one handed in the first timeline when it was due. In turn, the teachers questioned student effort. As the student teacher said, "Sometimes you are not that productive in class because of the different student interactions that are going on." Moreover, although the teachers highlighted the strengths of the performance-based curriculum ("You're not doing work over. You just have to add to the structure you've already created"), students expressed a different view—it was more work and it was confusing ("[Y]ou said we could do it like this and then when we did it, we got confused"). Finally, even though the professor sought student input regarding what to do about students talking after the bell had rung for class, there was no reference to collaborative decision making.

November 5, 1987

INTRODUCTORY NOTE. *Nearing the end of the first quarter, students and teachers continued to negotiate what the performance-based curriculum meant in practice and students still completed few projects. While some students put little effort into their work, others seemed confused by the novelty of the course.*

The student teacher began class by asking those working on timelines to form a semi-circle so she could meet with them. She then outlined her plans:

Today, I'll do examples of timelines on the themes of the Age of Colonization and the Age of Discovery. This is not the only right way to do it but it should provide you with an idea for how to do a timeline. You'll need to keep track of how this was done so that you can use it to do your own timelines. So make sure you save these examples of timelines and essays until the end of the year.

Picking up on the topic of saving course materials, a student asked, "Can we chuck these papers?" The student teacher replied, "What papers?" Raising a fistful of crumpled handouts the student responded, "All of them." The student teacher remarked, "You'll need to learn to save and order these papers so you can use them later on. You need to see why these papers are important. If you haven't kept track of what you're doing in class, you'll be lost later on. I'll help you organize the materials if you need it."

After handing out copies of her timeline on the Age of Discovery the student teacher told the class, "You should be reading the timeline events now." As students read, she asked whether they still had copies of the handout, entitled Criteria for Evaluation of Timelines, since this outlined the teachers' expectations. Few did. She also noted, "On the timelines you didn't provide adequate descriptions of the dates you gave me. You should describe the event and why it was important somewhere. You need to explain why the event was important. You can't just say, 'Vespucci got to the New World in 1501.'"

When students finished reading, the student teacher asked, "How did I do this?" A student said, "You read." She replied, "It seems to me that you didn't read the text very closely. There's a difference between copying what's in the text onto your timeline and really demonstrating an understanding. What else do you have to do to produce a timeline?" Another student answered, "You have to take notes." The professor then told a student who appeared to be sleeping to get her head off the desk. The student teacher continued, "Take ten minutes, read my essay, and look at your essay, and rewrite it." One boy quickly expressed displeasure, "This is a waste of time." The student teacher responded, "You all need to work on your essays." A girl replied, "I ain't doin' it." Looking directly at the professor she continued, "This is stupid." Another girl voiced her concerns, "Why do we have to do this when we could be getting on to something else?" In response the professor asked, "Why do you think we're doing it? Does it feel like it's too much?" Without hesitation, she replied, "It is!" The professor explained, "We're trying to organize your work so that you don't forget it." The girl continued, "But you make us do it over and over." The professor then posed a question to her, "When will it stop?" She replied, "I don't know." Another student interjected, "When it's done." The girl went on, "At the rate we're going, we might never get through with it."

Eventually, students began rewriting their essays. After writing less than a sentence one girl said loudly, "I'm finished." Ten minutes later, the student teacher checked students' work. The first student she checked had written two sentences, one of which complained about the assignment. The student teacher then asked a student why she thought her original assignment had been inadequate. She responded, "Because I put something, then changed it, then put something, then changed it. I don't know!" Another student proclaimed to no one in particular, "I didn't do it." Somewhat exasperated, the student teacher reminded the class, "You'll have an incomplete if your timeline isn't in tomorrow. We have been giving you [optional] homework assignments that are designed to help you do the timelines. You should be skimming the text and taking notes. If there's any other way you think you can do the timeline, please tell me." A student then asked, "Can we work on our timelines without taking notes?" She replied, "You are going to need to take notes in order to do the timelines. The problem with the timelines so far is that you haven't understood what's in the book. Is the book the problem?" A student remarked, "Maybe we could see a movie on the period and that would help us understand the period." Another suggested, "Why don't we all write down the problems we've had with the timelines and compare them? You're saying people aren't doing the homework and we all have reasons." In response, one student volunteered, "I don't do the homework because I'm lazy." Another explained: "I keep putting it off and putting it off, then it's too late."

As the student teacher went on to describe her expectations for the timelines, a girl cut in to ask, "For all the homework we've had so far, how many have done it?" The student teacher replied, "None. I've typed out homework sheets and listed work you need to do to pass the timeline assignment. It's very frustrating to pass these out and then have no one do the work. What assignments could I give you that would help you do this?" The student who admitted being lazy answered, "Nothing. We just need to do the work." The student teacher continued, "The assignments should help you discipline yourself and get the timeline done by doing it with brief homework assignments—a little bit at a time so it won't seem like such a big thing that takes a long time to do. It's also obvious that a lot of you aren't prepared to do your interviews for the oral history project. I'll give you a sheet and have you write out hypotheses and questions.

You need to be clear on these issues now." The bell then rang for the mid-period break.

For the second half of class the teachers told students to work on their timelines while they helped individual students. At one point the professor explained to one of the few students who had turned in a timeline why she had to redo it. While the professor explained her incomplete grade, she kept insisting, "But I turned it in on time." The professor then attempted an analogy: "Say our principal ordered desks and chairs from a company and they arrived on time but some had the tops break when students leaned on them and the seats of others broke when people sat on them? Yet the manufacturer kept saying, 'But I delivered them on time.' Would you expect the principal to pay for them?" The student replied, "No." The professor went on: "Would it be appropriate to ask the manufacturer to repair them?" She answered, "Yes." He concluded his analogy, "So now do you understand what we're trying to say about your timeline?" She replied, "Yes, I know, *but I turned it in on time.*"

While the student teacher and professor assisted individual students, some of the class engaged in other activities. Three girls discussed their professional futures: life as fashion designers. Two boys sang lyrics to a heavy metal song. When the student teacher gave a sample timeline to one girl, she asked, "What is this?" even though the student teacher earlier explained its purpose in-depth. As the class continued, the noise level increased. A boy in the back of the room emptied his notebook of unneeded paper, another listened to a walkman. Over the noise the student teacher reminded students, "There are two things you need to do: First, the oral history project. You need to get your questions together for your interviews. This was supposed to be done this week but we'll give you 'til next week because we didn't get to practice the interviews." She continued, "Just give me a minute and I'll be done. Also, the next timeline segment is only a chapter and a half from your text. It isn't that long." As the period ended she told the class that their revised timeline essays were due tomorrow and, since the class did not meet that day, they should turn their work into the Essential School office.

After class and somewhat distraught, the student teacher told me that she had created a second timeline, for the Age of Colonization, but never shared it with students because of how they responded to the first—even though she worked over fifteen hours to create the two timelines. The next day, two students submitted the assigned work.

SUMMARY. Like the previous vignette, students completed few assignments and negotiation took up a substantial portion of class time, with "doing nothing" now part of the negotiation process. The class also revealed how student behavior began to influence the teachers. They postponed the oral history questions, provided students with class time to work on projects, and never shared a second sample timeline with the class. In addition, the teachers saw a coherence to the work assigned ("We have been giving you homework assignments that are designed to help you do the timelines") and seemed to assume that students could do the work. As the student teacher told students, "Take ten minutes, read my essay, look at your essay, and rewrite it," offering no further instruction as to how they should apply this example to their work. Students were also told they had not "read the text very closely" and that they needed to take notes, assuming students could follow the text and take adequate notes. These assumptions may have been reinforced by the student who said he was lazy.

Yet there were signs that students had little idea how to approach this work. When asked if they had their Criteria for Evaluation of the Timelines, few did, although the teachers expected that this handout would guide their efforts. One student wanted to throw out materials the team had prepared. Another asked whether he needed to take notes to do the timelines. When a girl was asked why she thought her work was inadequate she answered, "Because I put something, then changed it, then put something, then changed it," before finally saying, "I don't know!" Moreover, the sometimes hectic nature of classroom interactions made it difficult to assess student learning—in particular, what their problems were and whether they were legitimate.

December 21, 1987

INTRODUCTORY NOTE. *At this point in the year students still completed few projects—although homework was now mandatory, in part, because the teachers felt students were ignoring the work. On this day, the coordinator and professor worked with the entire class while the student teacher was completing her university exams.*

As students arrived to class, the coordinator gave each a paper. Even before reading the handout students reacted: "Please, no more papers!" "You're going to ruin our vacation by giving us homework." The coordinator explained:

> For those students in Western civ, I will give you a spreadsheet that outlines where you stand right now in terms of completing your

work. Right now, two people are ready to take the Western civ final. For you other Western civ people, continue with your work. Now for U.S. history, I created a matrix of the work that you've done and that you still have to do—not to depress you, but to give you an honest display of what you've accomplished so far.

The coordinator then reviewed the "seven performances that *had* to be completed in order to pass U.S. history," discussed homework students had yet to complete, and added, "Those of you who are ahead of the rest can continue working on the assignments that you still need to complete. That's why I gave you the homework sheet before vacation—so you can catch up on your work over vacation. Do take advantage of the time to get some school work done. . . . I'm trying to give you some kind of a map so that you know what you're in for during the rest of the year, so you can plan ahead."

Following this remark, the coordinator told the U.S. history students, "Take out your homework. You were to have written an essay that explained what the Industrial Revolution had been. Who has the homework?" Most students tried to avoid eye contact as the coordinator repeated his request. Some admitted to not having done the work. Two offered excuses: "I left it at home"; "I was absent." The coordinator and university professor then engaged the entire class in a dialogue that touched on a range of course-related issues:

COORDINATOR: I need your attention one more time. We have a problem. Do you know what it is?

STUDENT #1:   Homework.

STUDENT #2:   Yeah, we get too much of it.

COORDINATOR: There's not much happening in terms of getting work done in this class. If you've got so much work to do, where is it?

STUDENT #1:   I didn't say that. I'm just not working. That's my problem.

STUDENT #2:   It's so confusing in this class that you don't know what to do. It's so confusing you don't know where to start.

COORDINATOR: But if you have to read some pages and answer a few questions, why can't you do that?

STUDENT #3:   But we have oral history projects, timelines, and tests. We don't even know where to start.

STUDENT #4:   And we have other classes.

COORDINATOR: Everyone has other classes. That's what being a student is.

PROFESSOR: It is confusing, but at least you can always do the questions from the reading in the text.

COORDINATOR: Even if it is confusing, what can you always do?

STUDENT #5:   Get out of this class, like I've been trying to do all year.

COORDINATOR: What if you're stuck in this class?

STUDENT #5:   I'll leave the school.

COORDINATOR: What if you decide that's not a solution and you want to go ahead and try to make it in this class?

STUDENT #6:   Ask for help?

COORDINATOR: Do you wait?

STUDENT #6:   No.

STUDENT #7:   Sometimes we *have* to wait, because the teacher can't always answer your question.

STUDENT #6:   I get really angry when I don't understand something, so I don't do it.

COORDINATOR: You get frustrated. Well *I'm* frustrated right now.

STUDENT #6:   You don't get as frustrated as we do.

COORDINATOR: We have a problem. We're talking about something as simple as reading six pages and doing a few questions. Sometimes it's only one question!

STUDENT #4:   But it's a hard one.

COORDINATOR: Then see me! Come to my office! I worked on this until 12:30 last night from four in the afternoon. It goes both ways. What I need to impress on you is that you need to do the homework and do the reading before doing the timelines and questions so that you get to the point of being able to ask questions about other stuff.

STUDENT #2:   Why not do the questions and reading in school?

COORDINATOR: Because it's better to do that work at home. The confusion that you experience can be dealt with in school where you have other students and your teachers to help.

STUDENT #6:   But it's better to read in school because you can ask questions in class.

COORDINATOR: It appears that you have questions on the timelines and oral history projects. So do the things you understand outside of class and do other things in class. We've set up a schedule so you will finish the work. And you're behind schedule.

PROFESSOR: Does anyone have anything to add?

STUDENT #5:   Give us time to do work in class. Other teachers do.

COORDINATOR: We gave it to you last week. The idea behind the homework was simple: First, you'd read it. Second, you'd answer questions. And third, we'd discuss it in class. Instead, we're talking here of doing simple homework assignments that shouldn't be that hard—fifteen to twenty minutes to do the reading and ten minutes to answer questions.

STUDENT #5:   But we have other classes.

COORDINATOR: But other kids have classes too! This is a fact of life.

PROFESSOR [*to* STUDENT #1, *who had recently completed his first project*]:   Why'd you decide to do the work?

STUDENT #1:   I didn't want to get further behind.

STUDENT #8:   We're still wasting time. Lots of kids have got jobs.

STUDENT #3:   We've got cleaning and cooking to do.

COORDINATOR: It's a tension between having a job and responsibilities at home and doing the work you need to do to get a good, quality education. We need to move on.

PROFESSOR: We've only got four minutes till break. I disagree with people who say a class like this is a waste. Part of the problem is that we don't admit these problems are real. It's not a waste of time. For the U.S. history students, here's what we'll do. . . . [T]he coordinator will take those people who have to finish the timeline from 1800 to 1840 and they'll make up questions for their quiz. Those who haven't given their oral history presentations yet will meet with me.

During the between-period break the professor helped two girls with their timelines and two boys stayed in the room to work.

In the second half of class students were grouped according to the projects they were doing. When working with those writing oral histories, the professor explained, "Instead of getting information from history books, you'll work as historians do. You'll get information from real people and write your own historical narratives." He then outlined how students could devise questions to test hypotheses they had posed. The coordinator assisted those doing timelines.

Some students had their notebooks or texts open and were reading and writing. Others did little. One boy slumped in his chair and read a spy novel. Two girls continued a conversation begun at the start of class. When the coordinator interrupted their conversation and told them to "get to work," the conversation ended but, once his attention was elsewhere, it began again. Two boys added up their work hours and asked the coordinator a few "work-related" questions:

"Is there time-and-a-half over forty hours? . . . Double-time for holidays, right?" When the coordinator told them to work on their projects, they assured him they were. A student working in the professor's group moved his desk and joined two friends in conversation. Seeing one student doing little, the coordinator remarked, "Get your books out. There are still twelve minutes left in class." As soon as he helped another student, this student joined a group of his friends. Realizing this, the coordinator again told him to do some work. The student responded, "I need a pencil." The coordinator replied, "There's always a reason. It's just a stall."

As the end of class neared, the coordinator reminded students once more of the work they still had to complete:

> On Wednesday we'll have three people taking the timeline test. Others may be ready for the oral history presentation. Those who can't do your oral histories as planned will have theirs rescheduled. . . . People still have timelines to hand in and there are some who still need to complete their oral history projects. Also, we will begin the research paper project next month.

Shortly thereafter, the period ended.

SUMMARY. As in previous classes, many students did little required work. Of the seventeen U.S. history students, only one had finished the oral history—the year's first project. Of the three timelines and homework assignments that should have been completed, students collectively submitted about twenty percent of the work, some of which would have to be redone because it received a grade below 75. Only one student received a passing grade for either of the first two quarters. Moreover, students and teachers still expressed differing views of the performance-based curriculum, differences highlighted in the student-teacher dialogue that arose in the first half of the class. Students also continued to collectively resist the teachers' efforts—bolstering one another's arguments and adding new concerns for the teachers to address. And this negotiation appeared to strain faculty patience, although the teachers were never abusive or unconcerned with issues students raised. While the professor acknowledged, "Part of the problem is we don't admit that these problems are real," the teachers still seemed confident that students could complete the assignments. The coordinator, for instance, worked over eight hours to develop a matrix of the work students needed to complete, with less concern for delineating how to do the projects. Further, his comments were directed more toward motivating students to complete assignments ("Do take advantage of [vacation] to get some school work done"), than explaining how to do the work.

There were also signs that the teachers had restructured their assignments and adjusted their expectations toward more traditional conceptions of school work, in the coordinators' words, toward "something as simple as reading six pages and doing a few questions." Still, some students seemed confused. As one said, "[W]e have oral history projects, timelines, and tests. We don't even know *key* where to start." Students also characterized their situation as inequitable. One threatened to leave the class and school. Yet others had begun to complete assignments and a few remained in the *→ can* classroom during break to work on projects. And as in previous *be done* classes, with many different messages circulating within the classroom it was difficult to assess why students did little work— some were confused, some felt they were being treated unfairly, others wanted to avoid any work. Nonetheless, all three reactions intertwined into the same end: students completed few assignments.

May 23, 1988

INTRODUCTORY NOTE. *By the fourth quarter about half the class had begun to complete projects. Others turned in little work. In late April, the teachers stopped covering new material, as students spent most class time working on projects. There was also much less student-teacher negotiation. On this day, the coordinator and professor taught the class.*

The coordinator began class by reading a note from the student teacher:

Hello everyone! I'm still waiting expectantly for [the coordinator] to give me all the work you need to be finishing up. Remember, your written exam is only two-and-a-half weeks away! Now is not the time to slack off. Half of your grade for the year will depend on the work you do in the next few weeks. So get to it! Remember you are invited to my graduation.

A student then raised his hand and asked why he received a grade of P on his report card. The coordinator explained that the dean of students put Ps on report cards to let parents know that students were technically passing—with a grade between 60 and 74—but were incomplete for U.S. history.[5] Next, he handed out lists of the work each student had to complete to pass the course, "so all of us know what you have to finish to get full credit." While doing so he remarked, "A number of people are doing very well. It's tremendous to see the progress that's taking place with some of you." At the top of each page it read:

> You still have a large number of assignments to complete. If you complete them satisfactorily by June 10th, you will receive FULL CREDIT for U.S. History. If not, you will need to continue U.S. History with a half-year course in September.

Each sheet listed the projects and homework assignments students had to complete, followed by a section entitled, "A note about homework." It read:

> Please do your work on lined composition paper. Make it neat. Use margins on both sides of the paper, complete sentences, and good English. Skip one line after each answer. Also, make sure you have identified each assignment with a title and page numbers. Identify three themes, three people, three events, and three ideas which are most important within the pages of each homework assignment. Show why they are important to U.S. History.

At the bottom of the page it read: "I have received this paper and will show it to my parent/guardian. Furthermore, I will return a signed copy to [the coordinator] by June 1, 1988."

After distributing these lists, the coordinator addressed the class:

> What you have here is what's left for you to do in this course. You should keep a few dates in mind when completing this work. Today's objective is to work on the timelines. On Wednesday—it's probably a good idea to write this down—those of you still completing timelines can do so, but timeline number six should be about ready. Once this is done, you should prepare to take the oral test that will cover material you have created for your timelines all year, from 1763 to 1920. For this oral exam, you will have to identify twelve of fifteen events and two of three themes with four examples for each theme to defend your point of view.

The professor then noted, "When you're ready, bring the timelines with you because the exam will be based on your timelines." The coordinator added, "And you will be questioned on specific dates and why they were important." The coordinator continued, "For Friday, you'll work on the timelines again. Don't put it off! You *can't* put it off. It may be inconvenient but we're running out of time. On June first and sixth, you'll review for the comprehensive final that will cover from 1763 to 1920. That exam will be on June eighth and tenth." He then explained the difference between the oral and written components of the exam. A student asked, "How do we prepare for the oral exam?" The coordinator replied, "You've already been given handouts that explain that." He added, "You also have to do a special project . . . and lots of people are going great guns. The rest of you who are at different levels of completion have your work laid out for you."

At this point three students left the room with the professor to take their oral exams. The coordinator then showed students a "timeline assembly sheet" the team constructed to help students with the timelines. The sheets had two parallel lines that ran lengthwise and divided the paper into thirds. Each line was cut perpendicularly by equally spaced dashes, much like what one would expect two parallel timelines to look like if no dates were listed. Students were instructed to "pencil in the years next to the vertical lines, tape the pieces together so they follow chronological order, and pencil in your events." Following this explanation, the coordinator helped individual students. He told one that she should complete her second quarter work before beginning anything new. He told another she needed to improve the map included with her timeline. Most of the class appeared to be working, textbooks were open, papers were out, and students were writing.

The coordinator continued to circulate among students. He answered a boy's question about his map. He told a girl who joined the class after finishing Western civ, "You've still got lots of work to do but if you can finish it, you'll be halfway through the course and you'll be in a position to complete the course next year." During the second half of class, the coordinator balanced his efforts among working with students on projects, disciplining those whose attention wandered, and imploring students to complete their work. While helping one group of students he remarked, "You can still get a half credit if you finish this work. If you really want to push hard and finish the course, you can still do that." As the class ended he told students: "It's just a matter of doing it, getting in there and getting the work done."

SUMMARY. This class differed from the previous four in one important respect: there was little negotiation or disruptive student behavior. Various factors contributed to this development. For one, much of the work was more traditional and was structured so that smaller assignments built toward the final projects, as contrasted with presenting students with the final projects at the outset of the course. Also, some students had learned how to complete the work properly and the teachers allowed them substantial class time to do their work. Further, the teachers did not push those students who clearly would not complete the course that year. And even though the assignments had taken on more of a traditional structure, the coordinator, at least, seemed assured that students could do the work. The "note about homework," for instance, stressed procedural matters (use of margins and including page numbers), while never addressing intellectual strategies. His remarks regarding the timelines, oral exam, and the timeline assembly sheet were comparable—focusing on due dates and structural techniques and saying nothing about relevant academic skills. When a student asked, "How do we prepare for the exam?" he replied, "You've already been given handouts that explain that." When class ended he stated, "It's just a matter of doing it. . . ."

June 7, 1988

INTRODUCTION. *Nearing the end of the year, negotiation was virtually nonexistent. About half the class was working while the other half did little. For most of the period students worked on their projects.*

To begin class a student named Thomas presented his "special project." Although critical of the performance-based structure, as the year progressed he was one of the first students to complete assignments. Sitting in the front of the room, Thomas began by playing a tape of a symphonic overture. After a few minutes of music, students' attention drifted. Some socialized. One girl read the yearbook. Another read her text. Thomas responded, "If you're not going to listen to my report, I'm not giving it." From the back of the room the coordinator signaled with his hand as if to say, "Let's get going." Thomas then posed a question, "What is aviation?" After discussing the legend of Daedalus and Icarus, he chronologically listed a series of dates from aviation history: the first helicopter flight, breaking the sound barrier, the first flight into outer space, and so on. When he reached the present he played another song, "Rock Steady," by Sting. As the song played, many students directed their attention elsewhere. One boy took a girl's shoe and passed it to a friend. Thomas sat in front of class and listened to the music.

After a few minutes of Sting, the coordinator approached the front of the class, apparently to talk with Thomas. Seeing this, Thomas reacted, "Let's have a big round of applause for Sting." He then played a tape of a crowd roaring and announced, "Now, let's get back to the report." Before he said anything else, a student asked, "Why are you playing songs?" He replied, "It's my special project, I'll do what I want." He went on to mention the role played by aviation in times of war—from the use of balloons in the Civil War, to synchronized machine guns on propeller planes, to the aircraft carriers of modern warfare. After briefly describing the use of air power in World Wars I and II, the Korean War, and the Vietnam War he dedicated a third song to the pilots who fought in these conflicts— Bruce Springsteen's version of "War." When the song ended, Thomas announced, "That concludes my report." The student teacher, however, asked him to explain why he chose this topic. He continued:

> My whole family was in the service, the Air Force and Marines. They told me of the glory and the problems they had and the great feelings they had and I got involved looking at their scrapbooks, which included a picture of my uncle standing next to a B-52 bomber. I started renting movies and getting into that and I had some dreams about flying and was seeing it on TV and hearing about it from my family and that affected me. It was a dream to my relatives too, but they didn't have the technology. But I have the dream and the technology so I can make it work.

Thomas received a grade of 95 for his report.

For the second half of the period students divided into two groups: those working on projects and those reviewing for the final. The review group worked with the student teacher. She first described the types of questions on the exam: multiple choice, definitions, and matching. She reviewed for the final by reading questions from the exam itself while students called out answers. (For example, "The 'father' of national labor unions?" "Which of the following was NOT a provision of the Missouri Compromise?") In the next class, nine students took the final. It included twenty-seven matching questions, twelve multiple choice, and ten identifications. Students had heard each question at least once two days earlier during the review. Although two periods had been set aside for the exam, every student finished in less than one. One student finished in roughly twenty minutes; she received a 98 on the exam. Two others left shortly thereafter. No one scored below 75.

SUMMARY. By the fourth quarter the teachers appeared to have changed their expectations for student work, a development which, in part, explains the less contentious relations between students and teachers. Consider Thomas' special project. While the syllabus noted

that this project should fulfill three criteria—display in-depth understanding of a topic, illustrate a sense for the student's place in
history, and draw intelligent conclusions from the past about one's
own life choices—nearly half of Thomas' presentation involved
playing taped music. He cited no sources, read from a prepared text,
declined to answer a student's question, and had to be prompted to
explain why he chose his topic. Nonetheless, he received a grade of
95. In the exam review the student teacher covered every question
that was on the final. Also, students had considerable time to work on
projects. Those who chose to do so, did; others were encouraged to
work but not pressured.

WHY DID STUDENTS COMPLETE LITTLE WORK?

Certainly, some students in this class wanted to do as little work as
possible. As one student admitted outright, "I didn't do the homework
because I'm lazy." But motivation was not the only factor that came
into play. For one, the course was difficult and different from what
students were accustomed to. As the teachers wrote:

> We feel it is important to stress that the students were right in their
> assessment that the curriculum asked something of them . . . that
> they should have found frightening. The curriculum asked that they
> look for their own place in U.S. history, using the skills and methods
> that historians say are appropriate for the task.

In a fundamental sense, many students were ill-prepared to
succeed in this course. A lecture on the American Revolution, for
instance, revealed one student's deficiency in note taking. To begin
class, the professor outlined the topics to be covered on the board.
While lecturing, he and the student teacher interjected suggestions
about how to take notes and encouraged students to be diligent note
takers. As he constructed a timeline for the period 1763 to 1783, he
explained why he called it the "Age of American Revolution," because
various "revolutions" occurred—economic, political, and social. To
substantiate his point, he discussed battles, social changes, and
political developments and explained how each fit with the theme.
After twenty minutes of explanation, a student with a blank notepad
raised his hand and asked, "So what do we write?" Moreover, even
when the teachers restructured the course so that smaller, more
traditional assignments built toward the final projects, they were still
unclear as to how students would complete that work.

Students, many of whom were limited-English proficient, also had problems with reading comprehension. When a group of Western civ students were to act as lawyers for a trial of Robespierre during the French Revolution and write an essay either attacking or defending his actions, they did not know the meaning of "reign" from "Reign of Terror," "address" as in "you are addressing the jury," or "views" when asked how "Robespierre's views had changed." They encountered these problems reading the directions. Eventually, such terms as "absolute power," "guillotine," and "power in the hands of the people," among others, proved troublesome. Later in the year the following questions would be posed of some of these same students, as well as other students with weak language skills: "Define racism and explain its persistence despite the freeing of slaves and the passage of new civil rights laws"; and "Write an essay that shows how the following go together: the Compromise of 1850, the Fugitive Slave Law, *Uncle Tom's Cabin*, the Kansas-Nebraska Act, and the emergence of the Republican Party."

Student explanations for why they completed little work were also consistent with notions of the course's difficulty and their lack of academic skills. When the teachers administered an open-ended survey in late January to assess why few assignments had been turned in, six of eleven respondents explicitly said the work was "confusing." In an interview, one student linked her difficulties with the timeline to the novelty of the course, "The timelines are very different from the things I used to do. Last year, I answered questions in a book and took tests. Now, I have to read books, find important events and dates, do an oral history, and write essays. It's really different." Another explained, "The teachers never give assignments to you one at a time . . . so you mix it all up in your mind and you get confused. I've never had a course presented in this format before [i.e., told what to do for the entire year]. . . . I can never remember being given as much as two weeks advance assignments before." Even students who did well in the course encountered problems. Elena Santa Rosa (the student quoted in Chapter 1), received the highest grade of the class, 98, and described the course as "very challenging. . . . the hardest Essential School course that I've taken."[6]

Furthermore, some students said they completed little work because the teachers' expectations were unfair. As the following remarks suggest—relative to the other Essential School U.S. history class, classes in other Eastown schools, and their collective sense of reasonable expectations—students felt they were treated inequitably:

Everyone argues about this U.S. history class. They all want to go to Mr. Nolet's class [the other Essential School history class] because you just work from the book—read the book, answer questions, and have tests. We have tests on timelines and it's not fair. And they know it. Everyone in U.S. history says there's too much work and it's too confusing.

There's so much work . . . and [the teachers] have never explained much of anything. We're a pretty good class, but we're not perfect. We don't understand all this stuff. . . . It's not something you'd expect an average tenth grade U.S. history class to do. My cousins at Archibald High [another Eastown school] don't do anything like what we're doing. Why should I?

At the start of the year, we had to do so much in a little time, the oral history projects and timelines at the same time. And we were told we were going to have tests at the end of the year. . . . I never had that much information at once before. . . . There was just too much to do in such a little amount of time. They were piling it up and piling it up. It was too much.

Student feelings regarding the complexity and inequity of the course structure and requirements were exacerbated by a common student reaction to academic confusion and frustration: doing nothing. As one girl said during class, "[Y]ou said we could do [the timeline] like this, and then when we did it, we got confused. . . . [I]t makes us mad and we're so confused that we just might not do it." The pervasiveness of such reactions was evident in January when the teachers surveyed students and asked: "What do you think will happen if you don't hand in your homework and timelines?" Of eleven respondents, every one acknowledged that they would receive an incomplete, stay back, or fail the course. Some sample responses are revealing:

I probably would get an incomplete, but I don't care because their[7] rushing me to do everything, they never give you time to finish what you started.

Nothing. Just stay back. Never graduate until 1991.

I will fall behind and fail miserably.

I'll fail and have to complete U.S. history next year.

Given their feelings of confusion and inequity, students felt justified in this reaction. Doing nothing and accepting failure was a valid and common response. And one's peers were likely to validate such decisions.

STUDENT NEGOTIATION AND ITS CONSEQUENCES

As the vignettes revealed, students and teachers held different views about many aspects of this course, in particular, the performance-based curriculum. For the teachers there were clear connections between homework, class work, projects, and exams. They felt that the Essential School's incomplete policy meshed well with their goals. They expected that allowing students to be their own historians would motivate students. Yet most students viewed things differently. Many found the work overwhelming. They questioned the incomplete policy. To be told assignments were "inadequate" and had to be redone was difficult for them to appreciate. It was also beyond common expectations.

Because of these differences students and teachers spent much class time negotiating what the course would entail, a development which had clear consequences for the education students received. For one, there was simply less time for academics. Rather than educating students, the teachers directed considerable time and effort into addressing the seemingly endless concerns that arose.

Negotiation also strained student-teacher relations (Good and Brophy, 1987; Woods, 1983), and thereby reinforced a common faculty conception of Russell students—as disrespectful and intellectually apathetic (although each teacher did so to varying degrees). A co-authored document written by the coordinator and Russell's principal the year this particular course was studied, the "Russell High School Long-Term Planning Outline: 1987–1991," spoke to this perception:

> Within the classroom there is a feeling of frustration on the part of teachers, that they have no impact on students. . . . Many wonder out loud if these students are capable of learning anything. . . . There is an attempt by the faculty and administration to create the atmosphere of trust until abused, however, the condition of the student body is such that it may be difficult for us to feel this is really the way we operate. There are too many kids ready to skip classes, skip school, use obscene language, or show disrespect for teachers and staff.

Following a class she found especially trying, the student teacher voiced her frustration with student behavior:

It was like a torture chamber. . . . The hardest thing about teaching these kids is I feel like most of them don't like me. [The university professor] says that shouldn't affect my teaching. But if you feel students are hostile, it affects your teaching. . . . The thing that gets me maddest is their behavior, toward me and each other. I take so much abuse. . . . They send me very clear signals about their feelings. That's why I hated standing up in front of them. . . . Just giving them announcements, much less a lecture. That was the worst. I hate this adversarial role in the classroom. . . . And I've assumed responsibility for why they don't like the class.[8]

In late May the coordinator expressed frustration with student reactions to the team's most recent effort to get them to complete work—a detailed listing of assignments they had yet to complete:

[W]e handed out those papers last week . . . to let [students] know exactly what work they still have to do. We laid it out for students. We're saying, "This is what you've got to do." We tried as hard as possible to put together a precise accounting of what students need to do to pass. We did it for every student because we wanted to make it clear that this is what needs to be done. Some students are very good at deceiving themselves into believing that they've done enough work to complete the course. Kids try to weasel their way out. . . . I try to put the responsibility on the students. . . . [but] I think part of the problem is that they're students with low motivation levels, low work output standards. They have gotten by without doing work and they are not willing to keep up with it.

In a jointly authored article, the team alluded to a lack of student effort, which they linked to a flaw in their curriculum, the room for negotiation created by their course structure: "What was designed as an opportunity for students to determine their own work, was seen as an invitation to 'negotiate,' a chance to push to see how much students could get away with." In turn, such perceptions influenced students' education. Because the teachers often interpreted student negotiation as reflecting a lack of commitment, not a lack of understanding, they tended to react to the students' actions by trying to motivate them to complete assignments, rather than helping them understand how to do the work.

Perhaps the most detrimental consequence of students' negotiation was simply that it was successful. Students effectively avoided challenging academic work. They succeeded in not learning. Since students consistently united and challenged the teachers, the team came to expect less work and accepted work of lesser quality.[9] Whereas the university professor at first expected students to investigate a range of sources for the timelines, he later noted, "After dealing with the tensions and problems generated in this class, I'd be happy if students just listed ten events on their timelines and did brief essays using only the text as their source." And as the vignettes from later in the school year revealed, such reactions by the teachers led to a more peaceful classroom. In effect, students "rewarded" their teachers for easing up on their standards.

Juxtaposing the teachers' initial project conceptions with student performances reveals just how some expectations changed. In the syllabus the teachers outlined the oral history project: "Each student will do . . . background reading and interview at least four people to uncover a change that occurred over time, and to find answers to three hypotheses of their own devising." In the three presentations I observed, no student cited background reading or discussed "change over time." Most read primarily from prepared texts. A girl named Jessica, for example, began her oral history on "recent American immigrants" by asking students to close their eyes and imagine being tortured, leaving their homeland, and having their family separated. Jessica said this happened to a person she interviewed. She then read her report for about a minute before she began flipping through pages, saying she had lost her place. After briefly trying to continue, she asked, "Can I do this another time? I don't know what happened to my pages." The student teacher told Jessica to organize her papers while the class read an article describing a recent change in U.S. immigration policy. Ten minutes later, Jessica began again. For the rest of the presentation she read directly from her report but still had difficulty arranging her pages and organizing her remarks. She never stated an hypothesis but noted in conclusion, "Immigrants came to the U.S. to prosper; most immigrants want a good education before they will return home; and illegal immigrants will prosper if given a chance." She received a grade of 80.

Student performance on the timelines also suggested that the teachers found it difficult to hold to consistent standards. Some work, for instance, seemed to have been plagiarized and ill-informed. As one boy identified Theodore Roosevelt:

> Lieutenant Colonel. A excellent soldier in the Spanish-American War. *Roosevelt ordered commodore George Dewey to attack the Spanish Warship. He finished the Spaniards off in seven hours. These rests of the fleet in North America was bottled up in Southeastern of Cuba.*

Except for errors, the material in italics directly parallels the text. For the Fugitive Slave Act the student wrote:

> The Fugitive Slave Act was an act about city authorities and even plain citizens to assist in the capture and return of runaway slaves.

Except for errors, this is exactly as the text. The student received a 75.

For his Civil War timeline another student described General Lee: "Confederate General. A Genius at Combat Strategy." For General Grant he wrote: "Future president is credited with the slow painful decimation of the confederate forces." Other answers were similar. While none were copied from the text, the errors in grammar and capitalization and use of terms such as "slow painful decimation" suggest that an encyclopedia was used. He received a grade of 75. Moreover, these examples of student work represented appreciable portions of the course requirements. The special project in which Thomas played taped music nearly as long as he spoke was worth one-seventh of his final grade. The same was true for the final exam that was reviewed the class prior to its administration and Jessica's oral history project.

Although the teachers modified their expectations, this did not reflect a lack of effort. Throughout the year they spent substantial time developing their curriculum, coordinating efforts, and grading student work. Yet their work was hindered by a misunderstanding that points to a final consequence of student-teacher negotiation: negotiation made it difficult for the teachers to differentiate student apathy from ignorance and refusing to work because of perceived inequities—especially since all three student reactions often had the same end result: students did little work. Whenever the teachers solicited feedback on why students had difficulty completing course work, someone usually admitted to being lazy. When given class time to work, some students did little.

But classroom interactions were often hectic. When students provided feedback on the course, the teachers heard a range of ambiguous responses. To articulate their problems, students needed to understand both the course goals and learning processes in general. But these high school sophomores had little, if any, experience assessing their own learning. Consider the class when the student teacher asked a girl why she thought her timeline was inadequate and she responded, "Because I put something, then changed it, then put something, then changed it. I don't know!" Or when the student teacher asked, "Is the book the problem?" and

not able to assess own learning.

students offered various suggestions—from watching a movie about the time period to surveying students on their reasons for not doing work—but never addressed the issue of their ability to understand the text. This was the only course I encountered at Russell High where students were asked to assess their own learning and, not surprisingly, they seemed ill-equipped to do so. Thus, it was relatively easy for the teachers to interpret students' actions as a lack of effort since students could not effectively articulate their confusion but their resistance and failure to complete work were readily apparent.

CONCLUSION: LOW CULTURAL AND SOCIAL CAPITAL IN ACTION

One way to understand what occurred in this U.S. history course is to frame this experience in terms of students' cultural and social capital (Bourdieu, 1985; Coleman, 1990; Coleman, et al., 1966). That is, in terms of the degree to which they possessed the resources, knowledge, skills, attitudes, and social ties that are valued and linked with success and influence in society; phrased somewhat differently, whether their personal histories suggested they were likely to be a success in American society. Specifically, cultural capital includes one's economic well-being as well as how effectively one has internalized the behavioral norms of the dominant social group(s)—their speech, dress, beliefs, and so on. In this case, students lacked such fundamental academic skills as reading, writing, and note taking. Their interaction styles could be abusive. Comments such as, "This is stupid," and "I'm not doin' it," were unlikely to engender adult respect and understanding. And their attitudes toward formal education led them to challenge any additional work the teachers proposed. In the classroom, they were seldom inquisitive, deferent, or informed.

Social capital, a closely related phenomenon, derives from the "social networks and relationships between adults and children . . . within the family, but also in the community . . . that are of value for the child's growing up" (Coleman, 1990: 334). Such networks may include friends, neighbors, teachers, clergy, community leaders, and counselors. These people not only support you in your life's endeavors but they provide role models and inspiration. They may help you realize what is needed to graduate high school or get admitted to college as well as inspiring you to do so, creating possibilities in your world. But in this U.S. history classroom students' peers represented a source of negative social capital; they supported each other in

[handwritten: lack of equity (?)]

"achieving failure" (McDermott, 1987). And in many respects they made it harder for their teachers, a potential source of social capital, to develop productive, ongoing relationships with them. (Although analytically distinct, the concepts of cultural and social capital overlap in many respects. Where appropriate, I collapse these categories and refer to them collectively as "personal capital.")

Relative to Eastown's three other high schools,[10] Russell students were disproportionately likely to be a person of color and to have low family income levels, high residential mobility, limited-English proficiency, and low levels of educational attainment in their families.[11] All of these factors correlate with limited personal capital and all could influence students' educational experiences. (This topic is expanded upon in the next chapter.)

Yet there is an alternative and complementary way to understand this sociological phenomenon. That is, to consider low personal capital from the point of view of those who lack this resource. In their formal education, they probably haven't seen themselves or the people they identify with highlighted in the curriculum, teaching their classes, or serving as school administrators (although the teachers in this course explicitly sought to help students "define" their own place in American history). Their linguistic styles and language learned at home and in their communities may be unacceptable or ineffective in the classroom. Their parents likely have had little, if any, involvement at their schools as well as little understanding of the educational system (McLaughlin, 1993). Suspensions, failures, and dropouts may be more common in their educational histories than graduations, commendations, and awards. What they are asked to do in their classes may have little relevance to their lives outside school (Connell, 1993; Noddings, 1992). For many of these students, schools are alien places where "success" entails embracing, to some degree, linguistic styles, behaviors, and attitudes seen as "foreign, conflictive, contradictory, and denigrating" (Stanton-Salazar, 1996: 1).

In such situations it is common for students to generate a subculture with values that run counter to schools' official goals (Coleman, 1961; Cusick, 1973; Everhart, 1983; Ogbu, 1987; Steinberg, et al., 1996; Willis, 1977).[12] In effect, students define education as a secondary concern. At Russell, failing or ignoring work that was frustrating was appropriate for confused, rebellious, or lazy students. It is therefore not surprising that students reacted so consistently in their history class: they found the work confusing and it did not accord with what was expected of them or their friends in most classes.

Of course, students were not forced to react this way. One girl earned a 98 for the course. Still, students could not control the actions of all their peers. Since many students shared a common sense of confusion, frustration, and inequity, their collective resistance took a toll on the teachers and encouraged them to give students what they wanted: lower standards (Brophy and Evertson, 1981: 52; Good and Brophy, 1987; Page, 1987a: 96, 1987b: 451). Nonetheless, there were students in this history class (and the school at-large) who were diligent, respectful, and committed to learning. Yet for them, the consequences were essentially the same as for those who were disruptive and resistant.

As is argued throughout this book, culture highlights and validates; it can also obscure and undermine. Although from my detached perspective the collective and shared came to the forefront in this class, those enacting this social drama on a day-in and day-out basis saw things more in individual terms. That is how most Americans understand educational opportunity, and this cultural predisposition is difficult to displace. At the end of the year the teachers and many students still talked about educational success and failure in individual terms. In May and June, as some students had projects accepted, they attributed this to their decision to begin working, not that teachers accepted less demanding work and had given them increasing amounts of class time to finish projects. As one girl said, "I guess everybody seen that they was failing so they started doing their work. At first they all played around but then at the last minute *they decided to do the work*. They played around because some don't feel like doing the work. *They were just lazy*" (emphasis added). Another student accounted for his improved performance in similar terms, "I messed up the work at first. . . . I got fed up and did little. I stopped working and did no makeup because I kept getting things back. So my response was—'I won't do it.' At the end of the third quarter, *I started working harder because I had to get it done* or I'd have to do it again next year" (emphasis added). When asked about her incomplete grade, a girl who early in the year often questioned whether the teachers' expectations were fair, remarked, "I have an incomplete now but *it's my fault* because from all the frustrations I just said, 'Forget it. I'm not doing work for awhile.' Then I realized that it was hurting me not them, *so now I get it done* " (emphasis added). And Thomas, the student whose oral presentation was described and who teachers felt made significant improvements during the year, could suggest no reason but increased effort to explain his performance, "I don't know what made me turn it around. I just said, 'I don't want to waste any more time. *I just have to do it*' " (emphasis added).

Although during the year students maintained that teacher expectations were unreasonable and that their problems with assignments were tied to the teachers' inability to clarify their expectations, by the end of the year, like the teachers, many students said they were responsible for completing their work. When teachers accepted their assignments, they attributed this to individual effort, it was mainly a matter of deciding to do it.

Moreover, the teachers maintained that they had not lowered their expectations. When students began completing homework, they linked this to their willingness to design assignments that were, as they wrote, "a compromise between teacher-imposed structure and student responsibility to choose and interpret material from the text." Reflecting on their standards, the coordinator stated during a seminar on school reform that he conducted with the professor, "In the end, the kids did not play games. They understood the seriousness of the responsibility that we gave them." And the team wrote: "As teachers, we feel the best way to deal with . . . [those not doing work] is to maintain consistently high standards and to change student expectations about what it means to be in school." In many ways, the teachers and students still saw educational opportunity as available to those students who wanted to learn.

Two final points regarding student power in the classroom are worth noting. First, while the teachers sought to create a democratic classroom and to share power with students, many students felt they were treated unfairly.[13] Even though the teachers and students established a collaborative process for addressing issues that arose, neither group ever explicitly sought to resolve any tensions that surfaced that year through a democratic process. This is no surprise. Given the nature of American schooling, neither group had any experience doing so. Second, while students seemed largely unconcerned with the formal power teachers offered, they exercised an amazing degree of informal power. Yet given what transpired, it is difficult to envision that they in any way benefited from their actions. They had won the battle; the war, however, was another matter.

equality = standards same

equity = skills to achieve standards

3

LOW CULTURAL AND
SOCIAL CAPITAL, CONTINUED

Instead of the principals trying to set up activities
for us—a fund-raiser or something where we can
have fun—they're worried about whether you
have a pass or who's been suspended lately. . . . I
think if they would do things with us or make it
more fun, or have activities or something to get us
more into school, there wouldn't be any fighting.
They're always worried about somebody smoking
and fighting, or who's writing graffiti on the wall,
or something like that. They don't think about
what they can do to make us *want* to come to
school.

—A Russell High Student

The previous chapter provided a sense for what low cultural and
social capital could look like in a classroom setting. Making a similar
analysis from an institution-wide point of view, this chapter examines
how the effects of students' low personal capital reverberated
throughout Russell High, shaping school policies and practices in
ways that disadvantaged students. Again emphasizing the collective
nature of the school's population, this analysis of educational
opportunity in practice begins by considering the composition of
Russell High and its structural position *vis-à-vis* the Eastown School
System, a system which not only tracked students within schools but

which itself was essentially "tracked." As Jeannie Oakes found in her research on tracking within schools, "Despite meritocratic justifications and democratic intent, [there was] an unequal distribution of learning opportunities in a direction that favors the already privileged" (1986: 63). Certain Eastown schools, for instance, enrolled disproportionate numbers of the affluent and educated, those with high levels of personal capital; other schools enrolled mainly low-income, persons of color, those with low levels of personal capital.[1] And these differences influenced the education students experienced. At Russell, the administration's overriding concern—maintaining an orderly school—was shaped by prevailing perceptions of students as a collective: perceptions that reflected the school's past as well as its present. Every new class of students was guilty by association, their reputations blemished by the original sin imposed on all Russell students. This was a bad high school, so it must have bad students. Further, the school's population, because of its high level of residential mobility, essentially determined what guidance counselors would do: process students into and out of the school. And the apathy, belligerence, and intellectual shortcomings of many Russell students encouraged teachers to strike compromises with them. Order and peace of mind were given priority and preserved; learning was often secondary. In this chapter, I explore these developments and how they shaped educational opportunity for Russell students.

RUSSELL HIGH AND THE EASTOWN SCHOOL SYSTEM

Russell High is one of five magnet high schools in Eastown. The student body, which generally included about 1,000 students during my research, was quite diverse. In September 1987 (my second year of research), African Americans comprised the largest single student group, forty-five percent. Twenty-one percent of the school were Hispanic, fifteen percent were white, eight percent were Portuguese, six percent were Asian, and five percent were Cape Verdean. (This ethnic distribution remained consistent throughout my research.) Within Eastown's secondary school structure, Russell was designated an "arts and communication" magnet—offering courses in theater, chorus, art, photography, video production, and dance—with about fifteen percent of the school participating in the program. As a member of the Coalition of Essential Schools, Russell also had an Essential School that enrolled thirty percent of the school's students. A special education program enrolled six percent of the student body, and the English-as-a-second-language (ESL) program included nearly one-quarter of the student population. The remaining twenty-five percent of the student body were enrolled in a comprehensive high school program and tracked according to a three-tier system.

The Eastown School System implemented the magnet structure in the late seventies to address desegregation mandates voluntarily, rather than having a plan imposed by federal courts. Of the other four public high schools, Travis High is a science magnet, Archibald High is a business/vocational magnet, Latin High is a college preparatory school, and there is a small alternative high school.[2] Four schools have open enrollment—virtually all interested students are accepted. Latin High has an entrance exam. Those who elect none of these options are enrolled in comprehensive programs at their appropriate zoned high school—Travis, Archibald, or Russell. Although the school system adopted the magnet structure to improve educational opportunity for all students, the system itself threw issues of equity into question. Most upper-income, white students, those with high levels of personal capital, attended private schools, parochial schools, or Latin High, the only public high school with an entrance exam. During my research Latin enrolled on average a higher percentage of white students, roughly seventy-five percent, than any other public school in the city, not just high schools. Middle-to-low-income whites attended parochial schools or the science magnet, Travis High, which had a fifty/fifty mix of working class white students and students of color. Archibald High, the business/vocational magnet, enrolled about seventy percent students of color and thirty percent working class whites. From 1986 through 1991, Russell enrolled between eighty and eighty-five percent students of color.[3]

Within Eastown, Russell had a poor reputation. When teachers were setting up the Essential School and looking to recruit students, the school's reputation hindered their efforts. As *The Eastown Gazette* reported in March 1986:

> The image of Russell High as a poor place to learn has made it difficult to attract students to an experimental program there. . . . The program coordinator told the School Board, "I have found, to my dismay, that the image of the school is so low that it is difficult to get students to go into this program. . . ." He believes the image is a "hangover" from the school's troubled period in the late 1960s and 1970s. . . .
>
> According to an interim report on the Essential School. . . . "Russell once attracted many high-achieving students, but now these students turn their educational interests toward the city's college preparatory high school or a variety of private and parochial schools."

Indeed, many students sought to avoid Russell High. A Latin High graduate from Russell's feeder pattern expressed a common sentiment when he recalled Latin's entrance exam, "Forget college exams. They were nothing. The most frightened I ever was taking an exam was when I took the entrance exam for Latin. If I failed that, I would have gone to Russell."[4] In fact, few students from the affluent Lesh Park neighborhood, where Russell High is located, attended the school, the exception being a core of African American students from an enclave within the neighborhood. More than half the students were bussed to Russell from Nelson Heights, a low-income neighborhood.

THE ADMINISTRATION

If one never knew that Russell High was a school and you happened into the building you might think the school's administrators were actually a squad of police detectives. Wearing coats and ties, they walked the school's corridors, stopping students to question them, usually asking for passes. During lunch, one principal worked the lunchroom, another patrolled school grounds, the third remained in the main office. So they could communicate instantly with one another, they all carried walkie-talkies. Both assistant principals had their own offices and secretaries whose main responsibility entailed processing passes, lists, and disciplinary forms the principals generated. Because of all the paperwork, when possible, student assistants were recruited to help the secretaries. In brief, controlling students and keeping the building orderly were high priorities for Russell's administrators.

Early in their high school experience, students learned this. On the first day of school in 1986, the principal greeted freshmen at the orientation assembly:

> You are now beginning your high school education. This is probably the greatest opportunity of your lives. As a high school dropout, with no formal training, your chances of succeeding in life are next-to-nothing. You need to start on the right foot. . . . Come to school every day. Do your homework. Take school seriously. . . . Take advantage of the opportunities you'll have at Russell High for the next few years and you'll transform yourself from a child into an adult. . . . Also, you need to follow the rules. Don't be in the corridors without a pass. If you are and I catch you, you won't be at Russell long. Don't cut classes and head to "The Avenue" [a local commercial district and student hangout]. We have a special arrangement with police.

They know to be on the lookout for Russell students. They'll pick you up if they see you.

The following September, the assistant principals emphasized disciplinary matters during freshman orientation. As one addressed students:

Welcome to Russell High. I am Mr. Hartnett. I will be in charge of discipline for your class this year. I hope that I won't see you in my office. The last time I had a 9th grade class [as my official responsibility], I had almost 500 suspensions.[5] Let that be a sign that we won't fool around. If you don't fit in, you won't be here. Besides the 500 student suspensions, lots of others were forced to leave the school.

The other assistant principal also stressed school rules and the consequences for disobeying them:

Welcome to Russell High. I need to make a few things clear so let me run them down quickly: no one gets into the building until 8:15, unless you're in the [government-subsidized] breakfast program. You have to be in your homeroom by 8:25 and it's better to be on time than staying for Mr. Hartnett for an hour. If you're chronically late, Mr. Hartnett will deal with you in other ways. The real world wants you to be on time. Being late is not acceptable. People who don't sign-in to the late room are suspended. The other thing you'll find out very quickly is we don't like to see people in the corridor. We expect you to show us your pass. We don't expect to have to ask. We won't accept the excuse that you're late to school. Be on time. Be where you belong at all times, and you'll be fine.[6]

Control, order, discipline, and rules were prominent concerns for many reasons. In part, this preoccupation derived from a defining moment in the school's history: a violent demonstration by African American students in the spring of 1969 that caused extensive damage to the school as well as a few injuries. For many in Eastown, this signaled the beginning-of-the-end for Russell High as a reputable, academically-oriented school (a topic discussed further in Chapter 6). Over time, this perception intensified as the number of white students attending the school declined while the school system bussed increasingly more low-income students of color from Nelson Heights to Russell. Various occurrences during my research reinforced this perception as well as the principals' concern with order. In the fall of 1986, two Russell soccer players struck the game officials after losing a match. Initially, the league suspended the team for the following season. After two appeals, the suspension was lifted but, as *The Eastown Gazette* reported, it entailed additional responsibilities for administrators:

> [T]here will be a number of supervisors at all Russell games this year to prevent incidents such as the one that occurred last fall. . . . A Russell administrator [will] be assigned to all school athletic events and the school athletic director [will] be assigned to attend all games, home and away. . . . The principal [will] meet with the athletic director, coaching staff, and all team members of all sports to ensure that all rules and regulations are consistently and effectively implemented throughout each season. In addition, the principal will meet regularly during the next academic year with all head coaches, assistant coaches, the athletic director, and athletes to continually reinforce this requirement.

Problems at after-school social events became so difficult that administrators kept them to a minimum. A student editorial in the school paper in April 1991 provides a sense for why:

> ### Why Doesn't Russell Ever Sponsor After-School Events?
> "Why doesn't Russell ever sponsor after-school events?" This is a question that is often asked by many Russell students. The outlandish behavior which took place during the production and then the following party given by our school's multicultural awareness program accurately answers this question.
>
> On Friday, this group presented, "The Ebony Rainbow" in Russell's auditorium to a full house. The production's goal was to educate and create a bond amongst the culturally diverse audience. The show went smoothly, but was not as successful as hoped as far as education and creating a bond. The after-show party in the cafeteria started out as smoothly as the show. Parents, students, and children were dancing, eating and having a good time together. Unfortunately the ignorant conduct of two fights involving Russell students ended the party.
>
> Take heed: the attitude of Russell High students must change. If you fail to do so, you will continue to ask, "Why doesn't Russell ever sponsor any after-school events?"

Russell's administration also worried about non-students coming off the streets to cause problems. The following open letter from a teacher to faculty and administrators, in December 1989, suggests why this was so:

> To Whom It May Concern:
> At approximately 1:10 P.M., I noticed four young, black men cruising the corridor outside of my room. I immediately took the telephone into the corridor and reported their presence to the main office. I described them as outsiders because of their physical maturity and the fact that they were all wearing full-length quilted coats. I also said that they looked like major trouble.
> Five to ten minutes later, three of the four entered my room. Two of them stood at my desk defiantly and one of them swept everything off one end of my desk. I approached them cautiously realizing that their purpose was to at least threaten me. Their actions challenged me to a physical response. As I moved slowly toward the door hoping to keep any violence outside of my class-room, they stationed themselves on either side of my doorway. At this point, I was absolutely certain that I was about to be physically assaulted. There had been no dialogue to this time and as I tried to anticipate their actions by watching their eyes and hands, one or both said something to the effect of "kicking my f – – – – – ass."
> It was at this time that an assistant principal appeared at staircase five. As he slowly advanced toward us, they moved down the corridor. The assistant principal was in communication with the office via walkie-talkie and as I told him of the severity of the situation, he requested police be called. In subsequent conversation with administrators, I learned that as a result of my initial call, the four young men had been located in the gym area. They had been told to leave the building and it was thought they had. Obviously, the three who appeared in my room thought they could carry out their intentions toward me without being apprehended.
> I consider myself truly fortunate to have survived this con-frontation and have no desire to repeat the experience. . . .

As the student editorial and the teacher's letter make clear, maintaining order was not only an administrative priority; students and teachers shared this view.[7] And so did the American public. The 1990 Gallup Poll on the "Public's Attitude Toward Public Schools," for instance, asked respondents which of six "national goals for education" identified by President Bush and the state governors they considered most critical. Fifty-five percent of all respondents, the highest figure for any goal, said the most important was that, "Every school in America [is] free of drugs and violence and offers a disciplined environment

def = low capital

conducive to learning" (Elam, 1990: 42). In listing the "biggest problems facing local public schools in 1990," Gallup's findings were consistent with these emphases: thirty-eight percent of all respondents identified the "use of drugs" as the "most serious problem facing American schools," and nineteen percent said it was a "lack of discipline," by far the most prominent responses from a list of thirty-three (Elam, 1990: 44).

Clearly, Americans want orderly schools. Russell administrators were doing what people wanted; but this did not ensure educational opportunity because of how order was achieved. There were trade-offs, one being that the school lacked a sense of community. As Philip Cusick found at a "disruptive" urban school, control and order came at a price. This school had "no free periods, study halls, or activity periods. . . . [D]ances and parties were rare and later eliminated. Funds were allocated for security guards and almost all of the administrators' time was spent on discipline" (1983: 22). In similar fashion, Russell had no "free periods, study halls, or activity periods." The school hired a security guard to patrol the parking lot the first year of my research and retained the position throughout. While I was there, the school sponsored no after-school dances and few after-school events. Students and teachers mainly saw each other in classrooms for fifty-three-minute snippets of time. Compared with other Eastown high schools, Russell offered a limited number of extracurricular activities and few students participated.

Although the school remained relatively peaceful, students, teachers, and administrators seldom had a chance to learn about each other outside the regimentation of daily routine, to create relationships that might promote greater community, mutual understanding, and respect—those features which make good schools a place people want to be.[8] Quite bluntly, there were few reasons anyone—students, teachers, or administrators—would want to spend time at Russell High. For most of these persons, school was merely a place they came five days a week, 8:30 till 2:30. The hallways and parking lot emptied shortly after school ended each day. Russell High was, for the most part, lifeless and unwelcoming.

Moreover, when administrators emphasize discipline and order, schools may not only surrender a sense of community; academics may suffer as well. As Cusick found, when control is the overriding priority, it becomes "more important to keep [students] in school, in class, and in order than to teach them something and see that they learned it" (1983: 39). During my five years at Russell, administrators seldom participated in faculty professional development work, and I never saw or heard of an administrator ever visiting a teacher's classroom. Administrators therefore had few (if any) opportunities to discuss teaching and curriculum with teachers, and they had limited under-standings of what went on in classrooms. Moreover, they made little effort to influence that arena, even though teaching and learning are ostensibly the *raison d'être* of American schools. Still, the principals' actions were fully understandable: While ensuring control and order does not guarantee learning, enforced passivity, disengagement, and alienation are common in our country's schools. If this is the cost of maintaining order, so be it. From the prevailing American point of view, educational opportunity still exists, even though some populations experience such conditions more often and more intensively than others.

THE GUIDANCE DEPARTMENT

Russell students' limited personal capital also influenced the services they received from the guidance department, largely because of the mobility of the student population. During the 1990–91 school year, for instance, Russell's guidance department processed 910 students into and out of the school (87.4 percent of its student population).[9] That year, guidance counselors at Travis High processed 504 students (37.0 percent of the student population); those at Archibald processed 417 students (23.8 percent of the student population); and those at Latin High processed twenty-eight students (2.4 percent of the student population).[10] This relative trend held true throughout my research. Consequently, Russell's guidance counselors spent most of their time sending and receiving transcripts, matching students with appropriate and available classes, and establishing course credits. They had less time to disseminate information about college admissions, financial aid, vocational opportunities, or the military, to say nothing of helping students with personal or family matters, or difficulties they might have with teachers.

One guidance counselor, new to Russell at the time, said her colleagues referred to the school as the "revolving door," and she quickly found out why: "I spend most of my time tracking down student records from other schools." Because so many students transferred into and out of Russell during the summer of 1987, she spent the entire first quarter settling student schedules. She seldom took lunch or had a free period, but still spent little time with individual students discussing anything other than schedule changes. Describing his "typical day," another guidance counselor said much the same:

> There's no such thing [as a typical day]. I rarely have a set appoint-ment or a set schedule. A parent came in this morning at 9:30 and I

had to meet with him. I'm meeting with a representative from the Chamber of Commerce at 10:30. During lunch, I have to pass out bus tokens.[11] I'll be meeting with a group of Hispanic parents this afternoon. . . . I also have to deal with a 9th grader who wants to be in 11th grade. She says she should be a junior but her course credits were never forwarded. It's easy for that information to get lost in the shuffle. . . . If she gets the information to me, she'll be promoted. Then I have to put the Metropolitan Achievement Test scores on students' personal records.

What is the most valuable service you provide?

I think it's helping students further their education beyond high school. But a lot of times it's important that I just listen to kids and try to help them, however I can, to follow up on things for them. Students have lots of different needs. I try to help as much as I can by doing whatever I can. . . . It's important that I build up trust and respect with students. . . .

How much time do you spend with individual students?

I don't really spend much time at all with individual students. Most of that I do during students' homeroom period. That's when I'm real busy. . . . I try to see all the students in my class [he had 10th graders that year] but I never make it through to seeing every student. Sometimes kids are absent so they miss the meeting. It just hasn't seemed to work to set individual times to meet with students. When I schedule meetings with individual students, I usually only end up getting to see about one of five. . . . But I think most of the 10th graders know I'm their counselor. . . .

What do you feel are the biggest obstacles related to your work?

Paperwork. It's not that big a deal although it does take up a lot of time. It will always be an obstacle. Some people just don't do the paperwork because it can get in the way of doing other things.

What does paperwork generally entail?

The main thing is changing students' status, coming and leaving the school. Setting up schedules for new students that suit their abilities and interests. Sometimes we need to send for personal record cards. Students are supposed to get these cards when they leave a school. . . although that doesn't always happen. I have probably done 300 transactions this year [the interview occurred in June] of a class with 225 students enrolled.

Because of their collective mobility, most Russell students saw guidance counselors only if they had a scheduling problem or during

how does a student enhance capital?

occasional visits counselors made to homerooms. In effect, all Russell students, even those who did not move, were less likely to enhance their social capital by connecting with a key institutional representative, a guidance counselor. Since many of their parents, siblings, and other close relatives and friends had little understanding of the public education system or college admissions process, the lack of time to meet with guidance counselors may have been especially damaging for these students.[12] In contrast, guidance counselors at Eastown's other public high schools, which had less mobile and more affluent students (and essentially the same number of guidance counselors per student), were more able to meet individually with students to help them identify educational goals and discuss strategies to realize them. The second guidance counselor interviewed exposed a contradiction in the structure of Russell High that speaks *inequity* directly to this inequity. On the one hand he claimed, "It's important to build up trust and respect with students." Shortly thereafter, he *not* acknowledged, "I don't really spend much time at all with individual *able* students." In this context, the school system "structurally" restricted *to* Russell students' opportunity to enhance their social capital, while *truly* more affluent and better educated students at other schools faced a *guide.* more advantageous situation.

THE FACULTY

The collective nature of the school population also had an impact on faculty. A small minority of teachers were blatant about the consequences for them. Usually justifying their decision in terms of perceived student apathy, they stopped trying and attempted little in class. But this was a handful. Still, even well-intentioned, hard-working teachers were encumbered by the challenges they faced. Excerpts from interviews with four teachers, selected because they were experienced and conscientious professionals (Hargreaves, 1996), illuminate how they saw working at Russell High and how their perceptions influenced their teaching and relations with students. All had advanced degrees and were widely respected. Two directed extracurricular activities. In the classes I observed, they were prepared, considerate, and seemed concerned with student learning and their general well-being.

EmmyLou Griffith (May 1987)

Ms. Griffith, a Spanish teacher, had taught for ten years at Russell High. In visiting her classes, she appeared to get along well with students. Some came to see her during their free time before school. When she entered the classroom, students often greeted her warmly. She regularly encouraged students to come for extra help whenever they could, before or after school. In observing her teach, I noticed that certain students consistently came to class, put their heads down on the desks, and did little but rest their heads and occasionally talk with neighbors. EmmyLou said nothing to them. One day, without my asking, she told me that she had battled with these students since September to get them to attend class and participate, with little success. After many frustrating days and aggravated nights, she asked herself, "For what?" Instead, she decided to work with those students "who want to learn," a decision that nonetheless troubled her. While "describing herself as a teacher" in an interview, EmmyLou touched on many of the same tensions we discussed that day:

> I'd say that I'm conscientious, sincere, concerned—sometimes too serious and intense because I want to be good. I'm frustrated and definitely determined. But I'm at the point where I need to explore different ways of teaching because what I've been doing on my own has worked but only for a percentage of students. The frustration is that each year that percentage lowers. I become less effective as a teacher as far as the growth and development of my students are concerned. I see kids with fertile minds and I can't motivate them. I can definitely turn some around, but I see so many that are lost in a system that says, "I don't care."
>
> I think much of this is tied to society. I feel that so many of our kids feel that this society will never provide them with anything. They're hopeless. Education is not the answer for them. Time and time again, bright kids don't see education as their way. And this is complicated because it's more difficult to make a living and get ahead now. While money is seen as the answer for them, they don't think that they need an education to get it. And that's what we're competing with. I feel that learning, curiosity, and creativity are almost dead in many of them. It may be due to the fact that many of them are children-of-children. So many are emotionally deprived, they haven't been loved. Their emotional development is really stunted.
>
> This makes me very upset because I don't know the answers. . . . It kills me to see kids sleep in class. They'll just say, "I'm tired. This is boring. Leave me alone." They resent you when you try to get them to participate in class. This past year the apathy and hostility were the worst.

EmmyLou also voiced concerns about her colleagues and their attitudes toward teaching at Russell:

> We need to create a consistent environment for our students. I think it's criminal to say that students can't eat in class or listen to walkmen, and then turn around and ignore that behavior when it occurs. The message is that you don't really care. You're just a hypocrite. And the teachers who want a healthy, good environment bear the brunt of that burden. My kids get angry and resent me because I truly want them to be students. And they say, "Why don't you just leave us alone?" I live with a lot of pressure because I correct student work. Some of my colleagues question me for doing this. They say, "The students don't care anyway. Why do it? Why do extra work?" It's a sad story to have to live with resentment from some colleagues who have given up, or almost given up, and from kids who tell me to leave them alone.

Hoping to improve her teaching situation, the following year EmmyLou joined the Essential School. A year later, she received a national award for teaching excellence and was named chairperson of the foreign language department.

Jody Golden (February 1988)

A relative newcomer, Ms. Golden was a business teacher with six years experience at Russell. We began the interview by discussing why she chose to get involved with a reform effort recently initiated at Russell, what was termed the 1992 Committee (discussed in Chapter 5), an effort separate from the Essential School:

> Personally, I was getting an overwhelming feeling of negativism. . . . And I saw it as tied to the attitude of the faculty and staff. There seemed to be no adults you could talk with who had anything positive to say about school. . . . Accordingly, it wasn't a healthy environment for learning. There was too much confusion and lack of cohesion among faculty, especially with regard to the goals of the school, our disciplinary and academic standards. . . . And I guess part of it was looking at the seniors who were coming out of Russell and looking at their educational skills and I thought to myself that there was no way that they could compete with kids coming out of other high schools, in college or for jobs. . . . Also, the idea that certain things are accepted as normal here really bothered me, as a teacher and as a person. Other teachers will say, "You're too serious.

They'll only end up working at McDonald's. Don't be so serious."
They saw students as write-offs. . . .

What do you think the school needs to do?

I think there's a need for more organization. We need common
standards of behavior and discipline. New ones need to be set. Now,
there's no consistency and the kids pick up on it immediately. . . .
We need to work with the kids to get them to understand what is
appropriate behavior. They should be able to assert their opinions
but they need to learn to do it through an acceptable form. In class,
kids will say to me, "Count this again [the addition on an exam].
You made a fuckin' mistake." Or they'll say, "Let me go to the
bathroom. I gotta piss." They need to realize that by talking like
that, they really turn off teachers. . . . They can raise questions but
need to do so appropriately.

I'd also like to see a change in teacher attitudes toward
students. . . . Teachers can be very disrespectful talking with
students. We need to judge discipline cases more fairly. In some
classes, kids get thrown out of the room very easily. Nothing's
tolerated and no attempt is made to understand the student's
situation. . . . If a student doesn't have a book or pencil, they're out
of the room. . . . Yesterday, a teacher came into my room while
students were doing a make-up exam and he said, "Why do you let
them make that up . . . ?"

Why do you think you're successful working with students at times?

Lots of it is just taking the time to listen. . . . We need to know
where these kids are coming from, to look for the "why's" behind
their behaviors. . . . It sounds idealistic, but it's not. It's practical. It
helps to be a counselor as well as teacher with these students. I have
very few classroom management problems. I don't kick kids out of
class. . . . But it does get hectic. The past two or three weeks I've
been really drained because of all the make-up I'm letting students
do. . . .

How would you characterize Russell students?

This is a population in need, in need of more structure, in need of
being re-educated in terms of their morals and values. They need
role models, to see other ways to live. Many are caught in the cycle
of feeling in a rut and never getting out of it. They have a negative
attitude toward life. They need to recognize that there are other
ways to live. . . . And because of that attitude, they have limited
academic skills. . . . Also, many probably don't have a very positive
home life.

Jody kept involved with the 1992 Committee until the committee and its related efforts went defunct during the 1991–92 school year. She remained at Russell High throughout my research.

Daniel Hand (June 1988)

Daniel Hand, an Eastown veteran, had over fifteen years experience as an English teacher. When I interviewed him at the end of the school year, he felt professionally dissatisfied. To address his disaffection he had recently made two decisions for the following year: he became yearbook advisor and he joined the Essential School. As yearbook advisor, he was released from teaching one class; in the Essential School, so he could collaborate with colleagues, he had an extra non-teaching period. Both decisions lessened his classroom responsibilities, the main source of his disillusionment. In the following remarks, Daniel, clearly frustrated, offered his impressions of the Russell population, in particular, A-level students, the school's lowest track:

> In teaching A-level students I can't but say to myself, "How did these people get here?" When reviewing for finals, students act like you never did the material. Nothing seems to stick with them and it seems to be getting consistently worse. A lot of factors seem to contribute. And it starts with the home environment. That's not very good, usually. There's not enough control over what students do. They're not nurtured to read or do enlightening activities because they watch too much TV and they're so influenced by TV. They certainly don't do anything educational because it seems that they get nothing educational outside of school. And so many come from single-parent families.
>
> So this causes practical problems, like you can't assign homework in books because the books that go out of the school disappear. We have large numbers of books missing. And the budget just gets to a point where you can't afford to replace books anymore. You can give homework to the C-level classes [Russell's top track] but not A-level classes. They don't have enough sense to bring pencils or notebooks to class, so that's an extra little thing that you have to do with them everyday before beginning class, give them papers and pencils.
>
> Also, the number of latenesses is incredible. A few hundred kids a day are late. And absenteeism is incredible. Look at the daily attendance sheet. Trying to maintain discipline with these problems is beyond any individual.

What solutions would you suggest for the A-level students?

On the high school level, none. They've already missed the boat. They can't spell. They can't capitalize. They use no punctuation. One kid couldn't even make capital letters. Where do you go with a kid who doesn't respond to any convention of good writing? If students can't do that, where do I go? They can't even understand why they should know how to write a sentence. And they got to 9th, 10th, and 11th grade without having to do it. . . . As for their study habits, even with books, three kids will do an assignment. Others profess ignorance or say they left it in their locker, or it's not completed yet, or they forgot it. Imagine how this is for a teacher. Believe me, it's very discouraging. Finally, you say to yourself, "What am I doing here? Why'd I go to college to do this? Why'd I get a master's degree?"

ESL   Two years later, Daniel left the Essential School to teach in an ESL program at another Eastown school, a change he found quite fulfilling. As he wrote four-and-a-half years later, "During the first year, I thought I had died and gone to heaven. . . . [T]hat year turned out to be undoubtedly the happiest and most rewarding I've ever had, by far. It recharged my batteries, rekindled my enthusiasm. I've fallen in love with the job and have been teaching LEP [limited-

LEP   English proficient] students ever since."

Stan Norwood (June 1989)

Another English teacher, Stan Norwood, taught for over twenty years in Eastown, eleven at Latin High. During the 1988–89 school year, he transferred to Russell to join the Essential School and work in the theater program. In comparing Russell High with Latin, Stan noted various differences between the school populations and how the differences influenced him:

At Russell I find there's more raw [theatrical] talent. They're equally capable as Latin students and, in some ways, more gifted. But it's more difficult working with the theater group here, in terms of merging creativity with responsibility. I have found that to be true in class as well. I may want to assign a number of chapters for students to read but I have found that many have jobs and family responsibilities, so they just don't have the time. I'm trying to develop the proper amount of tolerance for student needs, without shortchanging them academically. That's the problem: preparing them for the real world. I constantly have to ask myself, "What *are*

realistic expectations?" I don't want to be too intransigent. I'm trying *uncomprom-*
to negotiate that still. . . . [T]here is also the fact of having a lower   *ising*
socioeconomic base [at Russell] so that means students don't have
the material things that other students have. There's also more
connections with one's peers, there's likely to be more travel time to
school since they'll have to rely on public transportation. Plus, you're
trying to reach kids from very diverse backgrounds who often have
less proficiency with English. And the problems build exponentially.

It's not the same [as Latin High]. You're still teaching kids, but
you face more kinds of problems. That's why it's so exhausting. Not
only are you a teacher, but you're a social worker. At times, I have
offered students medical advice. To reach some of these students, it's
not enough just to disseminate information in class. You need to
really get to know the students. And *that* takes its own toll. *That's*
why it's so exhausting. And then it becomes very hard to leave
school and make the night yours—because you either have work to
do or you are thinking about students.

There are some kids that I know I can't reach. And I do think
about that. To preserve my own sanity, I have to recognize that,
because there are so many problems and they are so pronounced
with this population. Yet you realize that this does represent a last
chance for many students. It's tiring.

After teaching at Russell for two years, Stan left to become
English department chair at Latin High. Three years later, he left
Latin to help start a public school founded on community service.

Summary of Teacher Interviews

One way to understand these teachers' remarks is to see them as an
analysis of students' low personal capital and how it influenced
educational opportunity. Throughout their comments the teachers
identified attitudes, behaviors, and academic shortcomings that suggested low levels of personal capital. EmmyLou Griffith maintained
that many students "don't see education as the way . . . learning,
curiosity, and creativity are almost dead in many of them." Instead,
they confronted her with "apathy and hostility" and asked, "Why
don't you just leave us alone?" Jody Golden felt that students needed
"to understand what is appropriate behavior . . . [and learn] to assert
their opinions . . . through an acceptable form." Because they "really
turn off teachers," these students lost opportunities to enhance their
personal capital. Daniel Hand was frustrated by students being
chronically late to school ("a few hundred kids a day") and deficient in

basic skills ("They can't spell . . . can't capitalize . . . [and] use no punctuation"; one "couldn't even make capital letters"). Summarizing his position, Stan Norwood stated, "[T]here are so many problems and they are so pronounced with this population"—including low income levels, limited-English proficiency, and negative peer influences.

The teachers also described how students' low personal capital influenced them and their colleagues. EmmyLou Griffith, for instance, was discouraged because she couldn't reach all her students: "I see kids with fertile minds and I can't motivate them." Others challenged her so aggressively that she had given up on them and focused on those "who want to learn." She also noted that some colleagues reacted to students' lack of effort with apathy of their own, claiming "they don't care," so "why do extra work? . . . Why grade homework?" Contrasting herself with teachers who are so disenchanted that "[n]othing's tolerated [in their class] and no attempt is made to understand the student's situation," Jody Golden felt "[i]t helps to be a counselor as well as a teacher." Accordingly, she sought to listen to students and accommodate their needs, but found herself "really drained because of all the make-up I'm letting students do." Moreover, her colleagues, some of whom "saw students as write-offs," told her, "You're too serious [about your work]" and asked, "Why do you let them make that up?" rationalizing their indifference by saying, "They'll only end up working at McDonald's."

Daniel Hand gave his A-level classes no homework because "books that go out of school disappear." He had even reached the point where he felt he could do little to help these students since most had "clearly missed the boat." He was left wondering, "What am I doing here?" Likewise, Stan Norwood, new to Russell, was already asking himself, "What are realistic expectations?" Along these lines, he believed that many students, because of their economic predicament, "have job and family responsibilities [and] just don't have the time [for schoolwork]." While he saw going beyond classroom teaching as necessary, establishing such relationships proved draining: "It's not the same [as Latin High]. . . . You face more kinds of problems. That's why it's so exhausting. Not only are you a teacher, but you're a social worker . . . [and] it becomes very hard to leave school and make the night yours." Acknowledging how difficult he found this work, Stan admitted, "There are some kids I know I can't reach. . . . To preserve my own sanity, I have to recognize that." Nonetheless, he found this reaction unsatisfying: "[Y]ou realize that this does represent a last chance for many students." His final comment was simple but poignant, "It's tiring."

These teachers' remarks point to various implications for students' educational opportunity. For one, their jobs were demanding, and coupled with the attitudes of their colleagues and students, maintaining one's commitment and academic standards were a challenge (much as described in the previous chapter). This is not to say these teachers had given up. All four struggled to make their classes productive and all became involved with school reform at Russell. Although studies of curriculum development for "lower-track" classes (Oakes, 1985) and "working-class children" (Moll and Diaz, 1987) identify a common trend—"reducing or 'watering down' the curriculum to match perceived or identified weaknesses in the students" (Moll and Diaz, 1987: 301)—these interviews suggest that even hard-working professionals will struggle to maintain academic standards when they have compelling rationales for lowering expectations[13] and are rewarded for doing so by a decrease in professional frustration. Indeed, it seems significant that two of these committed and respected educators left Russell High. Moreover, the teachers said that many of their colleagues had given up. Some did not grade homework. Some restricted students' make-up opportunities. Others tolerated nothing in their classes and made no "attempt to understand the student's situation." In great part, these were reactions to the student population as a collective, and these reactions disadvantaged Russell students.

RUSSELL STUDENT PERFORMANCE

Thus far, I offered some understanding of how Russell students, as a collective, influenced administrators, guidance counselors, and teachers; and in turn, how these developments influenced students' education. In effect, I sought to add an ethnographic perspective to James Coleman's classic finding: "The fact that the social composition of the student body is more highly related to achievement, independently of the student's own social background, than is any other factor" (Coleman, 1990: 119; excerpted from Coleman, et al., 1966). To see how the previously discussed conditions translated into student achievement, I present some collective and comparative measures of student performance. As previously mentioned, in the late eighties Russell High had a failure rate in the area of forty percent—two-fifths of all courses students took, they failed. From September 1986 through June 1991, the school's dropout rate averaged 56.6 percent.[14] A comparative analysis says a great deal: during the 1990–91 school year, Russell had 147 students drop out of school, 14.1 percent of the total student population. That was forty-seven percent more dropouts than Travis High, 156 percent more than Archibald, and nearly 7000 percent more than Latin, which had two dropouts.

Russell's scores on the Metropolitan Achievement Test (MAT), a national exam administered every two years to Eastown 10th graders to assess reading, mathematics, and language skills, provides another perspective on student performance. In 1987, the average of math, reading, and language scores for Russell's 10th graders placed the school in the 24th percentile nationally, the lowest ranking among the state's forty-plus public high schools. Archibald High's 10th graders scored in the 26th percentile (the second lowest ranking in the state), and Travis' were in the 31st. Latin High scored in the 84th percentile, nine points higher than any other public school in the state. In 1989, the scores followed the same pattern: Russell's 10th graders had the lowest score in the state;[15] Archibald High had the second lowest; Travis placed in the 34th percentile; and Latin High had the highest ranking in the state. The "1989 SAT Profile" for these schools had a comparable distribution. At Russell, SAT scores, verbal and math combined, averaged 679. Archibald students averaged 650. Travis students averaged 653. And Latin students averaged 1028— 368 points higher than the average total for Russell, Archibald, and Travis.[16]

AN ALTERNATIVE VIEW: "CAUGHT IN A CROSS-FIRE OF OPPORTUNITY"

Although I maintain that Russell students were disadvantaged by their structural predicament, that their disproportionately low personal capital undermined their education, some saw things differently. In an interview for a cable TV program produced by Russell's media magnet, two guidance counselors (not those cited earlier) discussed with a student moderator their perceptions of educational opportunity at Russell High, specifically, students' chances for attending college.

GUIDANCE COUNSELOR #1: At Russell forty-five to fifty percent of the students generally apply to colleges and universities. . . . We find that many schools try to recruit minorities. There are programs in the state universities that try to help minorities specifically.

GUIDANCE COUNSELOR #2: There are even programs for minority students when they are in school, such as Upward Bound. Actually,

I think our students, especially our minority students, are caught in a cross-fire of opportunity. A day or week doesn't go by that some community agency, or one of the state universities or even a private college are not actively seeking out minority students, recruiting them just as a coach would recruit a ball player. Financially, a student with strong need could get as much as $4,000 in a combination of state and federal grant moneys to assist him or her in paying for their education. Expenses at the state university are about $7,000 a year. So a student, in terms of need, would have more than half of what he needed to pay for a university education.

GUIDANCE COUNSELOR #1:   The community college only costs about $1,000 a year and the state college's tuition is between $1,500 and $1,600 a semester. There are also college-based scholarships as well as state and federal scholarships available. Now, we also have a financial aid counselor who is working to make students aware of the forms they need to complete and the scholarships available for different ethnic and minority groups. So there is a lot of money to be given to students who are in need. Along with that, it is my understanding that many scholarships go untouched because people do not apply for them.

STUDENT MODERATOR: Why do you think this occurs?

GUIDANCE COUNSELOR #1:   They may think that the competition is too steep or that the money isn't worth the effort. . . .

STUDENT MODERATOR: Given the situation so many Russell students face, would you say family situations and things like peer pressure and teen pregnancy have a strong effect on whether they apply to college and to some of the special programs that are administered through the school?

GUIDANCE COUNSELOR #1:   That's an excellent question. To answer it directly, the answer is, "Yes." I would never wish to be a teenager today or to be going into high school today. The pressures—the peer pressure, the drugs, the alcohol, teen pregnancy—yes, it definitely has an effect on students. In fact, we often see that it's not the right thing to do, carrying books to school to get the As and Bs. It's sometimes looked down upon by a student's peers. It is very difficult for students in that situation to achieve. But we have many who fight peer pressure and are strong independently and will achieve. And that's where it's an individual who has to fight it and they need as many support services as possible.

individual effort

GUIDANCE COUNSELOR #2:   In addition, many students find outside employment more attractive than studying. It's immediate gratification. And very often, our students sacrifice long-term goals, long-

equity

term gain, for short-term of having money in the pocket. That's something else we have to deal with.

STUDENT MODERATOR: In certain situations, say a home with only one parent and say that parent works and you have brothers and sisters you have to take care of after school, do you think that in the long run the student will be able to handle that situation? I mean, having to come home from school and dealing with young kids when you see your friends going out to have a good time and you have to go home and your only companionship is a younger brother or sister?

GUIDANCE COUNSELOR #2:   Your question is well taken. That's a problem a number of students have to deal with. And the outcome, of course, is dependent on the individual. Some students are very strong. They can handle dual responsibilities. Others can't. Yet we can't criticize those who don't because it's simply too much for them. . . . It is extremely difficult. It's an added responsibility. Many of them, yes, will give up. Some are very strong and are determined to get their education. It may mean sacrificing some immediate pleasures in life and working very hard to get their education. Some will come home after school, clean their house, take care of their baby, try to put the baby to bed, and then start their homework. And that may not be until after eleven. It is very difficult.

STUDENT MODERATOR: How does the guidance department deal with this?

GUIDANCE COUNSELOR #1:   We have a special counselor for drugs and one for families and teen pregnancy, two special counselors.

STUDENT MODERATOR: What advice would you give such students?

GUIDANCE COUNSELOR #1:   I'd tell students, be determined to get your education. Don't let outside influences get in your way. The common saying today is to "say no." That's not just to drugs, but to anything that may affect your future plans. You do have opportunities to go to college and, in many cases, to get financial assistance. Be determined to get it. . . .

GUIDANCE COUNSELOR #2:   There's not much to add. I'm a firm believer in a student, in any person, being responsible for himself. One has a free will. He or she is capable of making choices. The choices should always be thought of in terms of, "What is best for my own life in the long run?" I should actively seek those means to obtain that end and, in many cases, education is the key, some kind of education. It doesn't necessarily mean college. It could be a technical school . . . even on-the-job training, apprenticeship, for example. But a student should constantly be seeking to improve himself so he or she might live a much fuller life.

In line with prevailing American conceptions of educational opportunity, these guidance counselors felt substantial opportunities for further education existed. There were "programs for minority students when they are in [high] school" and "college-based scholarships as well as state and federal scholarships [were] available." Russell had a financial aid counselor "working to make students aware of . . . scholarships available for different ethnic and minority groups." Indeed, "many [colleges] try to recruit minorities," to such an extent that students of color were "caught in a cross-fire of opportunity." If one failed to take advantage of these opportunities, it was largely a shortcoming of individual students, "sacrific[ing] long-term goals . . . for short-term of having money in the pocket," or who "think . . . that the [scholarship] money isn't worth the effort." Likewise, success was mainly a matter of individual initiative, where the "outcome, of course, is dependent on the individual." With this in mind guidance counselor #1 advised students: "[B]e determined to get your education. Don't let outside influences get in your way."

But individual determination may not have been enough at Russell High. How does an individual student get administrators to focus on academic priorities rather than control and discipline when students, teachers, district administrators, and the community want an orderly school? How do students who want an orderly environment create a sense of shared community when classmates have little in common with one another? How can an individual student prevent teachers from lowering their standards when other teachers validate such actions as a reasonable response to the student population, and when students themselves challenge teachers who seek to raise their expectations? And how can an individual student get a guidance counselor to see her or him for "guidance," not just setting a schedule, when the counselor has to place all students in classes?

Russell teachers, guidance counselors, and administrators were, for the most part, neither inept nor ill-intentioned. Administrators had to maintain order. Guidance counselors had to enroll new students in appropriate classes and process those who left. And teachers had to somehow resolve the challenges presented by their students, colleagues, and the institution itself, even though doing so might involve compromising academic standards. In the context of Russell High, all of these reactions made perfect sense. But as a consequence, the institution did not allow itself to enact educational opportunity. The structure of the school system and the organization of Russell High were ineffective, and therefore inequitable.

4

ONE STUDENT'S WORLD

AT RUSSELL HIGH

*A (School) Day in the
Life of Rafael Jackson*

At school, [students] are inducted into a functionary
world of utilitarianism and manipulation among
roles. . . . They are exposed to a number of new
experiences and phenomena, such as individual
teachers, aspects of school organisation, problems of
work and knowledge, class cultures, teacher and
pupil cultures, peer groups, toward which they are
required to make a response. Through this maze of
activity and encounters the pupil negotiates his way,
making the most of his power and abilities in
furthering his interests, often in company with his
fellows, discovering and inventing strategies of
infinite number and complexity. It is arguably the
pupil's most valuable lesson.
— Peter Woods, *Pupil Strategies*

As has been argued in the previous chapters, many aspects of
American secondary schools are understood in individual terms.[1]
Russell guidance counselors, for example, spent considerable time
placing students in appropriate classes to meet their individual

83

individualism— behaviorism (modifying behavior)
↓
interactionism

needs. In the U.S. history course, the coordinator saw students' failure to complete assignments as a matter of individual effort: "They
have gotten by without doing work and they are not willing to keep
up with it." And as the principal told freshmen, a Russell High education was key to individual self-fulfillment, "probably the greatest
opportunity of your lives." One additional manifestation of individualism is especially popular in American schools: behaviorism.
That is, the use of behavior modification—defined as the "deliberate
and systematic use of [positive] reinforcement (and sometimes
punishment) in attempts to modify behavior" (Lefrancois, 1983: 178).[2]
Drawing on this philosophical orientation, a U.S. Department of
Education publication advises that "instructors can reduce disruptive
behavior and increase scholastic success by setting and enforcing
clear rules at the beginning of the year, consistently rewarding good
behavior, and promptly punishing misconduct" (1988; quoted in
Carlson, 1992: 202). In this conception, students are understood very
much as individuals. Although the goal may be to influence the
behavior of classes, teams, or an entire school, rewards and punishments are applied to individuals. That is the appropriate frame of
reference.

In the high school setting, behaviorism is pervasive and enduring
for two fundamental reasons: it is seen as being equitable as well as
effective. It joins the moral with the scientific (Geertz, 1973). That is,
behaviorism—whether involving positive reinforcement, punishment,
or both—accords with the moral tenets of society. It is just and fair.
Rewards and sanctions are not applied broadly or haphazardly. They
are intended for specific individuals for specific reasons.[3] Moreover,
behaviorism is seen as effective, as scientifically sound. Not only
should notable achievements (e.g., good grades, drama presentations,
athletic victories, and so on) be commended because they are
inherently worthy of praise, but because praise makes these accom-
plishments likely to occur again. Conversely, if students transgress
school rules, they should be punished not only for violating accepted
standards, but because doing so dissuades future transgressions.
Research has proven this (even though it may have been conducted in
contrived settings with hungry rats and pigeons).

While behaviorism represents a logical outgrowth of individualism, this popular philosophy is founded on two problematic
assumptions, at least as applied at Russell High. First, behaviorism
assumes that students realize what is in their best interest, that
rewards and punishments are seen as just that, rewards and punishments. Research on formal schooling, however, emphasizes that
what constitutes a reward or punishment, or a student's best interest

[handwritten: Individualist vs. collective ⟹ contributes to insufficient educational pss]

for that matter, is seldom unequivocal and likely to shift, often due to peer influence (Ball, 1980; McDermott, 1987; Woods, 1980). In essence, behaviorist practices ignore the collective dimension to motivation. While most Americans value a high school education, this chapter steps back from that assumption, adopts a student's view of this taken-for-granted matter, and asks: is this education really worthwhile?

And second, for behaviorism to be effective, rewards and punishment should be applied consistently. Yet studies of American schools reveal that differential application of school discipline according to students' perceived social status is commonplace (Cusick, 1973; Havighurst, et al., 1962; Leacock, 1969; Rosenfeld, 1971; Spindler and Spindler, 1988). American society may assert that "all are created equal," but all students are not treated accordingly. Moreover, students at most schools have a repertoire of strategies that allow them to circumvent institutional sanctions. In sum, behaviorist philosophy assumes that schools can influence and direct student behavior by rewarding and punishing individual students. But since rewards, the most fundamental being a high school education and its associated opportunities, may be of dubious value, and sanctions are applied inconsistently, both the logic and ethical basis of relying on behaviorist assumptions to inform so many school practices become problematic. (This observation is critical because the next chapter reveals how engrained was a commitment to behaviorism, mostly negative reinforcement, among Russell faculty.)

An alternative to the behaviorist point of view is offered by interactionism. Three premises underlie this philosophy: (1) humans act in terms of the meanings they ascribe to individuals, contexts, objects, and so on; (2) these meanings are derived through interaction; and (3) through an interpretive process, meanings are adjusted (Blumer, 1969: 2). Rather than expecting rewards and punishments will always remain just that, interactionism assumes that the forces which motivate and inform behavior may shift over time and in different contexts. Not to say people don't respond to rewards and punishment, but that what constitutes a reward or punishment may change. Good grades, teacher respect, and academic growth may not always be viewed positively.[4] For high school students, peer acceptance and social relationships commonly supersede their schools' official goals. Interactionism is therefore valuable because it focuses on interpretation by social actors rather than assuming behavior will largely reflect the prevailing "environmental pressures, motives, attitudes, or ideas" (Blumer 1962: 82).

Within this paradigm, it is assumed that people actively create their worlds, although they do so within certain boundaries. Culture and social organization, for instance, represent frameworks within which actions are developed, not determinants of action. In this regard, one element of interactionist analysis, the concept of "strategy," is especially valuable for understanding formal schooling. As Peter Woods suggests, it is insightful to view the high school student as "a deviser of strategies," "adjusting behaviour according to situations and contingencies, continually monitoring the process of action, checking and re-casting his own thoughts and intentions in line with changing possibilities and expectations" (1980: 11).[5] While Russell teachers and administrators often assumed that meanings were fixed and readily apparent for students, that the benefits of a high school education and the inconveniences imposed by formal sanctions were clear cut, I found these assumptions to be unwarranted. Rewards and punishments were meted out inconsistently, and even what constituted a reward or punishment (including a high school education), could vary according to circumstances.

To provide some sense for why behaviorism was in many respects neither equitable nor effective at Russell High, the following section details a "day in the life" of a lower-track senior, Rafael Jackson.

A DAY IN THE LIFE OF RAFAEL JACKSON
(December 13, 1987)

Rafael Jackson, an African American, was a Russell High senior who I met while observing his zoology class for a few days. While an Eastown student, Rafael attended three different high schools. He entered Russell High in 9th grade because his Nelson Heights neighborhood was "zoned" for Russell. He was suspended that year and required to transfer to Archibald High. During his sophomore year he transferred to Travis High. Later that year his family moved and he enrolled in a school outside Eastown. When his family returned to Eastown, he re-enrolled in Travis. Because he "bunked" [skipped] school so often, he had recently been transferred back into Russell. Since Rafael had failed all his courses at Travis— because he skipped classes and school so often, not because he lacked intelligence—he was placed in a number of Russell's lowest track classes, A-level. Despite his record, Rafael had good relations with most Russell teachers and, because of his placement in mainly lower-track classes and his persuasive abilities, he found school easy.

In certain respects, Rafael was an atypical Russell student. While the school's population was highly mobile, few students transferred to different high schools six times. Although Russell's suspension rates were high, Rafael was suspended more than most students. He also frequently skipped class. Yet in other ways, his experiences were typical. The classes he attended were like many I observed. In some, teachers expected students to work, and they did. In others, teachers expected students to work and students did what they could to avoid working. And in others, teachers expected little of students. Moreover, passive learning and teacher-centered instruction were commonplace. Although Rafael spent an inordinate amount of time roaming the hallways, others students did as well. While Rafael was a skilled negotiator with teachers and administrators, other students seemed equally adept at convincing faculty and administrators to reconsider decisions they had made.

My day with Rafael began before the official start of school, hanging out in the hallways with his "buddies" and his girlfriend. When the homeroom bell rang, Rafael's girlfriend went to her homeroom but he and his friends stayed in the hallways on the school's second floor. (Rafael liked the second floor because "the principals are always on the first floor.") During this time a faculty member noticed the group, approached them, and told them to go to their homerooms. As he did, a young woman walked past. Although the students had begun to move as the teacher approached, when he said nothing to the young woman, they stopped walking. When the teacher reached them and said to leave, one of Rafael's friends asked, "Why? You didn't make her leave or check for a pass." The teacher explained that this was because she was on her way somewhere but that they were just hanging around. Another of Rafael's friends interjected, "So if I'm walking, I can do whatever the fuck I want?" The teacher then told the student he would submit a report to the office for disciplinary action regarding his remark, and he left. After this incident another teacher told the group to report to homeroom. In apparent compliance, Rafael and his friends dispersed; shortly thereafter, they met in a deserted corridor on the third floor, never reporting to homeroom.

When homeroom ended, Rafael and I went to his first period class, zoology. We arrived a few minutes late. Before the class began any formal work, Rafael told the teacher he had no pencil. She replied, "I would have bet my paycheck on it." Rafael then got a pencil from a friend, quickly placed it in his pocket, pulled it out as though it had been there the entire time, and said, "See, I've got it." He then asked the class, "Anybody got any paper?" While a student passed a piece to Rafael the teacher took attendance and commented, "Well, let's see, we have seventeen absent today [ten in attendance]. That's not too bad, and it's not even a test day." While erasing the board, which was covered in Spanish, the teacher remarked, "Next year, they'll outlaw this stuff" (a reference to bilingual education). Rafael responded, "What, writing? Good, I hate it."

The teacher then began a review for an upcoming exam by asking, "What have we been studying?" Two or three students quickly answered, "Mollusks." She continued, "What are some examples?" Students responded, "Snails," "Octopuses," and so on. One student answered most questions, pronouncing "cephalopods," "gastropods," and "echinoderm" with ease. Seven students participated in the review. One girl did math homework and two students sat passively.

Occasionally, the teacher explored tangents related to students' questions. When one asked why humans don't hibernate, she said there was evidence to suggest humans have hibernation-like behavior: "When we have light hit our eyes, we secrete hormones that make us active." She added that scientists were exploring whether humans could learn to hibernate and use that ability in conjunction with extended space travel. Slipping back into the review the teacher discussed "crepdula fornicata," snails that stack on top of each other and change gender over time. Throughout the review, the teacher told students she was using the upcoming exam as a guide. The exam would therefore be much like the review.

For the last few minutes of class, the teacher discussed Rafael's chronic lateness with him. She said that each time Rafael was late, he lost ten points from his exam grade, adding, "You'll have to get a 100 [on the upcoming exam] to get a 70." When the conversation ended, Rafael told me that the last time this occurred the teacher threatened the same but later said, "Make up a good story for why you're late and I won't take off any points." And she didn't.

As class ended, it was announced over the intercom that the home economics teacher was absent. Therefore, her cooking class, Rafael's third period, would meet in a different room. Because the notice came as students gathered their belongings to leave, Rafael couldn't hear the room number. Unshaken, he smiled, "Another reason to be late." During break Rafael talked with friends near his locker. One student was the center of attention. He had cut the corners from a $20 bill and pasted them on a $1 bill. It looked impressive and he planned to pass it as a twenty. He said banks would refund his money for the defective bill because it still had the serial number. He'd just tell the bank his little brother had done it.

Rafael and I were two or three minutes late for his second period class, as were most students, many of whom arrived after us. That day, eleven students were in class. Walking to his seat, Rafael kissed one girl and waved to another across the room. The teacher then told the class they would have a dictation quiz today. While the teacher explained the quiz, Rafael conversed with the girl who had kissed him, discussing aspects of their schoolwork as well as social lives. When the teacher asked Rafael to sit down, he immediately grabbed a chair, brought it next to the girl, and continued the discussion, telling the teacher, "I'm helping her with her work." The teacher replied, "Let's get through the dictation quiz and then you can get back to helping her. That's fair, isn't it?"

As the class readied for the quiz, a student asked, "Is this tied to *Cold Cash?*" a book the class was reading. The teacher answered, "Yeah, I guess so. It has young people involved with music in it." The teacher added that the dictation would include four sets of homonyms: to, too, two; right, write; by, buy; there, their, they're. He also said there would be some "tough" words—"publish," "corporation," and "lyrics." Before beginning the quiz, he told the class, "Don't use abbreviations." A student asked, "Why not?" He responded, "Because I want you to spell it out." The student replied, "That's stupid!" Without responding to the comment, the teacher explained that the dictation would deal with quotes, apostrophes, capitals, and end points. He added, "There will be no commas, so don't use any. If you do, it'll be minus five points." Just as the teacher began dictating, Rafael asked to borrow a pencil from him.

In administering the quiz, the teacher first read quickly through the entire selection to familiarize students with it:

> Mitch and Larry (Hint: If you itch when Mitch comes in sight, you'll know how to spell Mitch.) spent July trying to write lyrics for the two boys' songs. Those guys tried to sell two songs by themselves. Right at the summer's end Wildcat Publishing Corporation decided to buy them. It was the thrill of their young lives. Do you suppose other companies will want their tunes?

He then read through the selection more slowly. After a third reading, the teacher told the class, "Watch capital letters, punctuation, end marks, and apostrophes. Remember, no commas." When the teacher completed the third recitation, most of the class had finished the dictation. As Rafael turned in his paper, the teacher took a quick look and remarked, "When I said, 'When you see Mitch you get an itch,' it was a clue." Rafael returned to his seat and made some corrections.

As a few remaining students finished the dictation, the teacher read the selection a fourth time to a student with limited-English proficiency. He also returned a student's paper and told him he had used capitals improperly. During this time Rafael worked on U.S. history homework, explaining to me he was doing this because his history teacher promised him a state university sweatshirt if he got a perfect score on an upcoming quiz.

As a few students continued working on the dictation, the teacher commented, "If you're trying to find out how to spell 'lyrics,' don't just look for 'l' followed by one vowel but try a few different vowels." While the teacher helped students still completing the dictation, Rafael discussed his next class, cooking, with me—saying he liked it because he could "have fun" and there were mostly girls in the class. With nothing to do, Rafael began writing on his desk. Turning to a student sitting in the back of class staring blankly, he asked, "You've been to two classes in a row. Are you going to next period too?" The student replied, "Yeah." Rafael responded, "Wow! A record! It's too cold to bunk anyway." Rafael and this student then struck up a brief conversation. As this occurred, another student completed a math assignment and three students shared a newspaper. With assistance from the teacher, two limited-English students kept working on their dictation.

After talking with his friend for a few minutes Rafael turned to me and said that after being at Russell for three months skipping class was easy: "It's not even a challenge to bunk. I stay in the basement and sit there all period, just chillin', watchin' everybody walk by. I know where to bunk, when to bunk, and how to bunk. But I can't bunk Mrs. Ries' class [his other English teacher]. She's a 'bulletin watcher.' She'll catch you."[6] As Rafael grew bored, he decided to go to the lavatory. When he asked for a pass, the teacher told him he could go but he would have to serve fifteen minutes of detention (a school policy intended to reduce the number of students roaming the halls during classes by discouraging them from leaving class to use the lavatory.) Nonetheless, Rafael left. Walking to the lavatory I asked if he planned to serve the detention that afternoon. He responded, "No . . . well, maybe I will. My girlfriend may have to stay." While we were out of the room, the period ended.

During break, we headed to Rafael's locker. On the way Rafael discussed how he had a "magical way around Russell High," how he could do pretty much whatever he wanted. He boasted, "I've got those teachers wrapped around my little finger. I know how to talk to them." When he got to his locker and opened it, a stack of papers fell onto the floor and a book nearly dropped out. I commented on how packed it was and Rafael explained, "I share it with six or seven other guys. You should see it when we've all got jackets in here." (At this time the lockers at Russell High were in such poor condition that the school assigned students no lockers. Nonetheless, many claimed those still in working condition, often sharing them with friends.)

Third period was cooking class. Since the teacher was absent, the class met in a regular classroom instead of the "home ec" room. In typical fashion Rafael arrived late but armed with an excuse, he couldn't hear the announcement in his zoology class. This time no excuse was needed. There was no teacher. In fact, when Rafael and I arrived, three students approached me thinking I was a substitute, and told me why they couldn't stay in class that period. Shortly thereafter, the substitute found the room and signed a flurry of passes for students asking to leave the room. Rafael and I took seats to one side of the room.

For the nine students who remained, the substitute passed out the day's assignment, a copy of a workbook page entitled, "Television Schedules." A listing from a viewer's guide of TV specials for Monday and Tuesday nights was at the top of the page. The directions read: "In the box below is information on television specials. Use the information to answer the questions." The questions read:

(1) What time does *Greatest Heroes of the Bible* begin on Monday?

(2) On what channel is *Bobby Vinton's Rock and Rollers* playing?

(3) Would you watch *The Immigrants* on Monday night if you had to work on Tuesday night from 4 P.M. to 11 P.M.? Explain your answer.

Two questions required students to list the time a program began and its channel. To answer the third question students had to realize they could watch the first half of *The Immigrants* on Monday but would miss the second half because of work.

The second part of the worksheet had another section from a television viewers' guide. The directions read: "In the box below is part of a television schedule for a Monday night. Answer the questions and follow the directions under the box." The questions read:

(1) What time does *Financial News* begin?

(2) On what channel is *Gunsmoke* playing? When does *Gunsmoke* end?

(3) What time does the *Mickey Mouse Club* end?

(4) Would you watch *Bionic Woman* if your favorite show is *Adam-12*? Explain your answer. [You could only watch half of Bionic Woman since it was an hour program and the second half overlapped with *Adam-12*.]

(5) Which program is meant to make you laugh: *Mod Squad, Gunsmoke,* or *Bewitched*? [Next to *Bewitched* the guide noted, "comedy."]

(6) Place a check to the left of each program that is for children.

Rafael went right to work on the assignment, completed it, and shared it with friends so they could fill out theirs. Throughout the period class was calm. After completing the worksheet some students read. One worked on her geometry homework. Others talked among themselves. Occasionally, students in the hallway stuck their heads in the room to look for friends. If they saw any, they usually greeted them and left. By the middle of the period most students were conversing with one another. This continued until the period ended.

Rafael and I then went to the cafeteria for "first lunch." We ate with his girlfriend. Walking to Rafael's fourth period class we passed the principal talking with a cafeteria worker. He looked perturbed. The cafeteria worker was walking beside him holding a one-dollar bill with twenties pasted onto the corners and saying, "I don't know where it came from. Someone found it in her cash drawer." Rafael smiled, "I know where it came from."

When we got to Rafael's history class we were again late but the teacher had not arrived either. Some students used the extra time to study for a quiz they would have that day. Others were entertained by a young man who performed a mock strip-tease in the front of the room. Five minutes after the bell, the teacher arrived and told the seventeen students they would have a five-question quiz. Flipping through the pages of his textbook, the teacher announced:

Question one, fill-in-the blank: A feeling of extreme loyalty to one's nation, what is the term? Number two: The short period of U.S. history after the War of 1812 when all sections of the country supported the president—the "era of good what?" Number three: Name given to tariff to keep out foreign products? Number four: Law natives are supposed to use in dealing with one another? And number five: President Monroe's warning to Europe not to interfere in the western hemisphere or establish colonies there is known as the "blank" Doctrine. Fill in the blank. I have a bonus question: Who is the principal of Russell High? I'll guarantee not everyone gets it right. Half-credit for the first name. I'll give credit for the first name and last initial.

After collecting the quizzes the teacher told students to take out their homework and exchange it with a neighbor. He then read the answers to the homework and students graded each other's work. The first questions were fill-in's. For instance, "Britain sold its goods in so many places that it became know as the [blank] of the world." (Answer: "workshop.") The next questions were matching and included John Quincy Adams ("His father was also president"), Henry Clay ("He was known as the 'Great Compromiser'"), and Robert Fulton ("He invented the steamboat"). After students graded one another's homework, that score, combined with their quiz score, which the teacher graded during the homework review, established one's grade-for-the-day. The teacher then told each student what he or she had earned for that class. Throughout these activities, ten students participated in the teacher-directed activities. Two read newspapers, three chatted quietly among themselves, and two others appeared to be sleeping.

Next, the teacher told the class, "Open your texts to the map on page 227. What states comprise the northeast?" Students responded: "Massachusetts!" "New York!" "Connecticut!" He then asked, "What states make up the West?" Students again shouted out answers. While this occurred a young woman walked into the room to talk with a friend. The teacher told her to leave. After talking briefly with the friend, she left. Shortly thereafter, another student entered the room to get a set of keys from a friend. Five minutes later, he returned them.

After completing the map exercise, the teacher had students identify symbols on the map that represented products produced by various states. He asked, "What states produced rice?" and, "What states produced cotton?" He then told the class, "Now you have to compare two charts. This is the tough one. How many times greater is the production of cotton [it was 47 million bales] than wool [21 million bales]? How do you find out how many times greater?" A student replied, "Subtract." The teacher said, "You divide." After telling the class there would be another quiz tomorrow and identifying the section of the text it would cover, the teacher asked me to cover the final ten minutes of class and left the room. Some students started playing cards. The girl who had been asked to leave the room earlier because she wasn't in the class returned and sat with her friend. Students wandered in and out. One young man appeared to sleep through it all.

When the period ended, Rafael returned to his locker, met his girlfriend, and walked her to class. Nonetheless, he arrived at his next class on time, his second English class, taught by Mrs. Ries, the "bulletin watcher." The class was writing short stories. Rafael had already written most of his, although the teacher told him it still needed an ending. Looking at her comments on his draft, it was apparent she had spent some time correcting Rafael's story. Mrs. Ries even suggested that those having trouble with their story might check with Rafael because he had already written most of his and had done a good job. Although she complimented Rafael on his work, he didn't enjoy the class. "This class is boring," he told me. When I asked why, he explained, "She makes us work all the time." Throughout the class most students worked on English-related projects. Some checked Rafael's work, others completed a capitalization worksheet, and others worked directly with the teacher on their stories.

When the bell rang for Rafael's final class, wood shop, he told me he wouldn't be going because he had been "kicked out of class for awhile." This was because in one class there was a disruption and the teacher took Rafael out in the hall and yelled at him. Rafael explained, "You know when someone's yelling at you, how you feel like yelling back? Well, I did." Consequently, an assistant principal removed him from shop for a few days so both he and the teacher could cool off. Instead, Rafael reported to an assistant principal's office during last period. On this day the assistant principal wasn't in and since none of his friends were in the office, Rafael left to wander the hallways. As we walked he remarked, "This is what I do all the time sixth period." "But what about when you *had* shop?" I asked. He answered, "I still did it." For much of the period we sat in two broken chairs stashed under a stairwell in the school basement. Rafael talked with friends and a few janitors who passed by. While there, Rafael said, "You know, sometimes I sit here all day and do nothing. Sometimes I go to sleep. Don't nobody come down here. That's how easy it is, man."

When Rafael got bored hanging out in the basement we strolled the corridors. Whenever we came to a section of the building administrators might patrol, Rafael stopped before entering and asked anyone passing by, "Is it clear?" At one point Rafael saw an assistant principal walk onto a floor so he asked a student coming from that floor, "Which way did he go?" Later, Rafael saw a student trying to sneak past the main corridor and told him, "It's clear. Go ahead." As the student started down the hallway, Rafael imitated the principal's deep, guttural voice and boomed, "Hey, where are you going?!" The student immediately stopped, only to turn and see Rafael laughing.

Throughout the period, we returned to the assistant principal's office to see whether any of Rafael's friends were there. On one occasion Rafael encountered a friend, talked with him for a few minutes, and then left. We also went to the gym and watched a gym teacher and student shoot baskets. After a brief stay in the gym, we once again walked the corridors. When Rafael heard the principal's voice in a hallway we were approaching, he turned into the nearest stairwell and ran up to the next floor. On one visit to the assistant principal's office, as Rafael looked through the door to see who was there, a secretary opened the door and surprised him. Rafael immediately turned to the nearest locker and pretended to be opening it. The secretary passed by and said nothing.

Late in the period, Rafael turned down a hallway monitored by the assistant principal who had removed him from shop. Since the assistant principal clearly saw Rafael, he could not turn around. Under his breath he muttered, "Ah fuck, I'm busted," but continued walking toward the administrator. Along the way he devised an excuse: "I'll just say I'm going to guidance." When we got to the assistant principal, he used this excuse and the assistant principal told him to hurry and not to linger in the hallway.

With the end of the day nearing, Rafael headed to his girlfriend's classroom to see whether she was there so they could walk home together. Because posters covered the windows on both doors to the room, Rafael couldn't tell whether she was there. Yet he was certain that a girl he knew well, Susan Husted, would be in class since he had already seen her that day. With this certainty in mind, Rafael opened the classroom door and asked, "Is Susan Husted here? Mr. Hartnett [an assistant principal] wants to see her." As the teacher dismissed Susan from class, Rafael signaled to his girlfriend that he'd be in the hallway after class. After leaving the room, Susan thanked Rafael for getting her out of class. Rafael waited in the hallway until the bell rang. When his girlfriend came out of the room, they said good-bye to me and left school together.

EPILOGUE

Rafael never served his fifteen minutes of detention for using the lavatory during class and his zoology teacher never deducted any points from his exam grade for tardiness. Rafael passed all his courses that year and graduated, although he had one close call. For the first three quarters, he received grades of E, F, and F in one course. Combining an improved fourth quarter performance with some persuasive talking, Rafael convinced his teacher to give him a D for the year so that he graduated. Rafael then joined the army and served two-and-a-half years. During this time Rafael said three different sergeants called him "nigger" and he ended up fighting all three. While the army never disciplined him for these actions (although Rafael said the sergeants were reprimanded), after the third incident he went AWOL and left the army. He was given a dishonorable discharge.

Returning to Eastown, Rafael held three different jobs over the next year-and-a-half. He also began living with his high school girlfriend and together they had two daughters. In my last encounters with Rafael he was collecting unemployment, had no job prospects, and was supplementing his unemployment income through relatively minor but nonetheless illegal activities. Rafael's girlfriend was receiving welfare benefits and working toward her GED.

ANALYSIS

This vignette of a school day with Rafael Jackson sought to raise one question that is essential to this study, but which is too rarely asked: of what worth was this education? Why should Rafael value this opportunity?[7] In one class he analyzed a TV guide, in another he did a one-paragraph transcription. When he had trouble in shop, he was removed to spend time with the assistant principal. These were three of six major courses. In zoology and history, knowledge largely entailed factual recall and students relied on few skills other than memorization. Moreover, the institutional rewards offered Rafael, course credits, required little effort. In zoology the teacher used the upcoming exam as the basis for a review, thereby informing students of exam questions beforehand. During a dictation quiz the teacher provided students with hints regarding errors they might make ("There will be no commas"). Rafael's history quiz included bonus points for correctly identifying the name of Russell's principal. In wood shop he did nothing, and in home economics he did virtually nothing. Perhaps as a consequence of seldom being asked to do anything he couldn't already do with ease, when asked to do something intellectually challenging and significant, writing a short story in English, he disliked the class. Although but one day in Rafael's education, it would be absurd to claim that such conditions constituted "educational opportunity"—at least not an education "worth wanting" (Howe, 1993, 1997).

Futhermore, in terms of behaviorist assumptions, institutional sanctions were inconsistently enforced, which further throws into question the logic of relying so extensively and unreflectively on negative reinforcement to direct school life. While Rafael violated numerous classroom and school rules, he experienced no negative sanctions. During homeroom he and friends dodged a teacher who confronted them in the hallway, merely moving to another floor. An English teacher assigned Rafael a fifteen-minute detention for leaving class to use the restroom, but he never served that. Although his zoology teacher said she would subtract ten points from Rafael's test grade each time he was late, she never followed through on the threat. Rafael was supposed to report to the assistant principal's office during shop, but since the assistant principal was elsewhere, Rafael wandered the hallways. When he happened upon the assistant principal that period, he had a ready excuse that worked. And in one class Rafael's grades for the first three quarters—two Fs and an E—could have prevented him from graduating; yet he got a D for the course because he turned himself around in the fourth quarter and was rewarded for "trying hard" (Jackson, 1968: 34).

As the value of the education offered Rafael seemed dubious and his academic work offered few challenges or rewards, he approached school with indifference. He regularly arrived late to class and showed little interest in course work. The classes he enjoyed, home economics and history, were attractive for non-academic reasons, the opportunity to socialize with a number of young women and the possibility of winning a sweatshirt. Although his English teacher held him up for emulation, he was neither excited nor engaged in this class. For Rafael, school was a place to be with friends; accordingly, his interests centered on socializing. School work had little meaning. It was more a trial to be endured (or better, avoided) than a source of insight, growth, or empowerment (Carlson, 1992; Sizer, 1984; Steinberg, et al., 1996).

Still, in some respects, watching Rafael on this day revealed a measure of power, mastery, and satisfaction—all of which were tied to his ability to manipulate the institution. Rafael's actions were strategic, weighing options and taking good chances in a system with many points of vulnerability. In his own words, Rafael had a "magical way around Russell": "I know when to bunk, where to bunk, and how to bunk. . . . I've got those teachers wrapped around my little finger." But much as with the U.S. history students in Chapter 2, Rafael enacted his informal power in ways that were ultimately debilitating. Rafael, too, succeeded in not learning.

This glimpse into the life of Rafael Jackson also offers another view of control and order at Russell High. Despite popular images of violence, chaos, and overcrowding[8] in urban schools, Rafael's day was sedate; more accurately, it was boring. In most classes, work was trivial. Seldom were students asked to do something they didn't already know how to do. This kept life orderly, but again, order came with a price. As Linda McNeil found at two schools where administrators stressed discipline and control, "the strategies for instruction were quite similar: control students by making work easy" (1986: 184). At Russell High this was routine. Teachers didn't focus on control and order; they preserved it instinctively and unthinkingly. The teacher who left class plans for the substitute in Rafael's cooking class knew how to maintain control: give students something as simple as a TV viewer's guide to interpret. When Rafael wanted to talk to a young woman in class, the teacher instantly accommodated him: "Let's get through the dictation quiz and then you can get back to helping her. Now that's fair, isn't it?" When a student in that class called the teacher's rationale "stupid," the comment was totally ignored. Rafael's history teacher came to class late and left early. But he kept work simple and students were not disruptive. Because Rafael had a run-in with his shop teacher, to preserve peace, an assistant principal removed him from the class. Students, teachers, and administrators had struck their compromises. It was all routine and unquestioned; but it wasn't educational.[9]

PART II

THE RESILIENCE OF THE STATUS QUO

5

Reform that Reproduced

The 1992 Committee

The ad hoc responses [to problems characteristic
of teachers] are the responses of a group largely
constrained by their culture, that is, the responses
are devised and enacted within the confines of
limited, fixed, often unquestioned structures of
attitudes, beliefs, inclinations, dispositions, and so
on. For this reason, it is likely that they may not
solve problems in any genuine lasting sense.
—Elizabeth Hatton, "Levi-Strauss' *Bricolage*
and Theorizing Teachers' Work"

In the previous chapter I argued that various school policies founded
on behaviorist premises proved to be both inequitable and ineffective.
Yet such practices permeated Russell High. Behaviorism was at the
heart of the discipline system: if you violated school rules, you were to
be punished. Strategies teachers employed in their classrooms were
informed by behaviorist assumptions. Students commonly lost points
for late assignments. Good grades were thought to be a valued
reward; poor grades were seen as a reasonable means to motivate
underachieving students. The list goes on.

The question then arises: why? In part, this situation can be
understood as a reflection of the teachers' belief system, their culture.
Teachers saw behaviorism as an effective way to influence student
behavior. Indeed, as the student population was perceived to be
growing increasingly disruptive, teachers relied even more extensively on punishment as a source of leverage in their relationships

101

with students. As an independent study of the Eastown School System found, from 1983 to 1993 the number of students suspended in city high schools increased 200 percent.[1] In full accord with this finding, Russell's principal told a group of teachers during a 1988 school reform meeting, "Russell High has had more referrals for suspensions out of the system than ever before and the highest suspension rate ever of late." And as previously discussed, administrators devoted considerable attention to issues of discipline because so many teachers wanted the institution to impose sanctions on students. In part, a commitment to behaviorist premises may have proven so enduring because it offered faculty some sense of community. Within a faculty that had many points of divisiveness, it was a shared belief by which teachers could "honor the elements of a common faith" (Bidwell and Hoffer, 1996).

Yet there was no time during the normal school routine when Russell faculty could assess the consequences of their beliefs, in particular, the assumption that informed so much of their work: that punishment, by far the most common manifestation of behaviorism, was an effective and equitable means to influence student behavior. This accepted truth was never tested or challenged; it was only acted upon. In *The Structure of Scientific Revolutions*, Thomas Kuhn observed how scientific "paradigms"—models for explaining various phenomena, conceptions of how the world operates—predisposed their adherents to understand the world in particular ways and therefore not to understand it in other ways.[2] (When earth was thought to be at the center of the universe, night and day were caused by the movement of the sun.) Much as with culture, a paradigm can be a self-reinforcing system; you see what you expect to see. Change only comes about by the "failure of existing rules" (Kuhn, 1962: 68) to explain what is now known. (If earth were at the center of the universe, the planets wouldn't move as they do.) But at Russell High the "existing rules" were never challenged. There were no means to consider and resolve possible contradictions and inconsistencies in the prevailing paradigm. In terms of teachers' beliefs, the status quo largely endured.

To gain a sense for why this occurred, this chapter examines the work of the 1992 Committee, a schoolwide effort to "rethink the education provided students" that was charged with addressing a very open-ended question: "What should Russell High look like in five years?" Hoping to involve a broad cross-section of teachers in collaboratively defining future directions for the school, the 1992 Committee was created during the 1986–87 school year by Russell faculty and administrators, personnel from a local university, and some educational consultants. In this analysis I highlight one prominent aspect of the committee's work: while a range of topics was

Status quo = existing state of affairs.

discussed at most meetings, the committee's formal proposals reflected a consistent and limited view of education. They dealt with issues of control and order. Most aimed to strengthen existing policies for student violations of school rules. Nothing that affected classroom teaching, how curricula were conceived, or how the school was structured to promote learning was ever implemented. In effect, this effort to redefine Russell High for 1992 embodied the assumptions about educational opportunity that run throughout this study: The teachers defined their goals in individual terms; you could achieve order by consistently punishing individual students. Further, educational opportunity was unquestioned. The education offered students was assumed to be an opportunity worth wanting. There was no need for change. And student input was virtually nonexistent. No student ever served on the 1992 Committee, nor did students attend any committee meeting I observed, from January 1987 through April 1990.[3]

Often, teachers are blamed for the lack of change in our educational system. In this instance, Russell teachers certainly helped forestall one attempt at reform. But as this look at the 1992 Committee reveals, there was little reason why any of these teachers would change their beliefs or practices. Many issues arose during committee meetings but most were mentioned in passing. Few were treated in depth. When points of contention surfaced, they were often ignored or quickly passed over. Moreover, reform meetings never included the entire faculty and most meetings were an add-on to teachers' workday. They were not part of the official routine. Further, there was no guarantee that reforms adopted by the faculty would be endorsed by the administration. In fact, many faculty were openly skeptical of the administration's support for this work. With so many issues in question, where was the logic for change?

In analyzing the committee's efforts, I integrate two primary data sources. Vignettes of two 1992 Committee meetings offer a view of committee deliberations. Memos and descriptions of policies developed by the committee provide examples of what was formally enacted. Juxtaposing these two dimensions of the committee's work reveals how a reform initiative that encountered many ideas and proposals consistently distilled its formal actions to seeking more effective ways to enact the status quo.

THE 1992 COMMITTEE

The 1992 Committee initiated its work in January 1987, with a well-attended dinner meeting sponsored by a local university. Forty-three persons, from a staff of about seventy-five, attended. The theme for the meeting was, "Our Goals for the Future." That meeting proved encouraging for many and these persons agreed to meet again, to continue discussing how they could improve Russell's educational climate.

March 12, 1987: "The Road to 1992"
[title of the meeting listed on the faculty notice]

INTRODUCTION. *The second meeting of the 1992 Committee, another dinner meeting sponsored by the same university, was also well-attended. That week faculty had implemented a stricter policy about allowing students out of homeroom and had tightened the school's pass policy. Although only a few days had passed, there was a sense that school climate had improved. This meeting included about thirty teachers, the principal, and two representatives from the sponsoring university. It was chaired by Russell's representative to the Eastown Teachers Union. Following dinner, there ensued a wide-ranging discussion.*

ESL TEACHER #1:   My concern is that this will be a re-hash of our last meeting. I don't want to repeat all our grievances from then. I want to establish a committee to draft proposals by Monday. We need a declaration to show the community-at-large our ability and our ideas for reform, because the time is ideal now. There is a concern for a lack of standards in our schools, in the state, and across the nation. We need to tell people what a handicapped population there is at Russell.

ESSENTIAL SCHOOL TEACHER #1:   I think the best thing we're able to do here is get together to talk about these issues. I want to add that no one is handicapped by their ethnicity.

CHAIR: I realize that people took the night off to be here. So maybe we can put our heads together and do it tonight. But we should keep in mind that if we create a committee tonight, it might offend other teachers who couldn't make this meeting, or it might violate union regulations.

ARTS MAGNET TEACHER #1:   At Russell it's always been people saying, "Someone else is at fault." We need to take a drastic stand. . . . We need to mean what we say. We need a revolutionary attitude. Look at the building today [a reference to the new homeroom and pass policy]. Wasn't it orderly? Wasn't it revolutionary?

ESL TEACHER #2: Our curriculum does not reflect the population we serve. We have a diverse ethnic and socioeconomic population. If we're going to reform, we have to open up students' minds. We're just banging our heads against the wall to prepare our kids for something they can't achieve [i.e., college]. We need to give them something they can really use. And [students' backgrounds] don't have to be a negative factor, unless you won't acknowledge they exist.

UNIVERSITY REPRESENTATIVE #1: Are you recommending that Russell develop its own curriculum, rather than letting central office do it?

ESL TEACHER #2: Yes. We should have more input. We have the knowledge of what our kids bring to school. There's no sin in recognizing this fact, but it is a sin not to recognize it.

ARTS MAGNET TEACHER #2: Today was quite a contrast. We were keeping the corridors clear of students and that's a prerequisite for learning. I hope these efforts translate into an atmosphere where we ask what we can do beyond this. We should continue what we did today.

CHAIR: I hear discussions of order, discipline, and academic standards as recommendations. To learn you need order, and we all thought the school was beautiful today. Maybe we can also hit into curriculum issues. But we're not the whole faculty so we have to remember we need to bring ideas back to the whole faculty at some point.

ESSENTIAL SCHOOL TEACHER #2: I hear lots of good things today but there are lots of things we as teachers can't do because the power lies elsewhere. It's the nature of the beast. But we need to control what we can. I'm beginning to feel isolated. I don't know what else is going on in the building. As teachers, we could establish some kind of communication about academics and our curriculum so we know what is going on in other parts of the school and could support each other. We could teach ethnic groups about their ethnicity, because I'm proud of being where I came from.

LARGER SCHOOL TEACHER #1: How do you change a curriculum to fit the ethnic make-up of your school? I teach science. I teach "the principles of science" to "the kids." There's no such thing as Hispanic algebra. We need to teach kids what they need to know to go off into American society, into the real world.

LARGER SCHOOL TEACHER #2: Yes there is [Hispanic algebra]. It's algebra in Spanish.

LARGER SCHOOL TEACHER #1: We need to teach kids what they need to know to go off into American society. They need to be ready for the real world.

LARGER SCHOOL TEACHER #2:   All the data produced shows that kids taught in their first language transfer the skills they develop to their second language. Our prejudices might get in the way of interpreting that data.

LARGER SCHOOL TEACHER #3:   I went to a bilingual school in France and Belgium and I managed.

ESL TEACHER #2:   We can't change the laws of physics to make them relevant to our students. It's divisive to talk of bilingual education. I think there are areas and courses that could be devised so students would come to physics more prepared. Students don't need to start with physics. They need to start with classes that will prepare them for physics.

ESL TEACHER #1:   Let's not debate bilingual education. We're here to settle on how we'll change the school.

ARTS MAGNET TEACHER #1:   We have to work on our common threads. We need to make kids arrive here on time so I can teach them. [Essential School Teacher #2] is wrong, I feel, because we do have power.

LARGER SCHOOL TEACHER #4:   The time is right for change. We can take over control of the school now. All the research says that teachers need more control of what goes on in their schools.

LARGER SCHOOL TEACHER #5:   Let's begin the day by having a ten-minute homeroom period and using the extra fifteen minutes for more class time. [*Applause and seconding from others.* At the time, Russell had a twenty-five-minute homeroom period and many teachers questioned its value.] Let's schedule all our 9th grade English classes at the same time, so we can change students if there is a need, for reasons of discipline or appropriate level [i.e., track].

DEAN OF STUDENTS: Two-thirds of Russell students are failing one or more classes. The same is true at Travis High. Our average verbal SAT score is 290 [in 1987]. [Faculty and the principal then note that ESL kids take SATs and skew the scores.] We have to examine our curriculum and go to the middle schools and see why our kids are not being prepared.

ESL TEACHER #2:   We have to deal with what we have now. We can't cop out and blame middle schools. Let's concentrate on our 9th graders.

DEAN OF STUDENTS: Most of our 9th graders are at the lowest level of English competency.

UNIVERSITY REPRESENTATIVE #2:   Lots of people think of the Essential School as a structural experiment, with its double-periods and teachers working closely with students. But it's also very much a curriculum experiment. I suggest we engage in a discussion about this curriculum experiment. We can only gain from it.

LARGER SCHOOL TEACHER #5:   We can't have an impact until we have more parental involvement. We have lots of kids who just wander around all day. Where kids really achieve, parents are around. We need to *make* parents become more involved.

DEAN OF STUDENTS: True, but the parents need education as much as kids.

LONG-TERM SUBSTITUTE TEACHER [*who had been at Russell most of the year*]:   But we have some kids with no parents. It's different at Archibald High. Those kids are scared because parents are involved if you threaten suspension. At Russell, there's no one at home to direct kids.

PRINCIPAL: That's not totally true. [*To the coordinator of the Essential School*] Tell them how it's different.

COORDINATOR: In the Essential School we're working on simple skills—reading, studying, vocabulary. We have students taking exams more than once, until they pass. One girl recently took an exam three times before she earned a passing grade. But kids don't know punctuation or capitalization. I don't know what's going on in middle school. I've been there. They're trying too. The fact is, it takes a helluva lot of time to have an impact. Sometimes parents don't know what to do with these kids. We've got a girl who's grounded by her parents until June, but she's still skipping school. We also have advisory groups for our kids. It's a good idea but it's hard to pull together because there's so little time. We have a student leadership committee that sets the standards for our kids. [The students on the committee] want to require everyone to earn As and Bs before graduating from the Essential School. We also have teams [of teachers]. That may help. We think we're making a difference. We have less discipline problems and good attendance, but we still have trouble getting kids to do work. Lots of kids still have "incompletes" [a grading innovation adopted by the Essential School], and we're trying to find a way to convince kids they can't postpone reality.

DEAN OF STUDENTS: What are you doing about your incompletes, so kids have better study habits?

COORDINATOR: We keep them after class, we call their homes, we send them to the assistant principal, teachers send students to me. It seems kids who could have been hard-core failures are carrying books home.

ESSENTIAL SCHOOL TEACHER #1:   I never met with my kids' parents' last year, but this year I got one-third of them to come to parents' night.

ARTS MAGNET TEACHER #3:   In the magnet we have students for two periods a day, for four years. It may be wonderful or terrible, but you get a very intimate contact. Kids tell us things they won't tell their parents. You can act as a counselor as well as a teacher. I think it's important that we have a group of kids we are responsible for. We can't just pass them on to guidance counselors or administrators. We have to say we'll be responsible. I know it works.

ARTS MAGNET TEACHER #4: I have a bone to pick. I think you're missing the boat about the Essential School. Eight years ago [in the arts magnet] we had kids for all four years. We wanted our own guidance counselor and were told, "We can't do it." We wanted to have our own English, science, social studies, and math teachers. And we were told, "We can't do it." See, our teaching was ten percent music and ninety percent life. We saw kids mature with time regardless of ethnicity. You're wasting time figuring out what we already know: the kids are there because they love being with us. They don't love math, English, history, and science. So please don't keep this dialogue only in your four areas! Students choose to be in the arts magnet. They don't choose math, science, and English.

CHAIR: I don't think we should try to air all our frustrations. Let's get down to the concrete.

COORDINATOR: I'm not trying to set our work in opposition to the magnet.

UNIVERSITY REPRESENTATIVE #1:   I hear a terrific need for a sense of community. Some groups have created that, like the arts magnet. The school is working with kids who are failing and with parents who don't commit themselves to their kids' education. But somehow we need to consider if this high school needs to work as teams so you can have an impact on kids and get parents involved. We may have to do things differently, assume different responsibilities, create a different organization. We have a need for more intensive relationships with kids and their parents and other faculty members.

ESL TEACHER #2:   The Essential School is an experiment in curriculum reform. We all need to think about how we can give our population something relevant and important to their lives. Lots of kids don't buy what we try to teach.

PRINCIPAL: I think we could have a two-tiered Essential School, one connected with the arts magnet and one not. Intimacy seems to work. It gets parents to meetings. It's not always successful, but it's more successful. The comprehensive high school doesn't work for the alienated kid. Today proved that if we want to move and take control of this place, we can. With some common direction, we could do a lot more. If we want to change, the time is now. And I'm not talking about change for the sake of change, but in a well-ordered, systematic manner. What we've talked about here tonight is the real need for communication. When you get that in place, other things seem to happen.

UNIVERSITY REPRESENTATIVE #1: The population you're teaching is as needy as I've ever seen. I was bowled over by [the Dean of Students'] statistics. To deal with these problems, I'm talking about creating smaller units in the school and teaching in teams as the way to go, which leads me to see the need for real change, like people teaching beyond their certification. Maybe you should just offer two subjects, humanities and math/science. It would be a radical reorganization. But it is the only way you can do it.

CHAIR: We have no control over such decisions.

UNIVERSITY REPRESENTATIVE #1: It's a union issue as I see it. The State Commissioner of Education has let math teachers in the Essential School teach science.

ARTS MAGNET TEACHER #1: It sounds as though you're suggesting getting rid of things.

UNIVERSITY REPRESENTATIVE #1: No, there could be art, music, and other fine arts in the curriculum. You, as an art teacher, could teach writing skills too.

PRINCIPAL: We have a good chance to get something done here. [The local university] is a catalyst and we have the cooperation of the Commissioner of Education. But we have to get our act together and make realistic demands. We can't say we want twenty more teachers. This group has to be together.

ESL TEACHER #2: I'm having trouble getting from the abstract to the concrete. We have one proposal regarding a reorganization of homeroom. We have another to have all 9th grade English classes meet during the same period. Do we really know what our kids' educational needs are?

DEPARTMENT CHAIR: I feel it's hard to believe our kids are reading so poorly. I was told by people in the superintendent's office that only 100 kids aren't reading on grade level. Maybe we can show the superintendent we need help to get our kids up to grade level in reading.

CHAIR: So what do we do? Create committees? Any proposals?

ESSENTIAL SCHOOL TEACHER #1:   How about if we all come with specific ideas to the next meeting?

LARGER SCHOOL TEACHER #5:   We can write down suggestions, collate them, and share them with everyone.

PRINCIPAL: If we're going to change homeroom period, we need to do it quickly. It wouldn't be a problem if the union were involved all along. If faculty approve such a move, I could take it to the superintendent.

LARGER SCHOOL TEACHER #6:   I think we need to do a needs assessment before we can decide where we want to go.

COORDINATOR: Maybe the focus for the next meeting could be: how can we organize Russell to develop a more personalized atmosphere? The key to the Essential School is the extra planning time we have. I think it would be key to making the entire building work.

ESL TEACHER #2:   Tomorrow, let's have another day like we had today.

Subsequently, some participants took the "homeroom proposal" to the entire faculty, to see if they could take fifteen minutes from the twenty-five-minute homeroom period and add that time to the school day itself. At an April meeting, faculty rejected this proposal.

Summary

This second meeting of the 1992 Committee offers a useful lens for understanding Russell High, as well as the work the 1992 Committee would eventually undertake. Throughout this meeting control and order were prominent themes. An arts magnet teacher said that "keeping the corridors clear of students" was "a prerequisite for learning." The chair reinforced this point, "To learn you need order, and we all thought the school was beautiful today." When asked how the Essential School helped students develop "better study habits," the coordinator explained, "We keep them after class, we call their homes, we send them to the assistant principal, and teachers send students to me," all punitive actions.[4]

Yet control and order were not the faculty's only concern. An arts magnet teacher hoped this effort would translate into "an atmosphere where we ask what we can do beyond [issues of order]." An ESL teacher and the dean of students urged faculty to initiate a redesign of curricula. An Essential School teacher suggested the school "establish some kind of communication about academics and our curriculum so we . . . could support each other," and the coordinator thought faculty should collectively determine how they would create "a more personalized atmosphere." Various directions for school change were suggested by the university representatives.

Furthermore, a concern the chair voiced early in the meeting would continue to be an issue: What power did this group actually have? Could they make binding decisions even though not all faculty participated? As the chair noted, establishing a formal committee "might violate union regulations." Later, the principal felt a need to keep the union "involved" with the committee's initiatives. As committee work continued, concerns arose as to whether faculty could be required to enforce what the committee proposed as well as whether the administration would support committee proposals.

Faculty interactions at this meeting also suggested something of the tension that can accompany discussions of reform. When one teacher felt a need to make the community aware of the school's "handicapped" population, another took offense, saying, "no one is handicapped by their ethnicity." After faculty argued for the need to adapt one's teaching to the student population, one teacher remarked, "There's no such thing as Hispanic algebra," leading to a mini-debate on the relative merits of bilingual education. Feeling excluded from the conversation, a magnet teacher bluntly stated, "[P]lease don't keep this dialogue only in your four areas! Students choose to be in the arts magnet. They don't choose math, science, and English." Quite simply, tense meetings are unlikely to be fun. In these gatherings teachers commonly disagreed with one another in aggressive and potentially insulting ways. Over time, for many faculty it simply became easier not to attend meetings.

A final and revealing aspect of this meeting was its ending, revealing as to the uncertainty, inexperience, and lack of expertise of those participating. As the chair asked, "So what do we do? Create committees? Any proposals?" No one was sure of appropriate next steps. The chair, although knowledgeable in union matters, had no experience with school change, as did most everyone else at the meeting. When committee members subsequently sought to restructure the homeroom period, their inability to secure faculty support seemed to reflect a lack of experience. When the motion came to a vote the following April, many unanswered questions remained (e.g., Could faculty revoke this decision if it proved ineffective? Did the union support this action?). In large part because proponents of the change were unable to address these concerns, the motion was defeated.

Six Months Later (June 1987)

At this point, many involved with the 1992 Committee were frustrated. Meetings that thirty to forty teachers once attended, now had no more than seven or eight, plus one or two university representatives and perhaps someone from an educational consulting firm. Still uncertain of both their formal power and official charge, just before school ended committee members sent a letter to all faculty hoping to clarify their institutional status and renew interest in their work:

> As a result of the "Russell 1992" dinner meetings held in the last few months . . . a committee was generated to look into ways to improve the educational climate at Russell. This committee recently sent you . . . an outline pinpointing some of the more poignant needs of the Russell student population. We are attempting to get a consensus of opinion from faculty supporting the ideas set out in this outline and are therefore asking for your endorsement and comments. The committee will continue to meet during summer so your support at this time is crucial. Please sign the sheet in the main office before you leave and give us your educational and emotional support. Be optimistic about the potential for improvement— DON'T GIVE UP!

An attached sheet outlined the issues on which the committee sought consensus:

The Institutional Function of Russell High
Acknowledged Goal:
By example and instruction, to educate young people in good citizenship, as well as in academic areas as they apply to each segment of our population.
Facts for Consideration:
- Most obstacles which interfere with the accomplishment of our goal fall into one or more of three general categories: (1) citizenship; (2) curriculum; (3) physical plant.
- While acknowledging the interdependency of these categories, it is imperative to recognize that, without good citizenship, curriculum and physical plant have a limited impact.
- There must be consensus as to what constitutes good citizenship.
- There has to be a commitment by Russell administrators, teachers and staff to create and maintain an environment where the institution's goal can be achieved.

Conclusions:

1. The goal of the school must be stated and consistently promoted.
2. We must insist on good citizenship.
3. Clear, concise rules of behavior and penalties must be applied.
4. Prompt and consistent enforcement is essential.
5. Individuals who habitually disrupt the legitimate function of the school must be held accountable.
6. Alternative programs should be developed for those who do not function in our environment.

Although this memo acknowledged that the 1992 Committee was created to "look into ways to improve the educational climate at Russell," it is revealing of the teachers' beliefs that the committee emphasized issues of order and discipline so emphatically, framed in terms of "citizenship." Indeed, in outlining the school's "acknowledged goal," citizenship preceded mention of academics. Even though two "obstacles" to realizing the institution's goal included the curriculum and physical plant, nothing more was said about these topics except that "without good citizenship, curriculum and physical plant have a limited impact." There was no mention of changing students' educational experiences. From the committee's point of view, the school was not realizing its overall goal because existing policies were ineffectively enforced; the assumptions underlying these rules and policies were assumed to be effective and appropriate.

March 16, 1988: A 1992 Committee Meeting

INTRODUCTION. *Well into its second year, the committee designated a chair, a respected teacher who was selected for her reputation as well as her non-political stance; she was considered open-minded and tied to no particular faculty clique. As was true throughout its existence, the committee had difficulty finding time to meet as an entire faculty. On this early-release day (i.e., classes ended at noon) the afternoon was set aside for the 1992 Committee. A faculty memo described the meeting as: "Improving the Learning Environment at Russell, Part 1: Discipline and Teacher Unity." There would be three activities: First, participants watched a video that explored the issue of "teacher frustration." Next, they worked in small groups to "identify three actions all teachers could take that would make everyone's life easier at Russell." Third, the group reconvened and a department chair facilitated the process of "organizing and condensing the suggestions to three commitments of action to which all teachers agree to adhere."*

Thirty-one teachers, slightly less than half the faculty, attended the
meeting.

The chair began the meeting by saying, "At our last session, things seemed a bit disorganized. There was no unity. So we want to bring everyone together to watch this video on discipline. It will focus on teacher communication too. The video was made by the Eastown Teachers' Union and while it's not aimed exactly at what we want to address, it does deal with the issue of teacher frustration." A teacher asked, "Should the assistant principals be here?" The chair responded, "They were invited." Russell's union representative then noted, "We have reinstituted the Faculty Governance Committee [another reform initiative focused on setting discipline policies] if you want to join." Suggesting both skepticism and interest, a teacher asked, "What does it involve? Endless, tedious meetings or are we really getting something done?" The question was never answered.

Faculty then watched the video in which a science teacher encountered discipline problems in his class. In response, he relieved his frustration in his car on the way home, screaming about students, and honking his horn. The following day, the teacher's second day at school, he couldn't wait for the day to end so he could get in his car and relieve his frustration once more. By the third day, the teacher was so exasperated by his classes he put mustard in his coffee, thinking it was sugar. He had tried to be strict with students. He tried being lenient. He scheduled a parent conference. Nothing seemed to work. However, when he talked directly to the student with whom he had problems, he found it was not that the student wouldn't do the work, but that he couldn't do it. He needed assistance. After receiving extra help, the student did fine.

When the video ended, the chair remarked, "The point to this video is to highlight the frustration we're feeling, especially with discipline. So we want a general focus for all of us, and discipline seems to be key." She also said there had been a "general sense of euphoria" after earlier committee meetings because faculty had enforced "no pass" rules and required students who violated the policy to make up that time after school. She ended her comments by saying, "[The principal] will support three ideas immediately and implement them. The idea is to focus our ideas on three concerns . . . knowing we'd be backed up by the administration."

The teachers then got into small groups to determine three actions they could take to "make everyone's life easier at Russell." The memo teachers were given also said, "Please word each commitment of action so it is: (1) simple; (2) positive; (3) attainable; and

(4) unanimous." The group I observed included two English teachers, an ESL teacher, and a guidance counselor. The principal joined the group after about twenty minutes. This group focused on control, order, and discipline. Suggested improvements included imposing academic penalties for lateness to class and instituting an in-house suspension program. The group also spent a good deal of time clarifying policies related to control and order (e.g., how one teacher successfully stopped students from skipping his class; how the principal was restricted in suspending behaviorally-disturbed students). Some topics were not so tied to control and order. The guidance counselor asked whether "students really value what goes on in their classes?" Others questioned whether they really had administrative support to undertake their work.

Following these discussions, the chair asked each group to present its proposals, reminding faculty that these actions should have an "immediate positive effect." The first spokesperson said, "Number one, close the doors to your room during homeroom to prevent students from wandering in and out. Number two, students with walkmen will be sent to the office and the walkman will be confiscated and held until June. And number three, there will be no excused latenesses to class." The second group then reported:

> First, no teacher can keep a student out of another teacher's class without that teacher's permission, that includes the nurse and the Rainbow Center [the school's center for teen parents]. Second, teachers will uniformly and continuously enforce the policy on class cuts. The first time you cut, it's a one-hour detention; two hours for the second cut; the third cut is a suspension. Third, all teachers will move students into class as soon as they arrive at your room. They will be in class when the bell rings. We can't force them to be seated.

The spokesperson for the third group prefaced his remarks by saying his group had come up with "similar ideas": "First, one kid can be out of the room at a time. There will be a time limit on all passes. To make this work, all clocks in the building must work [at the time many did not]. And students have to stay in their seats until the bell rings at the end of class, instead of wandering around the room or out the door."

After hearing these groups, a teacher reacted, "We seem to be rewriting the discipline code. But the problem is compliance. It takes teachers to recognize the rules, then to help students follow them. And the most important factor of all, to apply the disciplinary rules to those who don't follow them. Do we have the *chutzpah* for that?" A colleague countered, "It's not a question of *chutzpah*. Do we have the stamina?" Another remarked, "A lot of people don't do these things." A fourth added, "We get tired. We need injections of enthusiasm at times."

The chair then recognized the final group whose spokesperson said, "Students will be sent to an assistant principal's office for all major infractions. Teachers will combine as a unit to cover areas in the building. If teachers hear noise in the hallways, more than one teacher will try to deal with it." One teacher added, "Unless it's special-ed students." Picking up on the remark, the principal said, "We can't suspend special-ed kids for more than ten days a year. . . . I have no authority to suspend a b-d kid [behaviorally disturbed]. I can't suspend a kid for having a walkman if he's b-d. Otherwise, I always suspend kids with walkmen."

The chair then posed a question, "What can we do tomorrow to make a difference in our lives?" A teacher replied, "Clear the corridors." Another responded, "But the entire faculty is not here to make the decision." One teacher asked the principal, "Is the 8:25 bell the signal to move to homeroom?" The principal acknowledged it was, and the teacher added, "So let's clearly define this for students. The students are always saying, 'It's not 8:30 yet.'" Attempting to summarize these remarks, the chair noted, "So we need teachers actively out in the corridors?" Another teacher asked, "If students are late to homeroom, they are to receive a detention, right?"

At this point, the bell rang to end the school day. Every teacher remained in the room. Offering another strategy, a teacher said, "One student is to be out of class at a time and there is to be a five-minute time limit on all passes." Another raised a concern, "I think we can only vote if we realize the significance of our vote. Will teachers acknowledge there are real discipline issues involved? We have to agree on what this means. Are these important concerns?" A colleague replied, "I think we answered your question by going through this process." Another teacher offered a different observation, "[What's being proposed] can't be done because kids can't be told what to do. I've been spat at too many times this year. I'm out in the halls everyday with [another teacher] and we tell them and we tell them and we tell them." A teacher then asked:

> But would these reforms improve the school? Let's suspend our disbelief for a moment. Also, will teachers assist in implementing these proposals? Will you try? If we'll try then a third question arises: Will teachers insist the policy be enforced by following through with proper disciplinary procedures—submitting cut slips,

disciplinary reports, and FTRs [failure-to-report slips submitted to assistant principals for those who skip detention]—to see what happens? If a kid doesn't comply with our legitimate requests, will we follow appropriate procedures? And if that's not done, will we question *why* the system breaks down?

The chair replied, "My understanding is the administration will follow through on our proposals." Those in attendance then voted unanimously to adopt the following: (1) Teachers will assume responsibility for keeping corridors clear during homeroom and classes; (2) students late to school will be assigned detention; and (3) one student at a time will be allowed out of class, with a five-minute time limit. The next day the following memo was distributed to all faculty and read over the intercom during homeroom:

> The following three actions were unanimously agreed upon at yesterday's meeting. We all agree to act on these three starting TODAY as a means of improving the learning environment at Russell and demonstrating our support of one another.
> (1) Teachers will clear the corridors during passings and before homeroom. Students are to be in their rooms *BEFORE* the bell rings. Teachers will assist one another to facilitate passings and prevent corridor disturbances.
> (2) Teachers will keep late students after school (late is coming in after the bell). Students late to school will stay for the appropriate assistant principal.
> (3) Teachers will allow only one student out of class at a time and will write on the pass a three- or five-minute time limit depending on the distance between the classroom and destination.

That day, I toured the school's corridors and found many teachers were active and visible, generally those who attended the meeting. Many students had headed to the less-traveled areas of Russell High and were on the look-out for staff seeking to enforce these rules. Two weeks later, things seemed pretty much unchanged. Students gathered in the corridors during homeroom and few teachers did anything about it.

Summary

In the small group sessions and larger meeting, control and order were prominent topics. The group I observed discussed actions they could take so students would follow school rules more consistently.

The larger discussion addressed no issue but order and discipline. These were proposals the small groups had unanimously endorsed. And all three proposals put forth by the committee were directed toward more consistent enforcement of existing policies. Nothing directly related to pedagogy, curriculum, or assessment was proposed. This was where teachers found consensus. Even though two other schoolwide meetings were planned, on curriculum and citizenship, they were never held.

Here again, teachers unquestioningly embraced behaviorist practices, largely punitive, that were thought to be "simple . . . positive . . . [and] attainable." These actions would "improve the educational climate at Russell." Further, the committee's proposals embodied an unproblematic view of educational opportunity. As one teacher said in her small group, "The most important things for students are: first, come to school; second, go to class. Everything else will fall into place if they do that." In the eyes of most faculty members, educational opportunity existed, regardless of whether students embraced this opportunity.

In terms of student participation, it says a great deal about Russell High that no student attended this meeting. Although the video stressed the value of listening to students to better understand issues of discipline, this topic was never addressed in the larger discussion nor the small group meeting I observed.

The End of the 1992 Committee

During the 1988–89 school year, the 1992 Committee received outside funding for its work when the State created "Governor's Schools." As a possible reform site, Russell High was awarded $20,000 to help the school investigate the feasibility of joining this initiative. A local educational consulting firm assisted the committee. To oversee this effort a steering committee was created. The committee published a newsletter and established subcommittees that dealt with issues related to school governance and departmental restructuring. Faculty visited restructuring schools, attended professional conferences, and reported their findings to the steering committee. The school bought books, subscribed to education journals, and purchased a copy machine. That year, over a third of all faculty either attended committee meetings, were involved with committee-related projects, or served on a subcommittee.

During the 1989–90 school year, the Governor's School funds ran out and interest in the 1992 Committee declined. A core of interested faculty and university personnel continued to meet. Occasionally, administrators attended meetings. By 1990–91, the steering committee and subcommittees no longer met and the newsletter was not published. Involved faculty attributed this inactivity, in part, to adjustments made to prepare for an accreditation study in that year, although the study was postponed. Since the school planned to subsume 1992 Committee work with the accreditation process, no time was set aside for the committee per se. By the fall of 1991, the 1992 Committee no longer existed.

CONCLUSION: REPRODUCING THE STATUS QUO

The 1992 Committee had a limited effect on Russell High. The initiative did succeed in involving a sizable percentage of the school—teachers, administrators, guidance counselors, and parents—in some reform activity. But these efforts, including the many initiatives aimed at tightening discipline policies, had little, if any, lasting effect. A team of teachers, for instance, were to develop graduation exhibitions—in-depth, culminating activities in which students "exhibit" mastery of multiple subject areas—for English, math, social studies, and science.[5] The committee met, but no changes were implemented. Some teachers sought to integrate the Essential School with the arts magnet program but the two remained separate entities. Projects to coordinate biology and health curricula, to develop an interdisciplinary game that "linked the central themes of Western civilization," and to create a "house" for 9th grade at-risk students were initiated, but never implemented. The committee did get a proposal passed that created time for faculty to prepare for the accreditation visit.

As is argued throughout, Russell High was not structured to promote educational opportunity; this was true for the 1992 Committee as well. While teachers embraced control and order as the means to improve education, there was no way to thoughtfully question this pervasive belief. There was little time for teachers to reflect on their work, aside from what they took from their personal lives. And when time was set aside to do so, issues of discipline and order dominated faculty discussions. Although schoolwide meetings were held, they were few and they were not truly schoolwide, as no more than three-quarters of the faculty ever attended any committee meeting.

Given the dismal dropout and failure rates of Russell students, as well as the institution's inability to maintain order, it seems amazing that the status quo proved so enduring. Yet, it also seems reasonable

to ask: Why *should* teachers have changed? They and their colleagues, a key source of professional validation (Bidwell and Hoffer,
1996), largely endorsed what they were already doing. There was
no conclusive evidence to substantiate the value of alternative
approaches to teaching and learning, at least none to which these
teachers had access. People were willing to consider change, as
evidenced by the many faculty who participated in some aspect of this
reform. But enacting reform was another matter, especially when the
institution provided so little support. Teachers weren't going to
change what they believed and what they did because of what they
heard at a few two-hour meetings. In addition, as they sought to
implement change, many teachers were uncertain how to go about
doing so (Sarason, 1990). Enacting power beyond the classroom or
department was new to virtually every member of the committee.
And this inexperience was undermined by the lack of clarity
regarding the committee's mission and formal power, leaving many of
those committed to reform unclear as to what they could undertake.

In an ironic twist, this change effort actually reinforced the status
quo. Most actions the committee initiated sought to intensify
practices already common to the school, not to rethink the nature of
education offered students. When the committee's work ended, the
following developments were apparent:

- A faculty already divided—the Essential School versus the arts
  magnet versus the comprehensive high school versus the ESL
  program—found little common ground. In a related vein, many
  teachers grew increasingly skeptical of their ability to collectively
  enact change (Sarason, 1971).
- The prevailing assumption regarding educational opportunity,
  that this democratic right was available for those who wanted it,
  was implicitly endorsed as the committee never considered
  changing the education provided to students.
- Faculty had their faith in behaviorism reaffirmed. It was the only
  topic that united teachers. And there was a ready-made excuse
  for its failings—people didn't enforce discipline policies consistently. Teachers endorsed this philosophy so willingly that an
  issue ostensibly resolved prior to the second committee meeting—
  that of students being out of homeroom and in the hallways
  during class—was, one year later, resolved again in the exact
  same fashion, by trying to impose more effective sanctions on
  students.
- Russell students had virtually no input into this initiative. In
  committee meetings such perceptions of students as "out of

control," and the school as being "under siege" were not only never questioned, they were regularly reinforced by participants' remarks. Student views on such matters were never explored. Moreover, throughout the committee's work faculty were reacting to students as a collective, in effect, defining their personal capital for them. And this was by no means an objective process. Russell students started with a "dirty" slate, and this reality had major ramifications for their education.

6

RESPECTABILITY LOST

An Historical Perspective on Russell High School

> We need to comprehend how the limits we all live
> within are historical limits. Thus . . . history is
> not to be relegated to the collection of "back-
> ground data," but rather becomes an integral part
> of the explanation of the regularities explored in
> any specific analysis.
> —Roger Simon and Donald Dippo,
> "On Critical Ethnographic Work"

[handwritten margin note: historical limits.]

When I was conducting research at Russell High (1986–91) the school had a poor reputation; but this was not always the case. Through much of its history, Russell was seen as an exemplary school, with many graduates going on to respected colleges and universities and students from nearby towns with no high schools enrolling because of the school's good name. By the late eighties and early nineties, perceptions of Russell High in Eastown were quite different. Many saw the school as a catch-all for the city's least desirable and least academic students. Although many factors contributed to this transition, one occurrence, a "riot"[1] by African American students in May of 1969, became a defining moment in Russell High's loss of respectability.

[handwritten margin note: 1969 riot]

While this event can be understood in various ways—as a reflection of unhealthy race relations, as students out of control, as the inevitable consequence of inequities in the school system, as a social tragedy with no winners—one point is indisputable: The African American students who initiated the "riot" had rejected

[handwritten margin note: reasons for the riot.]

123

traditional American beliefs and assumptions about educational opportunity, publicly and aggressively. Because of what was happening in American society at the time, these students began to see their schooling differently. Rather than being a purely individual experience, largely a reflection of the effort one exerted, they now saw a collective element to educational opportunity. As African Americans, they felt their educational experiences were qualitatively different from those of white students. Further, they wanted a say in defining educational opportunity. They wanted classes to reflect their interests and history. They asked for greater representation in student government. With the taken-for-granted challenged, the school system was uncertain how to respond. District and school administrators took no formal action on student demands until after the "riot." As momentum built behind the protest, Russell High was thrown into turmoil, and ultimately chaos.[2] In the words of *The East-town Gazette*, it was "Mindless, wanton vandalism and violence"—a characterization that seems appropriate for both the students and the school system. In one instance, the "vandalism and violence" were very immediate and very apparent; in the other, they were more long-term and subtle phenomena.

Yet in the opinion of many, African American and white, the school system and Eastown community responded in positive ways to this tragic, destructive event. Students gained a voice in educational matters. The school's curriculum was revised. The school department sought to hire more teachers of color. Russell's student government was restructured. Parents became a routine part of school life. Despite innovation and reform, with time and demographic changes, the school's reputation worsened. There was a sense that what had been gained was mostly lost. And this perception had clear racial and socioeconomic overtones, as increasing numbers of low-income, students of color were bussed to Russell after the "riot." Few students from the immediate neighborhood, aside from a core of African American students, attended the school. Russell became Eastown's least desirable high school.

A HISTORY OF RUSSELL HIGH SCHOOL

The First Sixty Years: 1898–1960

The original Russell High opened in the fall of 1898.[3] The school enrolled 500 students in grades six through twelve. At the time, Russell was one of the more impressive schools in the area, having an auditorium, science labs with the most up-to-date equipment, class-rooms that accommodated over forty students, and separate boys' and girls' gymnasiums. Even then, the school tracked students, dividing them between "classical" and "English" groups, each attending classes in separate wings of the building. The most prominent clubs were the Boys and Girls Debate Societies. When the U.S. entered World War I, military training for boys became part of the curriculum. Girls served as Red Cross volunteers. The school collected tinfoil for the war effort. The winning entry in the student essay contest was entitled, "Severing Relations Between the United States and Germany."

The twenties and thirties saw change at Russell High. Boys and girls competed on the same debate teams. The school instituted honors courses in English, science, and math, and further differentiated its tracking system, adding commercial, fine arts, and general tracks to its existing classical and English divisions. German and French clubs as well as a literary magazine were begun. There were boys and girls glee clubs, a band, and a dramatic society. In 1933 Russell had its first female editor for the school paper.

As part of Franklin Roosevelt's New Deal, in the late thirties the Works Progress Administration built a new Russell High. Relative to the original building, the school was immense. There was a large cafeteria, two gymnasiums, music rooms, and shops. Department heads had their own offices. That year the school instituted a student government that directed student activities but also made suggestions to the principal on "how to improve the school." In 1939, the school established its present tracking system, dividing students into three divisions—C-level (the highest), B-level, and A-level—according to IQ's and scores on a reading exam. *tracking*

When World War II broke out, the school again responded, adding courses on camouflage, aeronautics, and marine naval science to the curriculum. Students and faculty left to serve the country. The school's Victory Corps included over 500 students. Shortly after the war, Russell had its first African American class president, a student later to be the second African American to graduate from the U.S. Naval Academy. In the fifties and early sixties, Russell continued to expand and differentiate its curriculum, adding advanced placement courses in English, foreign languages, mathematics, chemistry, and physics.

For most of the sixties, Russell High was a respected school. Its graduates, usually about a third of each class, attended good colleges and universities. In the Eastown vicinity, only Latin High sent more students to Ivy League and other select schools. Nearly one-quarter of all students participated in band, choral, or theater organizations. The athletic program had a solid reputation. Russell's graduates included three Rhodes Scholars, an ambassador to Great Britain, a president of Chase National Bank, a prominent news correspondent, and a general who commanded the first divisions to enter Manila during World War II.

The "Riot" of 1969

In the early sixties, many Eastown schools were racially divided, a reflection of neighborhood segregation coupled with a school department policy that "allowed parents a free choice of schools, provided they assumed responsibility for transportation."[4] In a city that was ten percent African American, three-quarters or more of the students at seven grade schools were African American. Every high school was out of compliance with guidelines set by the Eastown Desegregation Plan, the city's self-initiated effort to integrate schools. Latin and Travis High enrolled too few students of color; Archibald and Russell enrolled too many. At this time, Russell High served many students from the city's wealthiest neighborhood, Lesh Park, as well as many working-class whites and a sizable number of African Americans, about thirty percent of the school.

On the national scene civil rights and racial issues were visible, highly charged concerns. Malcolm X was assassinated in 1965; Martin Luther King in April of 1968. Black Power, the Freedom Marches, and riots in Watts, Newark, and Chicago were national news. Prompted by these and related events, some African American students at Russell grew skeptical of the education they were being offered. They maintained that the school's curriculum ignored African American contributions to American society. They grew sensitive to the fact that African American students were under-represented in honors classes and over-represented in the school's lowest track. They questioned why few African Americans held offices in the student government. They began to see educational opportunity as a group phenomenon and they felt African Americans weren't accorded the same opportunities as white students.

To address their concerns, the students wanted a voice in defining educational opportunity for themselves. Specifically, a core of African American students submitted a list of demands to Russell's administration. These included developing courses in African American history and literature, hiring more faculty of color, allowing students to make up failed courses during summer school, and according African American students a greater say in school government. Later, these students demanded that three "racist" teachers at the school be dismissed. Over a seven-day period, students presented this list of demands to the school's administration; they boycotted classes and organized a protest; they mobilized community support for their action; and as tensions heightened, they reacted in utter rage and violence to what they perceived as the school's reluctance to address their concerns. In carrying out these actions, students consulted with African Americans from the community, African American students at an Eastown university, and representatives from the Student Nonviolent Coordinating Committee, an African American organization led by Stokely Carmichael.

One student who was integral in organizing the protest and who participated in the destruction that followed explained the event from his perspective, that of a young African American in the late sixties.

Why do you think the "riot" occurred?

My generation was the first generation of black Americans at Russell High to really find out what our history was, what our *true* history was. The sixties were a time when black history publications were coming out. Everything that black people were doing was covered by the radio and TV. There was Martin Luther King, Jr., the Freedom Marches. Young blacks at that time were a lot more aware of just exactly what was going down and what their history was and how their ancestors had been treated through the years.

When we began to realize what was going down, we didn't really have anybody to put it all into perspective for us, as to how to view it and how to take it. So we went through an emotional thing where, instead of blaming ourselves for the parts we played [in our social condition], or blaming the system, we tended to blame the people that were closest to us. And those were the whites at the school. Not to say that we didn't have white friends, but after going through elementary school and junior high and being told your people were nothing but a bunch of no good slaves and then you come to find out that your people have contributed something to history, a feeling of pride comes in, and a feeling of frustration. So we tended to lash out a little bit. As we had been hurt in the past, we thought maybe it was time for somebody else to feel some of it. But we really didn't have anybody to direct us along the right way. . . .

There was also a lack of understanding on the part of the school system and the teachers about black history and just what the movement was all about, a lack of concern when matters were brought up by students as to why we couldn't read a few more books in English by black authors. Or in history, why can't we learn a little

[handwritten margin notes: "true history"; "confusion on part of admin"]

more about ourselves, other than the fact that we were slaves? And a lack of concern on [the school system's] part, no action was taken, led to a lot of frustrations. Before the "riot," the school staff, the principal and vice-principal were informed as to how the students felt about this. . . . They told us that their hands were tied, that there was nothing they could do. They said they didn't control the school system and only so much money was allocated for certain kinds of books. . . . They felt as if there was enough black history included in the books and there wasn't. The only mention of blacks in the history books that we had was that blacks were slaves, and that covered maybe one or two pages. That was it. . . .

Was there any outside agitation or was this all done by Russell students?

The students weren't born in the school, they came from the outside. So anything the kids picked up on outside of school, naturally came into the school. . . . The major influence, I would say, was TV. Watching the sit-ins and the Freedom Marches and the March on Washington, Martin Luther King's speech, the Ku Klux Klan kicking people's heads, seeing that everyday. Things like that really sparked . . . the kids of that generation. It was a protest generation. The Vietnam War was just a sign of the times. It was something that just had to be. But as far as the Eastown Branch of the Communist Party [*chuckling*] or the Black Panther movement coming in and saying, "You should do this," it wasn't anything like that. It was the students themselves. . . . It all came from within Russell High. . . . It was kids. . . . What further shows that it was just kids doing it, is the fact that it's not there today. Because if there'd been some real structure behind it, we would have made sure that something lasted.

What was your role in the protest?

I helped to start it. I was into politics. I felt very deeply that great injustices were being done, not only at Russell but in the country in general. I was always interested in the political workings of things. And in talking with some students, I found others felt the same as I did. My main gripe was that black history was ignored within the school. There was no brutality on the part of the administration, no police coming in and messing with the kids. But we felt as if our ancestors had contributed something worthwhile to America and we felt as if they should be talked about within the school system, not neglected. . . . This is not to say that the teachers didn't care, because I believe they really cared. . . . It wasn't a protest against the teachers; it was a protest against the school system itself. I had very good times at Russell. I was on the football team, the basketball team. I had friends, black and white. . . . One of my teachers, my civics teacher, even brought me over to a local university a few times and bought me a few books. . . .

How did the "riot" come about?

It began with me and a few other people talking. We went to the principal first and explained to him what we felt. We gave him a certain amount of time to see what he could come up with. But nothing ever came of it and we felt as if he was putting us off. So one day we decided it was time for action and we called a meeting in the cafeteria. . . . From there we called for a strike. We said we weren't going to go to class. We didn't stay away from the school but we called meetings within the school. We wrote up a list of demands and presented them to the staff. . . . Still, nothing ever came of the meetings. The administration said there was nothing in the budget, that there wasn't anything that they could do, and maybe next year. But we just didn't want to hear it. We wanted things to be done right then and there. We felt if they really wanted it done, it would be done. So it just deteriorated from there and one day we had a meeting and all hell broke loose. Kids running through the school, tearing things up, breaking windows. I don't think anybody was hurt physically. . . .

People didn't sit around for two months planning this thing. It was just some kids who were immature and didn't realize there may have been a better way to go about doing these things. Maybe if we had sat down and planned it out, the things we had gained then would still be in effect today. Because a lot of those things were lost. I don't think they still have a black history course. We could have passed things on to the younger generations, something that would have lasted, a monument.

But it was just youth. It was pent-up energy and emotions. Just like if somebody had locked you in a room and told you that you were a dog all your life and that you were no good and your mother and father were tramps, and then one day you found out, no, it's not like that. You're going to have a lot of pent-up emotions. You might run around and break a few windows too. Not to say it would be the right thing to do. But if you were on the outside looking in, and you were objective, you would say, "Hey, I can understand. It's not the right thing, but I can understand why he's doing it." And that's what it was. It was just kids, trying to be grown-up and doing something that maybe our ancestors, black and white, should have done before us. There should have been black history days. We should have been reading James Baldwin and Richard Wright and other black

authors alongside Fitzgerald and Hemingway, because they all have
something to say. . . .

*history
is
history*

Really, the truth is, history is history. There's no black history
and no white history. It's just history. . . . That's the way I look at it.
If you're going to talk about Christopher Columbus, tell the truth
about him. He didn't discover anything. How can you discover
something when somebody's already there? That's like somebody
walking up to your car and saying, "Hey, look what I discovered."
The truth, that's the only thing that's going to work, the truth. . . .
We weren't just slaves. There were black inventors. There were
black sports heroes. There were great black politicians. . . . But
that's not the way it was taught.

And it means something. It really means a lot to a kid that his
ancestors had done something. Instead of just coming to one page in
a book and seeing some blacks picking cotton and saying, "That's it.
That's all folks."

Another African American who was central to the protest
reflected on his role in the event, and the reasons behind his actions:

It was May of '69 and I was graduating in June. We had a month of
school to go. . . . My question was: How do we make an impact at the
school? My sister was coming to the school the year I left. I wanted
to leave her something. . . . I didn't want her to go through four
years of school, of being part of that populace where they didn't care
if you got educated or got involved in activities. As a matter of fact,
certain activities weren't even opened up to certain populations in
the school. We didn't have very many minority students in the
Future Teachers of America [*laughs*]. We didn't have very many
folks in the drama club, on the debate team. . . . The Student
Council didn't have many blacks on it. . . . Most activities were
restricted to a certain population of the school. . . . Aside from
football and basketball and two cheerleaders, there were no blacks
involved in anything. It wasn't that you couldn't be involved, but it
was unwritten: you didn't get involved. They didn't want you
involved. If you got involved, you were out of there for one reason or
another. They made it uncomfortable for you to be involved. . . .

Say we graduated maybe 450 students, they only attempted to
educate maybe 150 of that 450. The rest, they didn't give a damn
about one way or the other. . . . Among minority students, you could
count the five selected to get an education, and everybody else was
left to fend for themselves. Guidance counselors didn't guide us to go
to college [laughs]. I applied to the Yale School of Drama and my

guidance counselor laughed at me. . . . He never spoke to me once about filling out a college application, never gave me the date when SATs were or anything else. He was a nice guy, don't get me wrong. . . . [But] I feel I was a pretty astute kid, but they weren't trying to educate me to go to college. They were trying to educate me to go to Vietnam. That was one of our protests: they're not preparing us for the world. . . . The law states that a kid under sixteen years old has to go to school. But the law doesn't state that the educators who collect the salary have to make sure that kid gets an education. . . .

How did the notion arise among students that something was wrong at Russell and with the school system? How did this evolve into a "riot?"

[The previously quoted Russell graduate] and I were both involved outside of school in various groups, speaking to black issues at that time. . . . So one day we said we ought to do something about it. So we sat down and drew up . . . a list of proposals that were patterned after the March on Washington. . . . Then we met with an assistant principal [an African American] and said, "What do you think of this?" And he said, "I don't think you should go about it like this, guys." But we were pretty high strung so we said, "We didn't think you would think that we should go about it like this but. . . . " What he was really trying to do was calm us down and let us know that there was only a month of school to go. He was ready to go on vacation. . . . But we wanted to make an impact. We wanted a change. So I walked into the principal's office and said, "We need to talk," and I gave him a list of demands . . . and brought up some issues about how we were part of the school from the community who were being ignored by the school. . . . And again, they were going to use the blanket of, "Well, here it is May. The school year's over. We can't do anything this year."

We told them what we wanted and they . . . said, "Well, let's think about it over the weekend," hoping it would blow over. But we went . . . down to a [local] university on that Friday night—a whole coalition of people who were going to see this thing through, guys and girls—and we met with some of the black leaders at the university . . . and went over some suggestions about where we'd go from here, different avenues that we might take this thing. We wanted to make sure that we had the people in the community involved, so we notified the parents. And before we knew it, we had a house full of people . . . and it got a whole lot bigger over the weekend than anyone expected. So when we went back Monday, we had a lot of ideas but nothing concrete. So we sat down and tried to put some structure to this whole thing: Where are we going to take it? What will we settle for? How can we get a commitment from the school system?

That Monday, when we went back to school, the administration said they respected our right to boycott, so they opened the auditorium for anyone who didn't want to go to class . . . and on Monday and Tuesday they let us not go to class, but they never met with us. So on Wednesday we decided to have another meeting with the community, parents, everybody. We went to one of the elementary schools in our neighborhood and discussed with our parents what we should do. Of course, their whole thing was, "You better go to school." And they were right, education is the key. But why go to school if no one wants to educate you? There's no sense in just putting in time. . . . We decided our passive resistance approach was not having the effect we thought it would. We had to do something else. So we got help from the Student Nonviolent Coordinating Committee [SNCC], Stokely Carmichael's group, and students at [a local university]. And we . . . had this representative from SNCC speak to us in the auditorium. And he gave a pretty powerful speech on Thursday.

It'd been almost ten days since the whole thing started and [the SNCC representative] made it perfectly clear to us that the administration was not interested in educating us. As long as the school was open, that was all they cared about. . . . As long as they were educating the select few who they cared to educate, they weren't going to do a damn thing about what we were talking about. So naturally we rebelled against that. And the rest is really history. We did $50,000 worth of damage to the school. . . . I distinctly remember seeing every window in that building broken. . . .

It was not intended to have it go that way, but that's the way it went. It got out of hand, I'll be the first to say that. But what we did was good for the school system. It put a jolt in them, and told them to wake up. Here are seventeen- and eighteen-year-old kids who are seeing what you're doing and are going to have some input in how you educate them. . . .

After the "riot" you met with the superintendent and school committee. What did you tell them?

What we basically told them was the truth—that people were frustrated with the quality of education they were getting and the bottom line was . . . we were the backbone of the school and we were being ignored. We didn't have any equal representation. We didn't have any say in anything. . . . Our protest was about getting the school back for the kids. . . . And the only way we got any say was to pull something like that. And they say "riot," but it wasn't really a "riot," it was just a group of kids caught up in the times. That's all it was. . . . All we wanted to do was close the school for awhile and let them know this was a real issue. . . .

After the protest and destruction, how did the school system respond?
After it reached that point, I think that everybody who had a negative reaction took that negative and turned it into a positive. I, in turn, got to see how school should work. After the "riot," they sat down and gave us a chance to voice our opinion. We set up a student coalition that touched every part of the student body. . . . We had student leaders from all the schools sit down with the super-intendent. Nobody ever met with the superintendent of schools as a student in Eastown. I went to his house and we discussed the issues going on at school. I have to say after this there was a real concern because that let them know something was dreadfully wrong with the system and something had to be changed. . . .

In an editorial published the day after the violence and destruction, *The Eastown Gazette* offered its view of the situation:

MINDLESS RAMPAGE

Mindless, wanton vandalism and violence. There is no other way to describe the outbreak of a group of young blacks at Russell High School and throughout Lesh Park yesterday in Eastown. They cut loose without provocation even as school officials were working for reasonable compromise on blacks' "demands."

Unruly dissidents, perhaps with eager help from nonstudents, had their thing in a dangerous and futile exercise in imitation of their elders on campuses of New York City colleges and else-where. . . . A minority—a tiny minority of almost 1,500 students— has forced the closing of Russell for a period of days and perhaps at the critical cost of suspension of the educative process for themselves and for the overwhelming majority, whites and blacks alike. . . .

Ten days after the protest erupted into mayhem and destruction, the husband of a Russell teacher outlined his perspective on the event in a letter to his daughter:

. . . The Russell story is roughly this: The black students all went to the auditorium on a Friday to make demands for Afro-American history, more liberal summer make-up work, and the removal of "racist" teachers. The administration was quite willing to negotiate.

Classes were called off on Monday and on Tuesday and the blacks were allowed to meet by themselves (but not all of them were Russell students) in the auditorium while a negotiating team met with officials in the office. Apparently some of them wanted a blow-up, because the demands eventually included one which could not possibly be met—that accused teachers actually be brought in to face the accusations of the group. Just about at the time this was reported back to the auditorium (that is, the rejection of this demand), there was an incident involving two white girls which gave rise to the rumor that some of the blacks would be charged with attempted rape. The rumor may well have been used for conscious effect.[5] Anyway, a rather large number of students (the papers said 200, but it was probably twenty or thirty who actually did anything), broke up the stage settings for a planned presentation of *Little Mary Sunshine* and using these as clubs, burst out into the lobby and down the corridor, smashing everything smashable. They did not set out to do bodily harm, apparently, but a few people were injured. . . . The teachers and students were sent home almost immediately and there was no school the rest of the week. The teachers met on Friday from 8:30 in the morning until 1:30 the next morning! School has been in session this past week, but very uneasily, with greatly reduced attendance. . . .

Throughout its existence, Russell High experienced change, most was gradual. Girls and boys weren't on the same debate team until 1920. The first young woman became editor of the school paper in the thirties. Student council was initiated in 1938. In the forties, Russell had its first African American class president. During national crises the school supported our national agenda—adding military training to the school's curriculum and creating a Victory Corps. In the late sixties some of Russell's African American students wanted change fast, and what they wanted did not accord with any national agenda. When the school system balked at student demands, a violent disruption ensued which caused substantial damage to Russell High, physically and symbolically.

The Aftermath: 1970–1975

Following the "riot," Russell High and the Eastown School System attempted to address many issues raised by African American students. That summer the school system offered seminars on the history and culture of African American students for all teachers in the state. There was a four-week workshop on curriculum reform for teachers from Russell and Archibald, the schools with the most students of color. The school system sponsored sixteen weeks of "sensitivity training" to promote understanding of racial and ethnic differences among teachers, administrators, and students. Parents were recruited to assist the school.

The fall following the "riot" Russell High implemented a new student government, one with a constitution that a committee of faculty, students, and parents created. Quoting an assistant superintendent, *The Eastown Gazette* noted that this reform had "unusual and exciting possibilities." A faculty member who helped draft the constitution told the *Gazette* that "student government should be operated by students and have self-determination and not just go through the motions." In the same article, a previous advisor to the student council acknowledged the students' lack of authentic power during her tenure:

> [In working with the Student Council,] we planned, we acted, but our hands were tied. The Student Council was correctly called a Mickey Mouse club. The student government should have the power to justify its attempts to reach definite goals. . . . The emphasis on student power is important today because I think the maturity of the individual student has gained immeasurably over the years.

In the following years Eastown teachers revised curricula and created mini-courses that offered students a less traditional view of history and literature. There was a course entitled, the "Modern Civil Rights Movement: 1954 to 1971," which sought to help students realize that "the modern civil rights movement . . . has a direct or indirect effect on their lives regardless of race, creed, or color." Another course, "How 'Free' Is Freedom?: A Study of the Development and Application of the First Amendment," was designed to help students "understand the history . . . of the First Amendment through an examination of the historical background, cases, court decisions, opinions, precedents and principles of freedom of religion, speech, press, assembly, and petition."[6]

A Russell teacher who became the school's principal after the "riot" saw this period in a positive light:

> After the "riot," Russell High and the school department really tried to pull things together. . . . Two or three years later, the school was a totally different place. Kids were peaceful. There were few fights. The staff was working together well. . . . Change was especially apparent in our curriculum. We developed different scheduling

schemes. We were able to offer students more courses. . . . We experimented with our schedule. . . . We gave more opportunities to the kids. . . . The parents became volunteers—they served as tutors and clerical staff. . . . We had committees with teachers, administrators, students, and parents on them all studying reform within the school. We had summer workshops. We all took this very seriously. . . .

An African American woman who was hired by Russell High to diversify the faculty in 1972 shared the principal's opinion:

> By the time I got there . . . the school was making an effort, as a result of the "riot," to be more multicultural. They had finally taught black literature. . . . We really had a great time there because it was a very exciting environment. . . . The structure of what we were trying to do was very much in tune with what I've later learned was a real reform of how we were teaching. But I didn't know that at the time. I just thought it was really pretty exciting that every nine weeks we did new courses. . . .
>
> So when I came they were really right on the edge of change, they were trying to address those needs that had come out—the need to have more multicultural curricula. . . . What was exciting about it was that I had to get started right away reading more contemporary stuff and getting caught up. . . . I thought Russell was really the greatest thing since sliced bread at the time. It was energetic. . . . And a lot of it had been initiated as a result of the social upheaval that had gone on.

Despite this period of vitality, over time, innovations fell by the wayside. Teachers grew tired. School system policies and local politics undermined some gains. In a letter to me, a professor from a local college who had two children graduate from Russell and who served on the parent-teacher organization from the late sixties to mid-seventies reflected on the school and his efforts to promote change:

> The sixties and seventies were exciting times at Russell. . . . There were some great teachers there and some great guidance counselors. . . . The budget was lean (no uniforms for the band nor the teams, no yearbook). Morale was low. . . . Latin High was the source of most of the problems, draining off the last pool of highly motivated, college bound students. . . . But there were good things and bad things. The school's musical productions were great. Teachers from [a local college] helped with costumes and sets.

People made their own connections and "did their own thing" as the school structure floundered and administrators chased after federal grants just to get a little extra money. Students attended meetings of the School Committee with their parents and learned about the way "the establishment" works (or fails to work). . . .

My view in a nutshell is that there were lots of good students at Russell, but most were turned off. There were a few active parents, who found the bureaucracy too tough to cope with. There were a lot of good teachers who were frustrated by regulations from "downtown," "upstairs," and "the union." There were good principals whose hands were totally tied. As a parent I found the teachers and principals eager to work with parents, but we spent all of our time at the superintendent's office. The superintendents were eager to help, but they told us to attend School Committee meetings. At School Committee meetings we found political appointees each loyal to a particular constituency and concerned with their own neighborhoods. On top of it all, we found the mayor who cut what little budget additions we could get through the Committee. The result was frustration on a grand scale. My kids all graduated, getting the best they could from the teachers they had and their own initiative, before my group of parents could make the slightest dent in the bureaucracy and political structure.

The teacher who became principal after the "riot" also felt the vitality, attention, and commitment that immediately followed this event subsided and that things took a turn for the worse:

[Over time,] parents started to disappear. From that point on the school went downhill again. By 1975–76, Russell experienced lots of difficulties. The parents lost contact with the school and other parents became disenchanted and sent their kids to private schools in ever-increasing numbers. . . . There was a new student population. Lots of changes that occurred in the community were reflected in the school. Russell's feeder pattern changed. Two of Russell's feeder schools were not within the "Russell neighborhood." That makes it hard to feel part of a community.

A guidance counselor who worked over twenty years at Russell described the period in a similar way:

After the "riot" there were lots of changes at Russell—lots of fear and excitement. Lots of teachers felt they were doing new things. It was really exciting. . . . Courses changed every nine weeks. We instituted heterogeneous grouping. The kids chose the units they wanted to study. The teachers felt they had the opportunity to experiment and kids felt they had choices, especially in their English classes.

What happened to that energy? Why does the school have such a poor image now?

Gradually, all sorts of problems just crept in. The teachers had good academic students and poor students in the same classes and eventually the teachers lost the willingness to handle the discrepancies inherent in such grouping. We decided to go back to the year-long system rather than offering quarter-long mini-courses. There were also lots of changes in the administration. And then the downtown curriculum office got into behavioral objectives and standardized testing so that was incompatible.

A teacher with thirty-five years experience at Russell provided another view of the school during the early seventies, one that was less positive:

Desegregation came in at that time, and they bussed students into Russell from all over the city. The school became a magnet school in the seventies. And then we had lots of immigrants coming to Eastown. The magnet attracted a different group of students. . . . Russell definitely began to change. It began to reflect our permissive society of that time. We offered students lots of electives. We almost catered to students. I think the school may have started to go downhill then. . . .

Another faculty member with considerable tenure at Russell shared this woman's perception, pointing to the "riot" as precipitating the school's fall from grace:

[After the "riot,"] the school went downhill. The teachers there were the finest group of teachers that I've ever seen. But lots of them left because of that incident. . . . It had been like one big family. . . . I can sincerely and honestly say that if we patterned our nation's democracy after Russell High it would be the greatest thing, because it was everyone working together as a happy unit, the rich, the poor, all the different ethnic groups, Italians, Portuguese, blacks, Jewish. . . . The changes were radical. Of course, the student population and education itself changed then too. Little by little, the quality of student declined. Disciplinary actions became bad. The quality of the teachers changed. . . . They lowered themselves to the students'

level rather than having students rise to the teachers' level. . . .
After the "riot," we had a different principal every few months. . . . It
was very difficult, very difficult. Disciplinary-wise, all idealism was
gone. The teachers were shaken and those who remained didn't care
too much. No group can be better than its head but there was never
a single principal at this time.

Russell High in Contemporary Perspective: 1976–1991

Following the post-"riot" period, Russell High faced a series of
challenges presented by its increasingly multi-ethnic student
population, which included sizable numbers of African Americans,
Hispanics, Asians, Portuguese, and whites. Thirteen different languages were spoken at the school and many students were non-native-
English speakers. In response to this demographic shift, the school
undertook various efforts—developing an ESL program, becoming an
arts and communication magnet, and initiating a school-within-a-
school program based on the philosophy and practices of the Coalition
of Essential Schools. Despite such reform, Russell experienced many
problems during this time. Administrative turnover was high. There
were twelve principals in thirteen years. One supposedly left the
building in tears, another was convicted of arson and sentenced to five
years in prison. The building fell into disrepair, becoming so bad that a
fence was erected around the school to prevent passers-by from being
hit by falling bricks. The dropout rate rose while daily attendance
worsened. Faculty grew disenchanted and divided. More and more
students of color were bussed to the school from low-income neighborhoods. Russell became less and less a neighborhood school and its
reputation citywide declined precipitously.

"Typical Day" Essays by Russell High Seniors (April 1987)

The following essays, written by three young women and four young
men from Russell's predominant racial/ethnic groups (Portuguese,
Hispanic, African American, white, and Southeast Asian), offer a
student-centered dimension to this more contemporary point of view.
The assignments were done by seniors in a "functional writing" class,
many of whom had been ESL students. To help them describe "a
typical day at Russell High," the teacher posed the following questions:

1. How do you get to school. Do you come by yourself or with
    friends? Do you get here on time? How often do you skip school?
    Why?

2. What do you do during homeroom? Listen to announcements? Stand for the Pledge of Allegiance?

3. What is your schedule? Describe your classes? Are your teachers good?

4. What do you do for lunch? What's the food like in the cafeteria?

5. Besides classes, what else do you do at Russell? Play sports? Hang out with friends?

6. Do you ever come back to school at nights or on weekends? Do you come to games or other school events?

7. What about the physical condition of the building? The leaky roof? The bathrooms?

8. How would you describe the attitude of teachers and administrators? Friendly? Bored? Hostile? Caring?

9. How would you describe the attitude of students? Do they fight a lot? Do they like school?

10. Finally, is Russell basically a good place? Do you learn things here?

Portuguese Female

Every morning my sister the one I live with takes me to school. I don't come with non of my friends cause I don't think non of them live close to me. anyway most of the times i come early. I said most of the times because I already been late like three times. Since I came to Russell I only bunk once and it was because it was bunk day, but I really don't like to bunk cause then I miss lots of things in class. While I'm in homeroom I just check if I have something to do or read something cause I really don't have someone to talk to you know like a friend, when they give the announcements they all shout their mouth and when they give the pledge of allegiance they all stand up. . . . I like all my classes but English and Biology are very hard for me cause I don't know that much English but I'm really hoping to pass. The teachers are nice and they try to help when somebody don't understand something.

At lunch time I just set down and talk with the girls I know. . . . Besides taking classes I hang around with my friends, just to bug out. . . . Lots of people say Archibald High is a better school I really don't know, but for me I think RUSSELL is better and as long I stay in Eastown I'm going to stay in RUSSELL HIGH SCHOOL, that's what I think about the school. About the building I think it's all fuck up but if they fix it and the bathroom these school would be great.

About the students in RUSSELL I think they all right even thought there always somebody trying to pick on you but I don't paid to much atention cause I don't like to get in trouble, but if somebody hits me I won't stay just like that. Well about RUSSELL I think its a great school and I will like to finish high school right here.

Hispanic Male

Everyday after I wake up I take a shower, get dressed up, and walk to the corner of Weir Street and Garcia Ave to catch the school bus along with dozens of friends around my neigborhood that attend Russell High. I usually arrive on time for breakfast so that is really early. [Russell High had a government-subsidized breakfast program.] I never oversleep unless I don't feel well or just don't feel like coming to school. I never bunk no matter what the circumstances are.

After I finish eating breakfast I hang out with my friends, go to my locker and get my books. . . . When the bell rings we start walking to our homerooms. I say good morning to my homeroom teacher and sit down waiting for the bell to ring. In a while John Padden, one of my good friends, starts saying the announcements on the loudspeaker. Most people in my class forget and keep talking but a few others and I listen attentively. I usually get up for the "Pledge of Allegiance" but sometimes I stay seated if I can get away with it.

My schedule is not that good. For first period I get Algebra. Not too many people like that class. I get Mr. Erdman for my first period class. He is a very good teacher, he tries to help students do well in math and understand your problems. For my second period class I have Science 1, I have Mr. Daley for this class. Now Mr. Daley may be an asshole in class because he is very strict, but I get along fine with him and I guess a few other students in this class have the same opinion. Third period class is a boring class, I don't like it a bit because the teacher doesn't put any excitement into our work. We get a lot of test but I usually cheat or I know the answers. For my fourth period class I get José Meyer for history. Usually all the kids bunk half period of the class including me even though I said earlier I don't bunk but this is for a special cause. Any way this is José's free period because he never teaches. That is why many people bunk his class. After this class I go to lunch. . . . After this I go to English for fifth period. Now Mr. Golden is a teacher that is easy to understand so everybody likes him. He is bright and smart, (he can tell you the definition of a word without looking it up in a dictionary) everybody has fun in his class because he usually tells a few jokes. For sixth period I have two classes. On Monday, Wednesday and Friday I have this class which is Writing and Study Skills. . . . On Tuesday and Thursday I get gym. This is the class I like the most because I get to workout and play basketball.

African American Female

I get to school from my father. He drops me off every morning, mainly because I'm too lazy to take the bus. . . . Oversleep? No, I usually never oversleep. I'm always bunking. I love it! It sorta makes me feel relieved knowing I'm not forced to attend a class if I don't hand in homework, or I don't like a particular teacher. . . . Anyway, I usually don't stay in homeroom too much, first of all it is definately to boreing and much to long. [Homeroom lasted 25 minutes.] I occasionally listen to announcements if it is something I want to hear.

My schedule is: 1st period I have English, 2nd I have the assistant principal's office [she was a student aid in an assistant principal's office], 3rd I have psychology, 4th is W. Civ, 5th is math, and 6th I have Gym and computer. My classes are what you would say a mixture of fun and boreing. Particular classes the work is hard, others I just sit back, chew my gum and relax. . . .

Russell's activities are very fun. Especially basketball, because I "LOVE" beating Melissa. She's good BUT—I'm better! Drama is also something to get into. I like it, it gets people's attention.

The school's appearance is terrible!! nothing ever seems to get repaired or fixed in this school. In the bathrooms, some toilets don't flush, the gym has broken windows, the ceilings leak, etc.

Attitudes of the teachers and staff are fairly close to very concerned about students. I understand that if a student does not want to learn what more can a teacher do, but I feel as though a teacher is there to teach, understand, discuss, be reasonable, and hear how students feel about certain situations. About students, there are so many students who could care less about an education and what life is all about.

My conclusion about RUSSELL is that it is just as good as any other school. I did get an education here and I will continue to.

White Male

. . . The first thing I would do on a normal day of school is go to all of my classes except for the last two. The reason why I might bunk is because I might one, be tired and want to make up my own early dismissal, or two, just because I want to socialize with friends. During homeroom I socialize and so do my friends, so we very rarely listen to what the loud speaker has to say. But there is one thing we do, and that is stand for the plege of the legions. . . .

All of my classes are O.K. I guess but I would rather not have school at all. I have between 20 to 25 students in each class. The teachers are all good or halfway decent except for one I wouldn't recommend. But I can say sometimes I like school work. I like the math but the rest is no good.

When I go to lunch I buy a meatball sandwich and some fries and a carton of milk. The food in the lunchroom isn't too bad but I would rather go home and eat. . . . I bunk classes sometimes so I can get some extra playing time in basketball. I like to play basketball a lot. And I like to hang around with friends. I leave school at the same time everyone else does. And I never come back. I hate school. . . .

The structure of this school is good but it wasn't made to stand eternaly if you know what I am saying. I think all of the fasilities of the school are shot to hell. Mostly all of the teachers are friendly but then again you get a few of those burnt out teachers who will give you the boot just for saying hello. The attitude of the students is more or less animal like in comparison to other schools. Russell is basically a good place to go to. And I think I learn things here whether I am distracted or not.

Hispanic Female

I take the bus to school with some friends and we get there on time and if we don't it's because we've planned it that way. I don't oversleep. I just don't come in just for the fun of it. Once I get here I start to walk around and then I go to homeroom before the 8:30 bell rings. I don't have a chance to listen to the announcements because the boys are talking too loud. My schedule is: 1. Biology 2. Photography 3. Math 4. History 5. English 6. Gym/Computers

I got to lunch after Math class. My classes are fun except for Biology. It could be fun but it can't because of the teacher. I could enjoy the work if I didn't get tons of it all in one period. For lunch I gather up with my cousin and friends. . . .

Here at Russell I have fun. I just hang around friends all day. I leave the class then I go to my locker. Then I either walk downtown or take the bus. I don't play any sports. . . . The hallways aren't bad. It's just the lockers that make them look bad. Now the bathrooms could use some work like clean them, have mirrors, and also some sinks.

Some of the teachers here are caring, friendly if you really know them but there aren't too many nice caring, friendly teachers here at Russell. Now the administrators are some times hostile but they're really friendly. All the students have different attitudes but the ones I know seem to have a very nice attitude. . . . Others I know let any little thing bother them like if it was a big thing. Usually they fight but not here in school because if they do they'll get suspended. Some complain to much about "uh why do I have to come here? Why not Archibald? I don't like it here it's too boring." The others say something like, "Well I like it here mostly because my friends are here."

Southeast Asian Male

. . . My typical day at Russell High School begin by going to school in a school bus. I come with my cousins. I always get to school on time and I never bunk classes. During homeroom I read my book or do some homework. When the announcement came half of the students in the room did listen to it. . . . During the pledge of allegiance nobody wants to stand up, but the teacher wants everybody to stand up. After homeroom period some of the students went to their classes and some bunk. Some classes I have are horrible. The things I do besides classes is to hang out with friends in the corridor. I don't play any of the sports in Russell.

During lunch time I went down to the cafeteria to get the food. The food in the cafeteria is like it have been there for a month. After lunch I read or do my work until it is time to go to my classes. I usually leave school at 2:30. After I left school I never came back to see the school at night or on the weekend or any of the games and other school events.

Russell High School is basically a good place to learn. I learned alot of thing in Russell. I learned alot about History, English, and Math.

African American Male

My day starts when I get to the bus stop, there I meet up with a couple of my friends. We always get here on time unless the bus doesn't come. Once at school we go to breakfast. There I meet up with a few more of my friends then we go and chill on the first floor until the first bell rings, then we go to our lockers. Then to homeroom. When I get to homeroom I look at a few magazines, talk with my friends until they say the pledge of allegiance, we all stand and face the flag out of respect.

First period I go to math, I like this class better than all my others because I get along with the teacher and students. Second period I go to English, I hate this class most because I don't like the teacher. Third I have print, I don't like the class because the teacher is never in. Fourth I have science, I like it because it's very interesting and I get along with the teacher and the students. Fifth I have U.S. History and its O.K. Sixth I have this class and gym. There both alright but I wish they wasn't the last period because I always want to go home.

I think the school department should fix up the school and it's surroundings. The first thing they should do is fix the brick work on the building and take that fence down. [At this time, bricks on the building were coming loose and falling. To prevent injuries, the school put up a chain link fence.] They should repair the roof and fix the green house. They should put in new lockers, fix the ceilings and pave the student driveway, and repair the playing fields.[7]

Some teachers in this school are really nice and really do care, the teacher I have for English is a very careing teacher, how do I know? Because she took time out of her free period to go over a research paper with me. And Monday this teacher is going to the library with me to help me out some more. But some teachers don't give a shit about the students or the school. The administraters all care. The students here are all different. Some come just to mess around and take up time. Others come for a education. This school has just as many fights as any other.

Russell is like any other school, if you want to learn, you will. If you don't you won't learn anything. . . .

In their essays these Russell seniors voiced their perceptions regarding many aspects of school life—their classes, cafeteria food, the condition of the building, and their relations with peers, teachers, and the administration. Their comments also spoke to issues of educational opportunity, for the most part in positive ways. Even though she knew nothing of Archibald High, the Portuguese female felt Russell was a better school: "Lots of people say Archibald is a better school I really don't know, but for me I think RUSSELL is better . . . its a great school and I will like to finish high school right here." The Southeast Asian male wrote, "Russell High School is basically a good place to learn." The white male expressed a similar perception: "Russell is basically a good place . . . I think that I learn things here whether I am distracted or not." In her essay, the African American female noted, "if a student does not want to learn what more can a teacher do." In conclusion, she wrote: "RUSSELL . . . is

just as good as any other school." The African American male put it
plainly: "Russell is like any other school, *if you want to learn, you
will. If you don't, you won't*" (emphasis added).

SUMMARY

This historical overview of Russell High illuminates a series of
interrelated developments linked to educational opportunity in
Eastown. For one, in terms of the "riot" and events surrounding it,
there were competing efforts to explain what occurred, and these
differing perspectives accorded with race. While African American
students saw this event as a protest that emerged from years of
inequitable treatment, *The Eastown Gazette* defined it as a "savage
attack on property and persons" initiated "without provocation." A
white parent felt the "administration was quite willing to negotiate,"
but African American students involved in those negotiations
maintained that the principal "was putting us off." The theater
teacher characterized the school as a model for American society, an
ideal of educational opportunity: "[I]f we patterned our nation's
democracy after Russell High it would be the greatest thing, because
it was everyone working together as a happy unit, the rich, the poor,
all the different ethnic groups, Italians, Portuguese, blacks, Jewish."
An African American graduate saw educational opportunity differently: "Say we graduated maybe 450 students, they only attempted
to educate maybe 150 of that 450. The rest of them, they didn't give a
damn about one way or the other."[8] For whites, this was a "riot"
because, for most, that is what it had become by the time they
learned of it. For African Americans, it was first and foremost a
protest; the "riot" was a regrettable development.

These disruptures between African American and white points of
view are both revealing and discomforting, as these differences of
opinion were mirrored in the educational, socioeconomic, and neighborhood divisions within Eastown. Put simply, in 1969 whites had
higher income levels and more education and lived in different and
more desirable neighborhoods than most African Americans (as well
as other persons of color)—suggesting that, as a collective, they had
greater opportunities and greater influence. They were richer in
personal capital. But these persons also had few chances to
understand the African American point of view firsthand. Such
disjunctures then can promote a faith in educational opportunity
among those with power while never testing this assumption among
those disadvantaged by the status quo, those with relatively low

personal capital. Without seeking to validate either point of view, it seems that the nature of these divisions precluded finding a just and satisfying resolution to many issues that surfaced during this period of turmoil—since African Americans and whites had such different experiences and views on educational opportunity. (The issue of socioeconomic and neighborhood divisions within Eastown and the implications for educational opportunity are developed further in Chapter 8.)

This historical perspective reveals another development entwined with issues of educational opportunity: the resilience of the status quo. While the immediate aftermath of this violent disruption saw concerted efforts to address many concerns students raised, with time, few endured. Tracking returned. Mini-courses were eliminated. Parental involvement declined markedly. During my last three years at the school, there was no student council. As of May 1990, half of all Eastown schools (seventeen of thirty-four), including Russell and Latin High, were in technical violation of federal desegregation standards.[9] When I ended my research (June 1991), Russell High employed five African American teachers on a staff of sixty-six. African American students had challenged the prevailing conceptions of educational opportunity but, with time, their challenges amounted to little.

This long-term view of Russell High also illuminates how student perceptions of educational opportunity differed between two time periods, once more pointing to the tenacity of the status quo. In contrast to the comments by African American students from the class of 1969, the essays written in 1987 never explicitly questioned educational opportunity. It existed for those who worked for it. Yet, students expressed displeasure with many aspects of their education. The Hispanic male felt justified skipping one teacher's class since "he never teaches," and the Southeast Asian male wrote: "Some classes I have are horrible." Along the same lines, the African American male said he didn't like printing because "the teacher is never in" and that "some teachers don't give a shit about the students or the school." The white male claimed that some teachers "will give you the boot just for saying hello," and the Hispanic female wrote: "There aren't too many nice caring, friendly teachers here at Russell." Moreover, students were uniformly dissatisfied with the condition of the school. The Portuguese female put it most bluntly, "about the building, I think it's all fuck up." And no student mentioned participating in extracurricular activities; most said they had no reason to be at Russell outside normal school hours. As the white male wrote: "I never come back. I hate school."

Nearly twenty years after the "riot," these students, at least, did not question whether educational opportunity was real. Although they described a measure of exploitation and inequity, this was generally interpreted as an individual phenomenon—a burnt out or uncaring teacher—not an inequitable system. In what may be a related development, during my research there were no protests comparable to what occurred in 1969. No students ever attempted to organize themselves to change the school nor to gain a greater say in defining their educational experience.

The work of Clifford Geertz offers one way to understand why African American students aggressively challenged the school system in 1969 while eighteen years later students seemed largely unconcerned with such matters. As Geertz argued, good sociological analysis requires separating culture from social structure, what people believe from what they do. Although interdependent, the two are not mirror reflections of one another. Rather, it is most useful to view culture as "an ordered system of meaning and of symbols in terms of which social interaction takes place," and to see social structure as "the pattern of social interaction itself . . . the ongoing process of interactive behavior" (Geertz, 1973: 144–45). During the late sixties there were messages circulating throughout society that equality of opportunity was being denied many persons of color. What once may have been seen as personal affronts or accepted as "the way things are in school," was linked with a larger system of exploitation in America. African American students' values had shifted. Now they saw educational opportunity as not only an individual phenomenon but as a group phenomenon as well. And students wanted a say in the education they received. Their change of beliefs had prompted action.

But the social structure—in this case, the school system—had no means to accommodate protest. There was no mechanism for student input, nor did any school department personnel possess expertise in this area. Consequently, some students no longer saw the school as serving their interests. Educational opportunity had become an illusion. And this disjuncture between belief and social structure, the incongruence between students' new conceptions of educational opportunity and the static school structures intended to promote that opportunity, figured in the mayhem and destruction at Russell High. In the late eighties, students made no comparable connection between inequities at Russell High and any larger sources of exploitation. For them, educational opportunity was seldom, if ever, questioned. The existing system, despite some flawed individuals, was seen as adequate.

PART III

PROMOTING FAITH IN
EDUCATIONAL OPPORTUNITY

7

Affirming the Myth of
Educational Opportunity

> If anarchy is to be avoided, the individuals who
> make up a society must from time to time be
> reminded, at least in symbol, of the underlying
> order that is supposed to guide their social
> activities.
>
> —Edmund Leach,
> *Political Systems of Highland Burma*

> Up till now it had been thought the growth of
> Christian myths during the Roman Empire was
> possible only because printing was not yet in-
> vented. Precisely the contrary. The daily press
> and the telegraph . . . fabricate more myths . . . in
> one day than could have formerly been done in a
> century.
>
> —Karl Marx, quoted in Cohen and Young,
> *The Manufacture of News*

In Eastown educational opportunity was a myth. Not that it was a
lie, but an idealized version of reality. What people want to believe.
Democracy as it should be. For some, the myth of educational
opportunity was true; for others, it was a partial truth; and for still
others, it had little validity. Yet I argue that educational opportunity
was seldom questioned. This was a folk tale most people had come to

believe. Although the lesson is not always explicit, in many different ways, Americans are regularly reassured that educational opportunity is real. And our faith in educational opportunity is so strong because often it is real. But not always.

To provide a sense for how this mythical ideal can be promoted—in this case, among students and in a city where educational opportunity was quite problematic—this chapter examines the messages conveyed about educational opportunity in two different forums, a school assembly and a television news special. Certainly, assessing the effects of mass communication remains problematic (e.g., Hartman, 1981; Olson, 1989). Yet, situating these presentations of educational opportunity within a broader cultural context reveals how they accorded with the values and interpretations common to that cultural system, thereby reinforcing popular perceptions of educational opportunity.

In stark contrast to what Russell students heard from a representative of the Student Nonviolent Coordinating Committee at an unofficial assembly in 1969 and with what media deemed "news" at that time (recall the African American student comments in the previous chapter), a more contemporary and official Russell High assembly as well as a TV news special on the school offered a very different view of educational opportunity.[1] In these two contexts, traditional conceptions of educational opportunity prevailed: this was an individual matter in which hardworking people succeeded. Few questioned whether educational opportunity was real, even though the subject was treated as something defined for, not by, students.

In formulating their views of educational opportunity both forums transmitted and affirmed prominent cultural values, doing so both by what was said as well as who said it. Accepted notions of educational opportunity were not only presented but prominent and credible spokespersons delivered these messages, many being persons of color. Further, these people drew on common assumptions and accepted values to create a credible view of the world, a view that fit with the taken-for-granted. This point is critical. As Edmund Leach wrote about the power of myth: "The significance of history lies in what is *believed* to have happened, not in what *actually* happened. And belief, by a process of selection, can fashion even the most incongruent stories into [credible narratives]" (1969: 81). In essence, people not only believed what they were told, but perhaps more importantly, they wanted to believe what they were told. It was the world according to myth. These were tales of hard work, optimism, and progress. Denying their validity would be to deny Bill Gates and Michael Jordan, Rocky Balboa and Forrest Gump. It would be un-American.

THE AMERICAN DREAM ASSEMBLY (MARCH 1989)

This assembly featured Lieutenant Ellis D. Jones, an African American and former Navy fighter pilot who told students: Education + Hard Work − Drugs = Success and the American Dream.[2] A local middle school hosted this event for three Eastown schools. *The Eastown Gazette* included the following description of the assembly:

Ellis D. Jones, a former Navy jet bomber pilot strafed Eastown high *fire upon as w/ a gun* school and middle school students with an anti-drug message yesterday, silenced their excuses and left them clutching at college, careers and the wild blue yonder. Students giggled, roared, fell silent and sometimes choked up as Jones piloted them through an hour of verbal acrobatics many had never seen equaled. Both soft and strident, Jones bombarded students with the endless possibilities a life free of drugs but full of education offers.

The assembly began with considerable fanfare. After students were seated, the lights were dimmed so the audience could view a videotape of Lieutenant Jones taking off and landing his A-6 jet on an aircraft carrier somewhere in the middle of an ocean, set to the music of the Michael Jackson song, "Bad." As students watched, Lieutenant Jones provided the voice-over: "I wanted to do something exciting. Something . . . people just don't do. Flying an aircraft off an aircraft carrier is the *crème de la crème*. It's number one. This is a video game where you just don't lose your quarter. If you mess up, it's the last game you play." Following the video, six students introduced Jones:

FIRST STUDENT: How many of you have seen the movie *Top Gun*? [Audience applauds.]

SECOND STUDENT: How many women did you see flying airplanes in that movie? [Audience: *None.*]

THIRD STUDENT: How many Orientals did you see flying airplanes in that movie? [Audience: *None.*]

FOURTH STUDENT: How many Hispanics did you see flying airplanes in that movie? [Audience: *None.*]

FIFTH STUDENT: How many Blacks did you see flying airplanes in that movie? [Audience: *One.*] And where was he sitting?! [Audience: *In the back!*]

SIXTH STUDENT: I'd like you to take a look at the back of the auditorium and see a real top gun, Lieutenant Ellis Jones. He's not Tom Cruise!

Wearing a blue flight suit, a yellow cravat, and mirror sunglasses, the six-foot-two-inch Jones entered from the rear of the auditorium and strode to the mike amidst the stares and chatter of students. Standing at the podium with lights reflecting off his sunglasses he began:

You know, they got these punks walking around here called the bloods and the crips. These punk gangs. THESE PUNK GANGS![3] Hold up! You got your PUNK gangs walking around here talking about they're bad. Even Mike Tyson, the heavyweight champion of the world, says he's bad. Michael Jackson has the *audacity* to say he's bad. [Audience laughs.] Guess what? They're not bad. *I'm* bad. [Audience hoots: "*Oooohhh.*"] I'm bad because I can fly 550 miles per hour, fifty feet from the ground and carry twenty-eight five hundred pound bombs under my wings. I have the expertise, the technology and the know-how not to just take out this school but to take out this *entire* neighborhood, and *that's* bad. [Audience: "*Oooohhh.*"] You see, if them PUNKS come bothering me with those 357s and 44s and shotguns and even their *colors* [audience laughs], if them punk gangs come bothering me, I'm in a gang too, and it's called the United States Navy. And if they bother me enough, I'll get my boys and we'll come take out Eastown. [Audience: "*Ooooohhhhhh.*"]

In this introductory statement Jones established a theme that ran throughout his talk. He was a hero, someone who embodied "fundamental and important themes of the culture, [thereby making] . . . . abstract principles, precepts, and moral judgments . . . more easily felt and understood, and more highly valued" (Warner, et. al, 1963: 210–11; see also, Kertzer, 1988). Certainly, he had achieved professionally, the video made that clear. Jones was also street-wise. Students responded to his language and pronounced style. Moreover, this "def" fighter pilot had attained financial well-being, making "$175,000 a year working eight to ten to twelve days a month" flying for United Parcel Service (after serving in the Navy). Early in his talk Jones also portrayed himself as a rugged individualist who, because of his military experience and patriotism, warranted student attention:

I PUT MY LIFE ON THE LINE FOR EACH AND EVERY ONE OF YOU SO I SAY EXACTLY WHAT I WANT TO SAY ANYTIME I WANT TO SAY IT! I WAS IN BEIRUT AND I WAS IN LIBYA AND ALMOST DIED FOR YOU! **I ALMOST DIED FOR YOU!** . . . WHEN I WAS OUT THERE, AND I WAS SCARED, I WAS NOT

FIGHTING FOR NO AFRICAN AMERICAN. I WAS NOT
FIGHTING FOR NO POLISH AMERICANS, NO WHITE AMERI-
CANS, NO ITALIAN AMERICANS, NO JEWISH AMERICANS. I
WAS FIGHTING FOR THREE COLORS AND THEY WERE RED,
WHITE, AND BLUE! [Audience applauds.]

By the end of his talk, Jones was unequivocal about his status. As he
proclaimed: "YOU ARE LOOKING AT THE AMERICAN DREAM!"

While asserting his credibility in various ways, Jones also stressed
individual autonomy, specifically, that students could influence
significant events in their lives:

individual autonomy

> You have to make the decision: either you're going to be like me and
> do the driving, or memorize this because you'll be saying it for the
> rest of your life: "Two-sixty-five, please." SEE, EITHER YOU BUST
> YOUR BUTT . . . IN HIGH SCHOOL AND BUST YOUR BUTT IN
> COLLEGE, and then be like me and *slide* for the rest of your life, or
> you can just slide now and work forever. . . . *It is up to you.*

Consistent with his stance on individual autonomy, Jones said
repeatedly that race and ethnicity had no effect on success and
failure: "LET ME TELL YOU SOMETHING: THERE IS NO WHITE
AND BLACK! THERE'S ONLY IGNORANCE AND INTELLI-
GENCE! SO TAKE THIS TO THE BANK: IF YOU BLAME YOUR
SUCCESS OR YOUR FAILURE ON YOUR COLOR . . . YOU ARE A
LOSER." [Audience applauds.] Later, he reinforced this point: "Don't
ever say your race or your creed, or your sex or your gender or
anything else is keeping you down. Because it's not. That's an excuse
and all children like excuses. . . . There is no excuse."

Jones dismissed financial constraints students might face in like
fashion:

> There are some of you who are going to say, "I can't afford to go to
> college. *I can't afford to go to college.* . . . " If you can't afford to go to
> college, you bust your butt in school, and people will make sure—if
> you have a three-point-eight, three-point-nine, or four-point-oh grade
> point average—you go to any college in this country for free. It's
> called a scholarship. AND IF YOU CAN'T GET A THREE-POINT-
> EIGHT, THREE-POINT-NINE, OR FOUR-POINT-OH GRADE
> POINT AVERAGE, THEN YOU GO WORK IN McDONALD'S, OR
> YOU WORK AT BURGER KING, OR YOU GET A LOAN, OR YOU
> GET A GRANT, OR YOU GO BORROW THE MONEY, OR YOU
> GO IN THE NAVY, THE ARMY, THE AIR FORCE, I DON'T CARE

WHAT YOU DO, BUT YOU TAKE YOUR BUTT TO COLLEGE
BECAUSE IT'S NOT THAT YOU CAN'T AFFORD TO GO
COLLEGE, YOU CAN'T AFFORD **NOT** TO GO TO COLLEGE!

Building on his assumptions of individual autonomy, Jones made
a link to responsibility. If individuals controlled so much of their
lives, success and failure were essentially personal matters:

responsibility I WAS THE ONLY BLACK NAVY JET ATTACK PILOT IN THE
WHOLE UNITED STATES NAVY at one time. . . . I was the only
one, but it wasn't the Navy's fault. IT WAS **YOUR** FAULT
BECAUSE SOME OF YOU IN HERE DON'T THINK YOU CAN
BE PILOTS! AND SOME OF YOU DON'T THINK YOU CAN BE
SAILORS! AND SOME OF YOU DON'T THINK YOU CAN BE
DOCTORS AND LAWYERS AND TEACHERS AND ENGINEERS!
WELL NOW I HOPE YOU DO. SEE, IF YOU DON'T FURTHER
YOUR EDUCATION, IF YOU DON'T BECOME SOMETHING IN
LIFE, IT'S NOT WRONG ANYMORE, IT'S A SIN! . . . IF YOU
DON'T MAKE IT, THERE IS NO EXCUSE! IF YOU DON'T MAKE
IT, YOU DIDN'T WORK HARD ENOUGH TO GET IT! IF YOU
DON'T MAKE IT, IT HAS NOTHING TO DO WITH YOUR
FINANCIAL BACKGROUND, OR YOUR PARENTS OR ANY-
BODY ELSE. IF YOU DON'T MAKE IT, IT'S BECAUSE YOU
DIDN'T CARE ENOUGH ABOUT YOURSELF!

effort This view of individual autonomy and empowerment closely tied to
a second theme: effort and determination, combined with education,
will lead to success. Lt. Jones, for example, told students, "I never quit":

I learned, from being a little boy, I don't quit anything. Why do you
think I'm a pilot? Do you think in the projects my father had an
airplane and he used to come up to me and say, "Come on son, let's
take a little spin?" Why do you think I'm a pilot? . . . I joined the
Navy and I studied I studied I studied I studied I studied. I didn't
even know how to spell "aerodynamics" when I got in the Navy. I
knew *nothing* about flying. But I studied hard. . . . I NOW AM AN
AIRLINE PILOT . . . AND THE ONLY REASON I'M AN AIRLINE
PILOT IS BECAUSE **I NEVER QUIT**!

Later, Jones again linked education with personal success:

You know the only thing that makes me bad? I HAVE A COLLEGE
EDUCATION! THAT'S WHAT MAKES ME BAD! . . . SINCE I

TOOK MY BUTT TO COLLEGE, MY LEVEL OF FUN IS UP HERE. When I party, I party in Paris. When I jam, I jam in Jamaica. I do the cabbage patch in Monte Carlo. [Audience laughs.] Since I went to college I'm so bad, I do the "butt" in the Bahamas. [Audience laughs.]

Concluding his presentation, Jones was explicit about the need for education:

The truth is that this is 1989, and if you don't plan on getting an education, I'm sorry to say this . . . [but] you're going to be a bum. . . . [T]hat's the truth. How did they keep black people down 200 hundred years ago? HOW DID THEY KEEP US DOWN 200 YEARS AGO? YOU THINK IT WAS WITH WHIPS? WITH CHAINS? WITH PICKING COTTON? THEY WOULDN'T LET US READ! THEY KEPT A WHOLE NATION OF PEOPLE SLAVES JUST BECAUSE THEY WOULDN'T LET US READ. . . . YOU BETTER WAKE UP AND GET TO THIS! THIS IS ONE PLUS ONE EQUALS TWO. IF YOU DON'T LEARN HOW TO READ AND FURTHER YOUR EDUCATION, YOU ARE GOING TO BE A SLAVE. . . . But if you do further your education, you can be anything you want in this life.

In his talk Lieutenant Jones reaffirmed many traditional conceptions of educational opportunity. Individuals were empowered and autonomous, capable of influencing critical aspects of their lives—including college and career choices. Effort invested in education offered a means to wealth, personal satisfaction, and social mobility. And one's race, ethnicity, or socioeconomic status should not restrict your opportunities. These remarks were received quite positively by many who heard Lieutenant Jones.

Student, Teacher, and Administrator Reactions

Commenting on the influence of heroes, W. Lloyd Warner and his co-authors wrote: "[The hero's] presence serves as a model for imitation and learning and for the measurement of [one's] own moral inadequacies. The hero arouses the hopes . . . of those who believe in him" (1963: 211). When Lieutenant Jones returned to Eastown the following fall for another series of assemblies, *The Eastown Gazette* featured students saying: "He's great," "He's an honest man. . . . He tells the truth," and "I like the way he gives a speech. It really got to me."[4] In fact, both articles that described the assembly (the morning and evening editions), ended with student testimonials describing a transformation in his or her attitude about education and career possibilities. As one read:

> When [Jones] asked Wayne Embry whether he planned to go to college, the boy looked down and said no. "You're not going to make it then," Jones said. "Look at me. Look at me. Look at me. Say, 'I'm going to be something and I'm going to go to college.'"
>
> Finally, while his classmates watched, Wayne Embry mumbled the words. Then someone asked Wayne what he wanted to grow up to be. "I wanna be an airline pilot," Wayne said. Why? "Because he said so," answered Wayne, pointing to the man in the blue jumpsuit.

To end another article, a student discussed her personal transformation:

> When [the assembly] was over Shalandra Scott, a tenth-grader at Archibald High, borrowed a piece of paper and headed down the aisle to try to get Jones' autograph. She has been "messing up" lately, she said, skipping school and thinking people would not let her succeed because she was black. But Jones changed that. "I learned a lot from what he said," she said, "I think I'm going to take his advice, try to finish high school and go to college."

After Jones' first visit, a middle school teacher had her students write letters to him. Of the 104 that I read, I came across one criticism, a girl wrote that Jones was "sorta conceited," but added that he had important things to say as well. The following letters are typical:[5]

> Dear Lt. Jones:
>
> I'm writing to thank you for coming to our school. I can't speak for everyone at school, but I can tell you that you are the best speaker this school ever had. It was terrific the way you could get everyone excited and then get them quiet. You are a great speaker. I could listen to you say your speach thousands of times and *never* get bored. It was a pleasure to hear you speak, but I think meeting you would be an even greater pleasure. You gave me a better view of life, I intend to live mine to the fullest, not giving up, and going through college even if I get really worn out doing it. Sir you are the best you know it, I know it, and everyone else who's every heard you speak knows it. Personally I think what you're doing by going

to all our schools and speaking to us you've given us all a new perspective in life, for this I thank you whole-heartedly.
Sincerely,
a fan

Dear Mr. Ellis Jones

I'm glad you came to my school because you really helped the kids. You are so cute. The way you came strutting down the auditorium with your dark glasses. I thought you were dope [cool]. My cousin butchie he really admires you. He use to think his father was bad. You helped me alot thinking about my career. What i want to be is a singer. I was going to work at McDonald's but when you said you were going to pull up in your black limo i was afraid that i was gonna be the one handing you the fries. If you can do the butt in the bahamas i can do the twist in college.
Dope on a rope,
Stacy Duke

Dear Lt. Ellis Jones

Thank you for coming to [our school]. I realy like your speech. Fore a couple of days after that people where talking about you. I want to go to Harverd law school and become a lawyer. I realy hope you come back realy realy soon.
Yours truly,
Antonio Sousa

Many administrators also found Jones' talk inspiring, accurate, and important—so much so that the school system invited him back and required all juniors and seniors from the city's public high schools to attend his speech—at a cost of over $10,000. During his two Eastown visits, estimates were that over 15,000 students heard him speak.

Many teachers also felt Jones had a valuable message for students. A teacher who helped arrange Jones' first Eastown visit, for instance, discussed her reactions in an article she wrote for a community newsletter:

Last summer, I saw Lt. Jones on the "Today Show." As I watched . . . I was impressed by his rapport with students. When I heard that Lt. Jones would again be on television, this time featured on a network special, I asked [my middle school] teammate to tape it. The next day, after seeing Lt. Jones for herself, she proclaimed, "We must have him!"

It was clear to both of us that Lt. Jones' message would be appropriate; he focused . . . on self-esteem, decision-making, and education. We also realized that a high-energy speaker could . . . have an impact on . . . the students. Furthermore, we knew the media would cover his visit, bringing his message to many more people than would see him live. . . .

Lt. Jones was able to establish a rapport with both students and community leaders in Eastown. He spoke to hundreds of students in a way they could understand, referring to problems and choices they all made on a daily basis. By addressing these young people with firm compassion and honesty, Lt. Jones got through to them in ways others could not. . . . Through this and other projects, we hope to improve the attitudes of our students about themselves, the value of an education, and remaining drug free.

In a "letter to the editor" in *The Eastown Gazette*, another teacher who helped organize Jones' first visit wrote:

Miracle in Eastown

Navy Lt. Ellis D. Jones spent three days recently in Eastown talking to about 4,500 students, teachers, and community leaders. Lieutenant Jones' gift of delivering a stay-in-school/stay-off-drugs message electrified his audience because it was not the hackneyed refrain students have learned to ignore. The sincere, powerful and inspirational message he brought to Eastown helped motivate students by raising their self-esteem and belief in themselves.

And then a great miracle happened here: Even before Lt. Jones left the city, some students re-enrolled in school, found employment, pledged to eschew drugs, and made a commitment to get an education and be successful. . . . As one of my students wrote: "The world needs people like you, Mr. Jones, to talk to all of us, including adults, to set things straight like education, drugs and discrimination. You made me realize that you have to believe in yourself and not stop until you succeed."

Anita Reagan
Eastown

Some Russell teachers also embraced Jones' message and felt it was something they should reinforce. Two days after his presentation a team of Essential School teachers reflected on his talk during a planning period, a twice-weekly meeting when these teachers and a university professor met to address program concerns. On this day, participants commented extensively on the

American Dream Assembly. In the first part of the meeting, the teachers and professor focused on how they might build on Jones' message:

TEACHER #1:   I cut out the newspaper article [on Jones] in the *Gazette* and hung it up on the bulletin board in my classroom because I want students to see it. I thought it was a super presentation.

TEACHER #2:   [The director of media services] taped it. We can show it to our classes if we want. Has anyone heard what students thought? . . .

TEACHER #3:   From all that I heard, they liked it.

TEACHER #4:   Mine, too. I asked students if he was a great speaker and they said, "Oh yeah!" But the effect won't be immediate. It will click into place later down the road.

UNIVERSITY PROFESSOR: It's too bad we didn't plan some follow-up questions to this, for after they returned from the assembly.

TEACHER #2: . . . It sounded great but I didn't know anything about it. . . . It's good that kids had the seed planted in their minds but if we don't do some follow-up, what's the point? It may save a few of them. . . .

TEACHER #5:   Kids can want to all they want, but they still have to do it. Maybe we should bring it up in a couple days, after some digestion.

TEACHER #2:   The kids told me, "He really understands kids." When Letitia told me, "He said you can get scholarships," I saw her eyes light up.

TEACHER #3:   I heard one say that too.

UNIVERSITY PROFESSOR: Can we follow-up on this?

TEACHER #1:   I can copy some "thought questions" on how students can develop their own potential and we could use it with advisory groups.[6] We can introduce the topic but relate it to Lieutenant Jones. . . . How about trying to address two questions in advisory? First, what do you want? Second, how are you going to get it? What will you do? Focus on the doing. Tell them Lieutenant Jones set up the target and now you have to develop the bow and arrow. . . . The students liked him because he told them they have self-worth. But there is no way to hang on to it for many of our students. The kid has to have a way, that we help develop, for the kid to feel good.

TEACHER #5:   But it has to fit within appropriate classroom behavior and good manners.

TEACHER #1:   We have to convince students that they have to do what we want him or her to do in order to get what *they* want. We have to communicate in a way students understand. So we have to talk from their viewpoint, like Lieutenant Jones did.

TEACHER #2:   Maybe we need to set up a dialogue so kids can talk about what they want and how they might go about realizing their goals. Lieutenant Jones said when he entered into his "common sense computer"[7] that he wanted to "make a lot of money and not work hard" his computer told him he could either be a drug dealer or a pilot. We could discuss that sort of dilemma in advisory groups. We can let them know we really care.

For the remainder of the meeting, the teachers and professor discussed what it would take for their students to be successful, including what role they, as Russell teachers, might play. [Picking up where the previous dialogue ended.]

TEACHER #5:   But how many kids know what they want?

TEACHER #2:   It's just important that we ask the question. . . .

TEACHER #1:   . . . We should want to know what they want and they should know they have choices. The point is, students need to leave their options open. Students should know to avoid any actions that may close a door for them so they can expand themselves if they want to.

UNIVERSITY PROFESSOR: We're getting at a fundamental point. It is crucial for all we do. When I say we can do this in class, I don't mean stopping class to do this, but that we send kids lots of messages through our verbal and nonverbal interactions, through the structure of our classes, through our whole persona. We're white, middle-class people. We have to face this everyday. They aren't kids we grew up with, but they can make it. They're our reason for being here. We have to believe in them.

TEACHER #1:   The main reason most people don't succeed is because they don't believe they can. I know a person who can't read and write but who owns an autobody business. He makes a million dollars a year. We have to help students find direction. Kids have to believe they can succeed.

TEACHER #5:   But we have to go one step further. Believing you can do it is not enough. You have to do it.

UNIVERSITY PROFESSOR: Yes, they have to believe it first. Then they'll be able to do it.

TEACHER #5:   We're dealing with kids without white, middle-class values and to be successful in the white, middle-class world they have to know how to succeed. So we have to show them this. . . . We have to model it.

TEACHER #2:   If we're role models, we need to create an environment where kids can succeed. If kids don't do the work, we have to ask why. Maybe our writing was unclear, maybe it was too confusing, maybe it wasn't broken down into small enough steps. *yes.* We have to set them up for success and they'll start to like class. We have to help them build their confidence.

TEACHER #4:   What bugs me is the failure to try. Even when the assignment I give is easy, some students will not do it and just shoot the breeze. They'll give you any excuse like, "I don't have a pencil or any paper." But it's just an excuse. What they're telling you is they didn't care. If you make it too easy, other kids will be turned off.

TEACHER #5:   If it's too easy, they won't make it in the world.

TEACHER #2:   I'm not worried about the real world but preparing kids for their next science class [chemistry]. We have to bring them along. Kids get excited taking chemistry now. And [the teacher] is tailoring chemistry to the kids and preparing them for physics. *That's* what we need to do.

TEACHER #5:   We need to do both things. We can't organize their assignments too much for them. They're not going to have someone take them under their wing in the real world.

UNIVERSITY PROFESSOR: But think how to organize your teaching differently. It's the way to start. We don't want to throw them into the real world in 9th grade.

TEACHER #5:   But some will be in the real world.

UNIVERSITY PROFESSOR: I think you expect too much from students. . . . We have to nurture them. We have to take them through different levels of cognitive development. . . . We are the nurturing group. . . . I think it comes down to, do we like the kids or not? This teaching team likes them. We believe in them. And we work as hard as we can to help them succeed. . . . [But] I think deep-down some teachers don't like the kids they're teaching. And we deal with their products. It's not because work is too hard. It's because they have no self-confidence. So first give them that. I think a lot of inner-city teachers don't like the kids they're teaching. . . . That's what we may have to confront.

Throughout this meeting teacher comments suggested that they shared many beliefs about individualism and success with Lieutenant

Jones. One remark sounded like it came from Lieutenant Jones himself: "The main reason most people don't succeed is because they don't believe they can. I know a person who can't read and write. . . . He makes a million dollars a year." There was also a sense, as Jones stressed, that "all children like excuses": "Even when the assignment . . . is easy, some students will not do it. . . . They'll give you any excuse." Underlying this reaction was student apathy: "[W]hat they're telling you is they didn't care." Moreover, educational achievement was an individual matter: "You have to do it."

Although many comments voiced in this meeting fit with Jones' message, there was a point of difference: some teachers and the university professor acknowledged that students faced some "real world" obstacles outside their control, including teachers who might not like them. Still, this point was addressed infrequently and arose only late in the meeting. Further, no one suggested any dissonance between this perspective and what Jones said: "IF YOU DON'T MAKE IT, THERE IS NO EXCUSE!" In addition, when questions about educational opportunity arose, they were often countered. After teacher #2 discussed a teaching strategy to help students succeed, another remarked, "What bugs me is the failure [of students] to try." Another added, "If it's too easy, they won't make it . . . they're not going to have someone take them under their wing in the real world." When the professor said that as white, middle-income adults they may send students negative messages in subtle ways, a teacher countered with her own interpretation: "The main reason most people don't succeed is because they don't believe they can." Moreover, alternative understandings of student failure were most often expressed by the university professor, an outsider to Russell.

An Alternative View

> See, you have the greatest thing that a country can have. You have something called "freedom." Not only are you free to mess up, use drugs, drop out of school and be a bum and not be successful, but you remember this: YOU ARE ALSO FREE IN THIS COUNTRY TO BE A DOCTOR, AN ENGINEER, A TEACHER, A LAWYER, A CONGRESSMAN, A SENATOR, OR THE PRESIDENT OF THE UNITED STATES!

In many respects this excerpt from Lieutenant Jones' presentation embodied his view of individualism and educational opportunity, a view many students, teachers, and administrators seemed to share (Hill-Burnett, 1969; Lesko, 1986). But Jones' message differed from the lived experience of many Russell students. His assertions applied to the ideal world, to the mythical. Consider the Eastown School System itself. One-hundred-eighty days of the year students were expected to go to school to be educated. But who were their teachers, principals, and guidance counselors? Who held positions of influence? It wasn't people who looked like them or lived in their neighborhoods. What messages might Russell students have perceived about opportunity given the following: while students of color comprised sixty-five percent of the Eastown student population in 1990, of the 1,178 teachers in the school system, eighty-six were persons of color, seven percent of all teachers. Of the system's forty-six guidance counselors, two were persons of color. In the city's thirty-four schools, three principals were persons of color. Of twenty-six full-time positions in central administration, three were held by persons of color. Although students were told they were free to be "A CONGRESSMAN, A SENATOR, OR THE PRESIDENT OF THE UNITED STATES," opportunity was more complex and problematic than that.

"Education, It's Everybody's Business" (April 1989)

This television news program presented an overview of Russell High and the Eastown School System by focusing on "challenges" faced by both—including high dropout rates, significant numbers of limited-English proficient students, a high incidence of teen pregnancy, and the mobility of the student population—as well as various ways in which Russell High and the school system were addressing these challenges. The special lasted a half-hour, by far the most extensive examination of Russell High by a TV journalist during my research.

In his opening remarks, the host for this television special, the station's news anchor, outlined the program's theme:

> Across the nation, our urban public schools are facing enormous challenges. The economic and social realities of the eighties have forced schools to take on more and more responsibility for fostering and developing our young people. As we near the nineties, it's painfully apparent urban educators need help. The more *you* know about the problems facing urban schools, the more *you* know we must not let them face these problems alone.

Walking through Russell's hallways, he described some challenges facing the school system:

The Eastown public schools serve 20,000 students. A mid-sized urban district, it shares many of the same challenges larger, inner-city systems face: a diverse and growing number of immigrants and minorities; an antiquated physical plant, and a *high* dropout rate. A thousand youngsters attend school here at Russell High, one of four secondary schools in the system. The last twenty years have brought ethnic and cultural diversity to what was once a neighborhood school.

Russell's principal then offered some historical perspective on this diversity:

The population prior to the late-sixties was mostly the population which existed then in the Lesh Park area [approximately seventy percent white and thirty percent African American] and it was pretty much a community school. With the latter part of the sixties, the "deseg" plan went into effect and Russell High opened its doors to youngsters who lived in other parts of town. That significantly changed 'the population. . . . We have a tremendous mix of youngsters here now. I consider it like the United Nations . . . it reflects what is known as the melting pot in American society. There are about nineteen foreign language groups [and] . . . we have a significant number of Hispanics, Asians, Cape Verdeans, and Portuguese.

The host then outlined the demographic characteristics of Eastown's school system:

Presently, forty percent of Eastown public school students are white, twenty-five percent are black, twenty-two percent Hispanic, twelve percent Asian, and one percent "other minorities." In just twelve years, the minority student population has grown twenty-four percent. The system's Hispanic and Southeast Asian population has grown dramatically. In 1978, Hispanics made up seven percent of the student population, Southeast Asians two percent. These two groups are now thirty-four percent of the student population.

The Superintendent of Schools described how these demographic factors influenced Eastown schools:

The social and economic status of our students is a major factor which leads us to have to design and implement programs specifically to address "special needs." Approximately 2,300 limited-English proficient students come into the system in any given year.

> These students have a wide variety of needs that have to be assessed. . . . Our intake process involves gathering demographic data, determining a dominant language, assessing basic skills acquisition, determining proper grade placement and instructional placement, determining what support services are needed—counseling, medical services, psychological services—determining transportation needs, food services and food programs. . . . And the population, overall, is very mobile. . . .
>
> So when you take the particular needs associated with a very mobile population . . . the variety of programs that have to be designed and implemented almost exceeds one's ability to comprehend. Because the needs of the students are so varied and so great, we, as educators, admit, and rightfully so, that we have reached the point where we realize we cannot do it alone.

After outlining these "challenges," the program examined how Eastown schools and their partners—a state university, parents, the Urban League, and a national school reform effort—were working to address these matters. The first discussion of a collaborative effort centered on Eastown's "forty-five percent dropout rate." The city's partner in this effort was the state university's Urban Field Center. Viewers were told that the Center had conducted "eighteen months of research and based on this study, the Ford Foundation presented Eastown with a $100,000 grant to pursue its fight to reduce the dropout rate."

In the next segment two "successful" African American Russell graduates, a man and a woman, were shown speaking to 9th-graders, those students most at-risk of dropping out. The man offered a testimonial to the value of a Russell education: "Russell High has allowed me to reach many of the goals that I set for myself. . . . [H]ad that not happened, I don't know whether I would have had the opportunity to go to Georgetown University." The woman advised students: "You've got to have your own mind-set, be confident that you're doing what you want, regardless of what your friends are up to."

An African American representative from the Chamber of Commerce then said that the business community was committed to addressing this problem since "its future is linked to the school department producing knowledgeable graduates to fill jobs." The director of the Urban Field Center reinforced this point:

> What's fashionable now is to talk about dropouts as an educational issue. It's an educational issue *now*, but in five years, ten years max, it's going to become an economic problem because the very

businesses that are coming into Eastown, the high-tech businesses, aren't going to have anybody to hire because they [need] a work force that's skilled enough to fill those jobs. . . .

To conclude this segment of the program the Superintendent again emphasized the need for community involvement:

We need the help of the business community, we need the help of higher education, we need the help of labor unions, we need the help of government officials. . . . If an urban district is to be successful, it will be because a community effort has been designed and has been put into place where everyone feels that education is their business.

Next, the program examined teenage pregnancy, "the single leading cause of female teens leaving school"—with a dropout rate, nationally, "between sixty and eighty percent." While viewers watched a health worker and a female student examine a model of a woman's anatomy, they were told that Russell High has a health center that "provides prenatal counseling, parenting classes, and other services" to pregnant teens. The director of the center explained:

We started in '84 and every year at least six to ten young ladies graduate. . . . We're working together and the families are great. They do want their children to finish high school. You're dealing with a fifteen- or sixteen-year-old who has to now deal with adult problems . . . you have to juggle a baby with you, sometimes they have to take two and three buses. They have to go to day-care centers or to a day-care mother.

In summary, the host stated, "Day care is one of the biggest barriers facing pregnant teens," but added, "Next year, the system's first school-based day-care center will open at Archibald High as a pilot."

The program then introduced Russell's "mentor program" which "brings together inner-city kids . . . with people who can offer guidance and direction." After introducing an African American student involved in the program, her African American mentor commented: "I enjoy it a lot because you basically do what you want to do. . . . The Urban League is there for guidance or if you have questions or if you just need to find out, 'Who can I get for this person as a tutor?'" The student said, "I get frustrated really quick. Like if there's something I can't do, I get frustrated and I like to quit. But then when I call my mentor and talk to her, she's down to earth with me and she'll say, 'Well look Doreen, c'mon, that's not a good excuse.'"

The show then moved to Russell High and introduced two African American students, fraternal twins—one, the senior class president; the other, an all-state basketball player. Both "are planning to leave their inner-city neighborhood for college." Each student discussed his social development. The basketball star commented:

> You have a different attitude . . . when you live on the streets where I live at. I see people stealing and stuff like that, because I was a part of that when I was small, but I grew up to know that that was wrong. . . . I didn't grow up with both parents. I grew up with just one parent, my mother. She did all she could do, she stayed on my back. She was my mentor. I looked up to her, she listened to what I had to say. I listened to what she had to say. She helped me in a lot of ways.

His brother, the class president, remarked: "As time moved on, people's morals and values changed. They became . . . lower [for some of my friends] and they stopped dreaming. I still love all my friends and stuff, but there comes a time when people move on."

After hearing these students, the Field Center's director reinforced an earlier point:

> There is no doubt in my mind, from all the research I've done and all the research I've seen over the last two-and-a-half years, the simplest, most powerful, most effective . . . dropout prevention program is an adult who cares about a child. What we're working on at the Center, what we see as our most important initiative for this year, is to increase the involvement of parents in the schools and in their children's education.

After acknowledging the value of such relationships, the program host added that "parent-teacher relationships have never been easy to cultivate." A representative of the Eastown Teachers' Union concurred:

> It's one of the most frustrating arenas that we engage in. It's very hard to engage parents in a positive way in their children's education. Parents generally don't come to school because they want to discuss their child's progress. They want to yell at the teacher for giving a failing grade or, in their view, not correcting enough papers, or doing whatever they feel is the deficiency of the teacher. And we have a lot of tradition that we've got to overcome if we're going to get a better relationship with parents.

The president of Russell High's Parent Association described her group's efforts to improve parent-teacher relations: "We have grant money to develop a parent handbook and it will be a handbook by parents for parents—"How to get yourself and your child through Russell High." We hope to have this book translated into Spanish and two or three Southeast Asian languages." The superintendent then commented on the parent-school relationship, calling it "the most critical partnership in education . . . [which] must be maintained at all costs."

The host next introduced Daniel Biscoe, a white student whose "relationship between his parents and a teacher changed his life's direction." Alternating between shots of Daniel at college and at home in his parents' living room, Daniel described his past: "I smoked marijuana. I stayed out of school quite a bit. I harassed teachers. I was against authority altogether—100 percent against authority." The teacher credited with "saving" Daniel, Ellie Drenan, then commented:

> Daniel was an outrageous student in my class. He was the class clown. He had an E average. He cut. He was six-foot-six in the ninth grade and, as such, other students looked up to him, literally and figuratively. And he proved to be a leader of the pack. If he misbehaved, others misbehaved. But the one thing that did seem to help for me with Daniel in getting him to perform in class was interaction with his parents.

Daniel's mother agreed:

> More times than not, Mrs. Drenan wanted to give up because Daniel is difficult at times, but she didn't. Thank God she didn't because she was our savior. She helped us. And if it wasn't for the efforts of the Eastown school department and teachers like Ellie, there'd be a lot more kids fall by the wayside.

The host summarized Daniel's experience: "The partnership between a caring teacher and loving parents paid off. Daniel is now in his third year [of college], studying architecture." In agreement, Daniel concluded the segment:

> If I had gone on the way I was going in the 9th and 10th grades in high school, I would say that now I wouldn't have some of the things I have. . . . Ellie started it all. If it weren't for her, I wouldn't be here. . . . I'd probably be working as a laborer for some contractor somewhere

banging my knuckles around and making ten dollars an hour for life. That's not what I'm looking to do. I'm looking for something more.

The show then examined Russell's Essential School, a school-within-a-school program that was part of a national school reform effort, the Coalition of Essential Schools. The host introduced the program by saying it was "an attempt to provide more continuity and less anonymity in the classroom." While viewers watched an Essential School class, the principal elaborated:

> The Essential School is an attempt to restructure the high school as it presently exists. And I think it's had a tremendous effect on revitalizing Russell High because there's a whole conversation about education going on now that didn't exist six years ago. People are really talking about the way we do business and how to make it better.

The coordinator of the Essential School offered his comments: "The Essential School . . . works hard at developing active student learning. . . . [W]e also work at personalizing the program for the student so there's strong interaction between staff and students. There's also a lot of strong contact between the staff and folks at home."
  The host then introduced Theodore Sizer, chairperson of the Coalition of Essential Schools and a prominent spokesperson on educational reform, who elaborated on the issue of student-teacher relations:

> [The Essential School structure] greatly reduces the anonymity seen in so many big high schools. It also gives real authority and emphasis to the essential core of education. The issue is not only small classes, it's the total number of students a teacher is expected to know. A typical urban teacher may be expected . . . to know 130 to 180 youngsters. You can't get to know kids, or anybody, very well with those numbers.

While viewing Essential School classes, the host observed that "Russell's Essential School is not specifically a dropout prevention program, but much of its philosophy and many of its methods address the kind of alienation felt by students who do drop out." Sizer added:

> Show me a school where the faculty has time to know students and to respond both to the stress those kids feel and to the hopes these kids may have, and I'll show you a school with a low dropout rate.

Show me a school where a youngster feels she is unknown and I'll show you a school with a high dropout rate. So in a very simple way, as kids say, "I am somebody." And "If I am somebody at school, I like it." But, if nobody seems to care, and if I pass through five or six or seven different adults in the course of a day—no one of whom knows me very well—I say, "Hey, they don't care, so why should I care?"[8]

The program's closing comments were optimistic. The Superintendent said: "[O]ne reason why Eastown can, in fact, turn itself around, is because we can still manage it. You can manage thirty-four schools, 2,000 employees, 20,000 kids. You can make an impact." While not as optimistic, the teachers' union representative added:

We are getting support. There's no question in my mind. The only problem is that it's not enough. In some instances, it's token support. In some instances it's more than token but it's not sufficient to really make a difference. The costs will be extraordinary—extraordinary problems require extraordinary measures for solutions.

The Director of the Urban Field Center remarked:

It's clear this is a city that can address its dropout problem and can significantly reduce it. There are lots of cities that are not in that position, that simply do not have the resources. . . . Eastown is in a fine position to make tremendous headway and to be, in some ways, the shining light of dropout reduction. We can have an impact. But what the city has to recognize and what the community has to recognize is this is not a school problem, this is a community problem. So every part of the community must recognize and must take part of the responsibility for reducing the dropout rate.

Concluding the special, the host remarked: "As we've seen tonight, there's a lot more to teaching these days than reading, writing and arithmetic. The more you know about the plight of our urban schools the more you realize that education is everybody's business."

Summary

As with Lieutenant Jones' presentation, this media presentation was upbeat and optimistic. While acknowledging that Russell High and the Eastown School System faced many challenges, much more attention was devoted to discussing programs devised to address these concerns as well as introducing individuals who, in spite of obstacles, had succeeded.[9] In doing so, the program created scenarios which promoted an optimistic but simplistic view of educational opportunity, in other words, culturally, these scenarios "made sense" to Americans. For example, the dropout rate was portrayed as a serious problem. This was followed by a description of what the school system had done to reverse this trend—grants had been secured, counseling and day care were available to pregnant teens, successful adults met with at-risk students, a parent handbook was produced and translated into various languages. A Chamber of Commerce representative told viewers, "[T]he business community understands . . . our futures are intermingled with the youngsters we produce in our schools." The program also presented a relatively successful cross-section of Russell High: a young woman and the mentor who was helping her through the frustrations of teenage life, twin brothers who had confronted the trials of urban living and had their sights on college education, and a graduate working toward a degree in architecture who was "saved" by a caring teacher.

The description of Russell's Essential School followed a similar pattern. The principal remarked, "[T]here's a whole conversation about education going on now. . . . People are really talking about the way we do business and how to make it better." The Essential School coordinator said the program emphasizes "active learning" and "strong interaction between staff and student body . . . and folks at home." The chairperson of the Coalition of Essential Schools told viewers that such programs "greatly reduce the anonymity seen in many big high schools." And closing comments to the program were hopeful. The superintendent noted, "Eastown can, in fact, turn itself around. . . . You can make an impact." The director of the Urban Field Center added, "Eastown is in a fine position to make tremendous headway and to be, in some ways, the shining light of dropout reduction."

Yet these optimistic scenarios selectively used data to promote positive views of educational opportunity. Perspectives and issues that could have complicated or undermined such interpretations, including critical comments, were seldom included—which points to the importance of "understanding not only what is there, but what is not there" (Apple, 1993: 105). Although the special stressed that "Education . . . is everybody's business," some key persons were excluded—the most prominent being classroom teachers. The program discussed business partnerships, teen pregnancy, parental involvement, and the Coalition of Essential Schools, but viewers never heard how any teachers felt about these issues and efforts, aside from a few comments by Ellie Drenan about her involvement with a student and his parents.

In a similar way relevant but problematic quantitative data were, at times, omitted (Dijk, 1988). For instance, the television host outlined the racial/ethnic composition of Eastown schools and the superintendent said the school system dealt with sizable numbers of limited-English proficient (LEP) and special education students. Although accurate, disaggregating these figures creates a different picture of the school system. During the 1988–89 school year, Russell High enrolled approximately eighty-five percent students of color, while seventy-eight percent of the students at the selective and more prestigious Latin High were white. Latin High also enrolled no LEP students and no special education students, while over one-quarter of Russell students were designated LEP and six percent were special education. The television special made no reference to these differences, their effects on Eastown schools, or any reasons why these differences existed.

This special also selected visual images that cast Russell High in a favorable light. When introducing the show the host used a row of lockers as his backdrop. Unlike most lockers at Russell, these were in fine condition.[10] As a teacher who watched the show remarked, "Where'd they find *those* lockers?" A researcher who worked at the school a year earlier offered a very different picture:

> The building itself is in terrible condition. The outside looks dirty and neglected. Inside, the most visible symbols of the school's fall from grace are the lockers. Painted in garish colors of orange, blue, green, and brown in some earlier, half-hearted effort to alter the climate, they have been wrenched and torn as though a gang of vandals had passed through intent on destruction. Nearly half of them have been rendered useless, and their twisted metal leaves a powerful impression on the visitor.

This news program also included no critical comments by Russell students. All of their remarks fully endorsed the status quo. While the student-teacher relations portrayed in the article were part of life at Russell High, so were less caring and less respectful relations. When two young women from another school visited the school in January 1990, they developed a different perception of some teachers and their classrooms. In a journal she kept during her visit, one of the young women described a Russell class:

> This teacher . . . takes the approach of trying to be more humorous with the pupil's in order to break the ice, while at the same time keeping an authoritative disposition. . . . During the first ten

minutes I was present in this class the instructor made at least three ethnic jokes and two jokes about where I live. The first that offended me the most was when we were told Dr. Martin Luther King Jr. did achieve something, he gave us a holiday when we do not have to work. That is one of the most ignorant statements I could hear from a teacher in 1990!

Then we heard about how the brother of Charles Stuart was very brave for standing up and finally admitting it was his brother that killed his wife, and we as black people should not be upset because he blamed it on a black male because black people were also known for blaming terrible crimes on white people.[11] While the teacher was grinning broadly, the class asked for evidence to support this claim, automatically a case still pending was presented, the Towanna Brawley case which involved a African American female who claimed she was raped by three white police officers. For certain reasons this case has never been brought to trial, but until it is brought to trial no one can say whether she is telling the truth or not. But to make the entire situation worse the class was told that police officers went and raved through the white community just as they did in Boston. That is out right lie and I do not understand how a teacher could try to make students believe such lies. . . . Lastly to put the icing on the cake we were asked "How many white-folks are there in your school?" What in the world does that have to do with anything?. . .

Being that this class was also majority African American this teacher forces them to build a defense wall, because every time the teacher says something they think some racial comment is going to come flying out. Most students have been forced to accept this behavior because this person is their teacher and someone who they feel has a big influence on whether they graduate or fail. So some smerk, some still get very offended and just shake their heads. But should they be forced to go through something like this?

During her last day at Russell, this student was again offended by how she was treated by teachers and an administrator:

> As a guest I found the students more helpful and comforting than one teacher . . . who never asked us questions about our school or ourselves, and never once tried to see whether we understood what was going on in class. . . . [On] our last day at Russell, my friend and I walked into the class. This would be the second time we sat in on the class in our four-day period of going to Russell. As soon as we stepped into the room the teacher became frantic and said

"We have no time to talk to you we have a lot of work to get done today, so just go and sit in the back." This was weird, of course, because first the teacher did not even take the time to say "good morning," or even "how are you?" Secondly, instead of explaining the situation to us we were made to feel we were just in the way. . . .

The second incident involving a staff member, which caught our surprise occurred in the fifth period class. My friend and I were present in this class the day before so this predicament should have never arisen, but it did. What happened was, our student guide at the time walked into the classroom. As soon as the teacher saw my friend and I the teacher began to scream "you are not a part of Russell!" We answered, "We know that, but we are visitors" the teacher replied "you are not visitors! no visitors!" The entire class tried to explain the truth but the teacher would not listen to students, and soon began to scream again "go to the office!" In order not to create a scene bigger than the one already created for us we just left. . . .

The third and last situation that occured happened when we complained about that class to an administrator. First the administrator listened to our complaint but then had to leave to complete a tour of the school for some visitors. We were told the administrator would be right back in three minutes when the truth of the matter was the administrator returned a hour later. Then the administrator offered no apology for lateness, or comforting words for us as students having gone through such a awkward situation. Instead, we were treated like we had no political or financial status compared to those in the tour group . . . and did not deserve any explanations but we were expected to keep quiet and smile at the absurd predicament we were put through.

The picture of Russell High created by the news special was also incomplete in terms of the students presented. Certainly, there were students who, with the help of teachers, friends, and families, accomplished much. But many students were not that fortunate. Some had no family, little idea how to apply to college, found school boring and unpleasant, and were more concerned with what their friends would be doing next period than whether decisions they made that day might limit their options in life. To balance these presentations, I introduce two students whose life circumstances differed from those presented in the special. The first, Diana Barros, enrolled in the vocational magnet program at Archibald High as a freshman. That year, she skipped school fifty-six times. No one ever called her home to determine why she was absent. Still, she passed all her courses but was expelled from the program for excessive absences. The next year, she enrolled at Russell because she lived in the school's feeder pattern. There Diana continued to skip school:

> I bunked [skipped school] almost all of third quarter. My mom and dad were going through a divorce. My brother was arrested and sentenced to the state prison. And I was having problems with my boyfriend. . . . Sometimes, when my mom went to court with my brother, I'd have to stay home and take care of my two little sisters. With all of these things going on, I just couldn't keep my mind on school. So most days my girlfriend would pick me up and something would be happening and she was having problems too, so we'd just never show up at school. . . . We'd spend a lot of time talking about our problems.

Unlike her previous school, when she was absent from Russell, administrators called her home. A concerned teacher who lived near her also checked up on her and urged her to attend school regularly. However, her parents were busy and distracted, so they could never make her go to school. Although she violated the school's attendance policy, Diana was never suspended for skipping school nor did she ever serve a detention. She passed all her classes except "basic math," a course where she refused to do any work because she felt improperly placed, since she had already passed pre-Algebra and Algebra I. Thus, although she found the work simple, she failed.

Diana never enjoyed much about Russell High. She found the physical plant "disgusting." As she once asked me, "Have you ever looked around this building? It's so dirty. Everything's falling apart. There ain't no chairs. They're falling apart too." In her three years, she never participated in any extracurricular activities. Still, she made a few good friends and thanks to their regular attendance and some teachers whom she respected, Diana remained in school and graduated.

I met the second student, Lorraine Benson, when a teacher asked me to help Lorraine complete an independent research project. I agreed and began meeting with her to discuss the project. More accurately, I *tried* to meet with her. Most often, rather than arriving at our prearranged times, Lorraine never showed up and I ended up calling her and arranging to meet another time. To do this, I had to call her aunt's apartment and leave a message because Lorraine's home had no phone. Eventually, we began to meet more regularly and, after working together for a few months, I came to see her as a pleasant young woman with a foot in two very different worlds. On the one hand, she was irresponsible about showing up for our meetings and her work was often superficial. She appeared to be consumed by her relations with friends. She was clearly excited to be in school but this excitement never translated into the work she did with me. On the other hand, she seemed too young and too naive to be facing the real world challenges that she did: She lived in a high-crime neighborhood. Her daughter was born during her junior year, when Lorraine was alone because her mother, her only parent, had left the country with her boyfriend, lost her passport, and was unable to return. Lorraine also had sickle-cell anemia and needed to go to the hospital for regular treatment.

In contrast to the stories of Russell students who succeeded, an essay Lorraine wrote as a culminating activity for her senior English class suggests that the possibilities in her life might be limited, especially given her academic skills.

"THE IMAGE THAT I SEE"

I Lorraine Benson was born on the month of August 5, 1973 in the city of Baltimore, Maryland. I, my mother, and sister leaved together in the city of Baltimore. We lived in Baltimore until 1984 the day that my mother decided to moved to Eastown.

I can just sit back and remember that day, it was a rainy day there was not a thing to do all of our friends were home. And me nor my sister could go and say goodbye for the last time. By the time we could ask Mama why didn't she let us say bye to our friends who we were not going to see for years, it was time to get in the car and leave. I and my sister cried mostly for our home witch we had lived in all of our entire life.

We arrived in Eastown around six o'clock, just like my sister thought there would be all kinds of different ways of dressing and way of talking. The only thing that was on my mind was how was the house going to look like, was it going to be better looking than the houses in Baltimore. I was right the house was and beautiful lime green with white around the balcony. The house and the kids started to grow in each day. My sister and I started hanging with our relatives and stared meeting different faces everyday. Then everything seem like it would be perfect everything was not perfect but it was better than we figure it would be. We went to school in September. School was very different for one we did not have to take the train to school every morning, for two there schools rules were real back than our were, last the thing that really hit me was that the way the dressed. But me and my sister had to get used to it and by us doing that we gathered more friends than we particle thought we could.

High school, I came to Russell Essential High School. I entered the ninth grade in September 1988, I was the shortest in the school. There were jokes made but it was just fun and games we all laughed at it and went on with our work. Tenth grade was the same as freshmen year, the teachers were great because knowing that we were in one class for two hours they tried there hardest to pay and listen to everything that we had to say.

My favorite teacher was Mrs. Martinelli. Mrs. Martinelli was very nice, not saying that the other teachers were not. Mrs. Martinelli took out time from the class and talked to you if she felt or something was not going right. Mrs. Martinelli always knew what was wrong no matter what you said. There is so much that I can not explain Mrs Martinelli is just outstanding.

The grade that I really loved was the eleven the third quarter. I had a beautiful baby girl named Whitney Monique Benson she brought wonders to my life. Some people thought the opposite of that but I did not care Whitney was my responsibility not no one else. Whitney has brought knowledge to me also, Whitney is just everything that I could had ever asked God to give me.

Now, this is my last year the teacher who pushed me was Rebecca Davis. Ms. Davis helped me through a lot of mistakes and many bad problems. If it was not for her I would not be where I am at today. This is how I see my image today.

The stories of students such as Diana and Lorraine were more complex and less hopeful than the vignettes featured in the news special. They also pointed to many problems with Russell High and the school system. This is not to say the news program was inaccurate; it was systematically incomplete and therefore misleading, promoting a view of education that located success (and implicitly failure) with individuals while downplaying relevant systemic factors. By stressing what the system was doing to address the challenges it faced and by highlighting persons who had succeeded within this system, these presentations promoted the belief that something was being done about these problems, that the solutions were effective and satisfying to students, teachers, administrators, and parents, and that students who wanted to succeed could do so. This observation is crucial since, as the previous chapter revealed and the next chapter explores in some depth, Eastown is a divided city and low-income persons and persons of color have little interaction with those more affluent and more influential. Consequently, those with political power in Eastown often have their understanding of what it means to be disadvantaged created by media presentations which, in this case, portrayed educational opportunity as largely unproblematic.

CONCLUSION

The American Dream Assembly and the news special on Russell High presented a selective and decidedly optimistic view of educational opportunity, a partial view of the school and school system. Both focused on persons who succeeded and on efforts made to improve the system (Lesko, 1991). The examples I juxtaposed were chosen not as alternatives but as complementary perspectives, a balance to the views of Russell High and educational opportunity that dominated the assembly and TV special. And such balance is critical if those interested in improving urban schools expect any success. To reform the urban high school, the institution must first be fully understood. Unfortunately, the American predisposition to honor exemplars and seek the optimistic distorts our understanding of these schools. What we seek to change, we don't fully understand.

While I believe educational opportunity was neither as simple nor as straightforward as the assembly and news special suggested, I should emphasize that their intent was not to deceive. The assembly sought to help students achieve academically by increasing their motivation. The news program hoped to involve the community in improving its schools. Yet by viewing student achievement through the lens of American culture—especially in terms of individual autonomy and responsibility—students, teachers, and administrators were predisposed to understand student success and failure as individual phenomena attributable, in great part, to individual initiative and determination, thereby distracting attention from systemic influences.

8

EASTOWN

A City Divided

. . . Eastown wants to be the Paris or Venice or (choose you favorite European city) of the East Coast. By building elegant bridges and river walks along its reopened waterfront; by breeding a Soho lifestyle of students, artists and young professionals among the eclectic architecture downtown; by encouraging a renaissance of art, entertainment, dining and shopping; by inviting thousands of conventioneers to enjoy this bohemian atmosphere . . . Eastown's economic development plan may be the boldest of any American city. . . . There is a real feeling that downtown Eastown is on the move. If that is true, then these could be the best of times. . . .

But what about the worst of times? What about the Eastown that its residents experience day in and day out? This is the Eastown that now seems destined to jump on the bandwagon of decline with Newark, Detroit, Los Angeles (choose the American city of your nightmares). This is the Eastown of the fleeing middle class, the growing poverty class, and the shrinking tax base. . . . Once thriving districts . . . are decaying neighborhood by neighborhood. The houses in some of these neighborhoods are emptying out as residents flee to low-tax, high-service suburbs. In Eastown's more prosperous neighborhoods, residents talk of the city's less stable sections as if they were trenches at some latter-day Verdun, abandoned grudgingly as block after block grows meaner and meaner in a losing battle for residential civility. . . .

Do these divergent tales truly reflect the same city? How can they coexist? . . . Is it possible that downtown could become a sort of American Venice while some of its surrounding neighbor-

hoods seem on the verge of becoming Detroit? The
fact is that they probably can: Wealth amid poverty
is as old as history. But who wants it to happen
here?

—*The Eastown Gazette*
(editorial, July 1992)

Ethnographies often begin with community overviews that set a
broad context for the ensuing study. In this case I use the community
context more in an explanatory fashion. That is, to show what is
happening socioeconomically within Eastown and how related trends
are mirrored in the school system; and to perhaps create a sense of
urgency since the trends I describe are growing more pronounced and
will grow increasingly difficult to counter.

While I conducted research at Russell High, Eastown was a city
in transition, a transition which, when viewed in terms of its shifting
racial and ethnic composition as well as its socioeconomic structure
and neighborhood distribution, created a divided city. Reflecting a
common trend among American urban centers during the seventies
and eighties, the city experienced an influx of low-income persons of
color, including significant numbers of immigrants, refugees, and
non-English-speaking persons (many of whom were school-aged
children)[1], while many middle-income residents left the city for
surrounding suburbs—what Thomas and Mary Edsall termed the
"suburbanization process" (1991a, 1991b). By 1990, the socioeconomic
polarization engendered by this demographic shift was clearly tied to
racial and ethnic differences and was manifest in many dimensions of
city life. On average, white residents earned higher incomes, had
more formal schooling, and lived in the city's wealthier neighborhoods. Persons of color had disproportionately low incomes, less
formal schooling, and lived in poorer neighborhoods.

CHANGE, PROSPERITY, AND POVERTY IN EASTOWN

Occupying twenty square miles of land, Eastown is an East Coast city
with a population of 160,000. In 1970 Eastown was ninety percent
white, with Italian-Americans, Irish-Americans, and "Yankees,"
being the dominant European-American ethnic groups. As of 1980,
whites comprised 81.2 percent of the city's population. According to
the 1990 census, 62.8 percent of Eastown's population was white. In
addition, after several decades of population decline, in the eighties

Eastown experienced its first growth spurt, an increase of 2.5 percent spurred by an increase in the number of low-income residents and persons of color.[2] Not only were persons of color a growing entity, they were an increasingly diverse one as well. In 1970, persons of color, mostly African Americans, represented ten percent of Eastown's population. By 1980 the percentage of African Americans increased slightly while the number of persons of color overall doubled, a consequence of growth in the Hispanic and Asian populations. This trend continued through the eighties as the number of Hispanics nearly tripled and they emerged as the city's most populous minority, being 15.5 percent of the population (25,000 persons). The Asian and Pacific Islander population experienced similar growth, increasing from 1,700 in 1980 to nearly 10,000 by 1990, 6.2 percent of the city's population. African Americans accounted for 14.8 percent of the city's population (24,000 persons) (U.S. Bureau of the Census, 1990).

During the mid-to-late eighties, the city and state experienced a period of significant prosperity. In 1989 Eastown was named as one of America's "hottest cities" by a national news magazine. The state's municipal bond rating rose to an "A" standing. As the regional economy flourished, real estate values increased sharply and construction projects sprang up throughout the city. The number of jobs increased. The professional service sector—in particular, fields such as law, finance, and advertising—experienced significant growth. This economic invigoration was symbolized by the construction of new office, hotel, industrial, and commercial development projects that transformed the city landscape, most notably, the downtown district.

Despite such growth and prosperity, many Eastown residents were financially, educationally, and socially impoverished. According to the 1990 census, 34,000 persons, nearly one-quarter of all city residents, lived below the poverty line—an increase of 14.0 percent from 1980 (U.S. Bureau of the Census, 1990). Thirty-five percent of all children below the age of eighteen lived in poverty, an increase of 22.5 percent from 1980. In addition, Eastown's median family income, $28,342, was nearly $11,000 below the state median, $39,172 (U.S. Bureau of the Census, 1990). Compared with comparable measures statewide, Eastown's public assistance figures reveal the pervasiveness of poverty in the city relative to other state communities. According to a State Division of Planning report issued in 1990, while the city's population made up only sixteen percent of the state's population, 42.6 percent of all Aid to Families with Dependent Children cases were in Eastown, 46.0 percent of all General Public Assistance cases, and 34.4 percent of all Supplemental Security Income cases.

Eastown also had a considerable number of single-parent and female head of household families, characteristics that closely correlate with poverty. In 1987 the State Health Department reported that thirty-seven percent of all Eastown families had a single-parent and over thirty percent of children born in Eastown between 1982 and 1986 were born to single women. In those neighborhoods designated as "extreme poverty," that figure approached forty-five percent.

In terms of education, the city's dropout rate—estimated at 46.6 percent in 1989—signaled further evidence of social dysfunction. Discussing the effects of a high dropout rate, the Eastown Dropout Prevention Collaborative observed:

> Several national studies have shown that dropouts have an unusually high demand for social services, medical care, welfare benefits, and job training programs. Dropouts require the services of the judicial and correctional branches of local and state government far more often than high school graduates. Moreover, although dropouts use more public services, they usually pay lower taxes than their neighbors . . . because they earn significantly less taxable income than high school and college graduates.

To make this situation even more difficult, by 1990 the region, state, and city were all experiencing serious economic problems. Due to mismanagement and corruption, many banks and credit unions were forced to close, depressing the local economy and throwing the future of some development projects into question. Unemployment rose to 9.2 percent and the state's bond rating dropped to AA. As the decade ended, a city with a relatively impoverished population, compared with the rest of the state, faced difficult economic times, in part, because so many middle-income residents had left the city.

How Is Eastown Divided?

As the suburbanization process unfolded in Eastown, not only did many middle-income residents move to surrounding suburbs, but the city's population grew increasingly polarized—in terms of income, race/ethnicity, neighborhood, and educational levels. According to the 1990 census, 34.0 percent of all city households had what the State Housing and Mortgage Finance Corporation termed "very low" incomes (less than $20,300 per year), and 21.5 percent had "low" annual incomes (between $20,300 and $32,480)—in total, over 55 percent of Eastown households. Further, 25.9 percent of city households were in the higher or highest income brackets. Those with moderate or middle incomes constituted only 18.6 percent of the city's population. Compared with 1980, these figures represent an increase in the number of households in the lower economic strata, a decrease in the number of middle and moderate income households, and a slight increase in the upper economic strata.

This economic polarization also correlated with ethnicity: persons of color, on average, earned less than whites. In 1990, the mean household income for African Americans in the city was $10,400 less than that of whites; for Hispanics it was $9,500 less; and for Asians and Pacific Islanders it was nearly $11,000 less (U.S. Bureau of the Census, 1990).[3] While in 1990 18.3 percent of Eastown families lived in poverty, when disaggregated according to race/ethnicity, 12.0 percent of white families lived in poverty while 29.1 percent of African American families, 36.1 percent of Hispanic families, and 41.2 percent of Asian families did (U.S. Bureau of the Census, 1990).

Looking at city census tracts revealed a second dimension of socioeconomic polarization, one manifest in terms of city neighborhoods. While the median family income in Eastown increased by 89.6 percent between 1980 and 1990, from $14,948 to $28,342, this increase was not evenly spread across city neighborhoods. Rather, the number of upper-income census tracts (with average incomes over 120 percent of the median family income in the city), increased from seven to ten; the number of lower-income census tracts (with average incomes of less than 80 percent of the median family income), increased from thirteen to sixteen; and the number of middle-income census tracts (with average incomes between 80 and 120 percent of the median family income), decreased from seventeen to eleven.[4] Again, as occurred with household income, Eastown grew increasingly polarized; the number of upper- and lower-income neighborhoods increased while the number of middle-income neighborhoods shrunk.

These socioeconomic divisions in Eastown census tracts reflected racial and ethnic differences as well. Those tracts with higher percentages of persons of color had consistently lower average household incomes; conversely, predominantly white census tracts had higher average household incomes. In the ten census tracts with the greatest percentage of persons of color (averaging 79.1 percent), median family income averaged $17,823—37.1 percent below the city average. In the ten census tracts with the highest concentrations of white citizens (averaging 91.4 percent of their total populations) the median family income averaged $41,605—46.8 percent above the city average. Moreover, all but one of the census tracts with high concentrations of persons of color are contiguous, and eight of the ten predominantly white census tracts are contiguous (U.S. Bureau of the Census, 1990). As the Eastown Department of Planning and Development noted in a 1990 report, this polarization by race/ethnicity and socioeconomic status along neighborhood lines was accentuated by the tendency of the city and state to locate government-subsidized, low-income housing in the city's poorer neighborhoods.

SUMMARY

In terms of educational opportunity, the very nature of the suburbanization process has endangered the well-being of low-income residents and persons of color, in Eastown as well as other American cities. With the demographic shifts of the eighties, those with lower incomes and persons of color are increasingly concentrated in specific cities, where they tend to settle in neighborhoods with populations much like themselves. For instance, the State Housing and Mortgage Finance Corporation noted in 1991 that, in the state as a whole, persons of color made up 10.7 percent of the population, but in only four communities did their numbers exceed a comparable percentage of the total population. Likewise, in a 1990 report the Eastown Department of Planning and Development wrote that in seven of the city's twenty-five neighborhoods persons of color accounted for seventy percent of all school children.[5]

What is critical to keep in mind is that these divisions within Eastown and across the state made it increasingly less likely that low-income residents and persons of color would interact with those more affluent as neighbors—in the communities-at-large as well as in the schools—and develop the kinds of understanding and relationships such associations may engender. Edsall and Edsall alluded to the consequences of such pronounced divisions:

> The contact between whites and low-income African Americans [and I would argue, most persons of color] has routinely violated every standard necessary for the breakdown of racial stereotypes. Most white contact with these groups is through personal experience of crime and urban squalor, through such experience related by friends and family, or through the daily reports about crime, drugs, and violence which appear on television and in newspapers. The news includes, as well, periodic reports on out-of-wedlock births, welfare fraud, drug-related AIDS, crack babies, and inner city joblessness. (1991a: 56)

Seeing how interaction (and therefore understanding and empathy) decreased between those more affluent and persons of color and low-income residents, it becomes apparent how the suburbanization process helped to promote the myth of educational opportunity, while coincidentally endangering this democratic necessity. When dissatisfied middle-income residents moved from the city to the suburbs, these towns could spend liberally on education, recreation, roads, and the general quality of life. Yet these persons could also represent a force for fiscal conservatism in state and federal spending, including urban school funding (Edsall and Edsall, 1991a, 1991b; Kozol, 1991). Therefore, suburban voters, those whose power increased during the eighties, could overlook concerns of the inner city as they and urban, low-income persons of color were less likely to interact in ways that could promote mutual understanding and empathy—at precisely the time when the numbers of urban needy increased and the city's ability to address these needs decreased. Alluding to this development—what he termed America's "residential apartheid"—Andrew Hacker noted how this trend influenced middle-income whites:

> [F]ew white Americans feel an obligation to make further sacrifices on behalf of the nation's black minority. They see themselves as already overtaxed; feel the fault is not theirs; and that money cannot achieve a cure. About the only funding the public approves is for more police and prisons. (1992: 214)

Steven Rivkin bluntly outlined the consequences for urban school students: "[T]he persistence of extensive residential segregation inhibits the realization of equal opportunity in the United States" (1994: 291).[6]

Further, the parallels between what occurred in the city of Eastown during the eighties and what occurred in the school system are striking: many of the disadvantages faced by low-income residents and persons of color recurred in the school system. Schools, both public and private, were polarized and segregated according to race/ethnicity and socioeconomic status. And certain schools were especially needy—enrolling disproportionate numbers of low-income, limited-English proficient, transient, and special education students. As the preceding chapters made apparent, concentrating these populations in particular schools promoted educational policies and attitudes among students, teachers, and the larger community that served to further disadvantage Eastown's already disadvantaged school children.

PART
IV

CONCLUSIONS

9

So What?

What the best and wisest parent wants for his
own child, that must the community want for all
its children. Any other ideal for our schools is
narrow and unlovely; acted upon, it destroys our
democracy.
—John Dewey, *The School and Society*

The question is not, Is it possible to educate all
children well? but rather, Do we want to do it
badly enough?
—Deborah Meier, *The Power of Their Ideas*

This ethnography offered a cultural analysis of educational opportunity at Russell High, an urban school. Accordingly, I propose a
series of reforms for urban secondary schools derived from this
cultural analysis and linked with existing research on promising
school reform practices. These proposals attend primarily to one
dimension of school reform, the cultural.[1] The intent is to improve
educational opportunity by getting people involved with urban schools
to see their world differently.

In recent works, Seymour Sarason (1996) and Kenneth Wilson
and Bennett Daviss (1994) advised that, given the systemic nature of
our school systems, reform should be undertaken systematically;
anything less will be overwhelmed by the status quo. In full
agreement I would add that those enacting reform need to realize
that being systematic requires attending not only to what people do,
but what they believe, to culture. Teaching styles, curriculum, and
assessment practices may need to change, but so do such things as
how educators approach issues of student responsibility, how

teachers think about student abilities, how students view academics, and how administrators define their work.[2] That is, values need to change (Cohen, 1995; Cummins, 1986; Fullan and Stiegelbauer, 1991; House and McQuillan, 1997; Weinstein, et al., 1995). But values are unlikely to change unless teachers and students alter the nature of their interactions. To change beliefs, you need to change experiences. The routine does not promote new thinking. The following proposals therefore have as a central aim to restructure the fundamental nature of the student-teacher relationship, to focus "change where it counts most—in the daily interactions of teachers and students" (Tyack and Cuban, 1995: 142).

Moreover, urban school systems will only change through markedly rethinking and restructuring what they do; their system. Thus, not only do school structures need to change, but these changes must be drastic enough to make school experiences qualitatively different from their present state. If old and comfortable habits can return, they will.

SMALLER SCHOOLS

The most radical change I propose is simple: make urban schools smaller. For one thing, doing this would acknowledge the collective nature of educational opportunity. Urban schools serve students whose families are disproportionately low-income, single-parent, non-English-speaking, and geographically mobile—factors which all correspond with low levels of student achievement and high dropout rates (Lippman, et al., 1996). In addition, most urban high schools are structured in terms of an industrial-efficiency model that has long since proven ineffective. School structures do little to foster learning, trust, or understanding. Most urban teachers see 120 to 150 or more students a day. Work is superficial because that fits with the schools' priorities, which often reflect greater concern for control and order than learning and growth. And many students welcome these practices, which effectively allow them to approach schooling with much the same impersonal detachment as shown them by the institution. The structure simply does not allow teachers to understand students as learners nor to demonstrate concern for their well-being (Noddings, 1992).

In contrast, findings from research on smaller schools are powerful. As Valerie Lee and her colleagues found in their analysis of restructured schools, "[S]tudents learn more, and learning is distributed more equitably, in smaller schools" (Lee, et al., 1995: 1; see also, Clune, 1995; Keedy, 1995; Sizer, 1992). This is what American education has set as an ideal for some time—equity and excellence. Likewise, Mary Anne Raywid's study of alternative schools points to the value of smaller school structures, as all schools judged "successful" by the study were small (Raywid, 1995: 131). And Raywid was unequivocal as to the basis for their success: "Human relationships within the school are the critical component, particularly the relationships between students and adults and, most particularly, between students and teachers" (Raywid, 1995: 133).

Kathleen Cotton's (1996) synthesis of 103 studies that examined the relationship of school size to various aspects of schooling were similarly positive. As she found, in small schools:

- Academic achievement was at least comparable to—and often better than—that of large schools.
- Student views of school life in general and toward particular subjects were more positive.
- Student behavior—including truancy, discipline problems, violence, theft, substance abuse, and gang participation—was more positive.
- Levels of extracurricular participation were higher and students described their involvement as more fulfilling.
- Attendance was better and dropout rates were lower.
- Students had a greater sense of belonging.
- Relationships among students, teachers, and administrators were more positive.
- Students performed as well as those from large schools in such areas as College Board scores, grade point averages, and college completion rates.

The factors underlying these positive developments are multiple and interrelated. At small schools it is harder for students to get lost and easier for their parents to become involved in their children's education. Students know each other better and are therefore more likely to take risks in the classroom and offer support to one another in their learning. Discipline and disorder tend to be less of a concern when faculty and students know one another (Meier, 1995; Raywid, 1995). Education becomes the focus, rather than control.

Faculty can benefit from a smaller structure as well. Reflecting on her work at Central Park East Secondary School, one of a number of schools of choice in New York City's District 4, Principal Deborah Meier wrote:

Only in a small school can deep ongoing discussion take place in ways that produce change and involve the entire faculty—even there, it's tough to sustain. For teachers to start thinking through the task before them, collectively and collaboratively, schools must be so small that governance does not become the topic of discussion but issues of education do, so small that the faculty as a whole becomes the decision-making body on questions of teaching and learning. (1995: 108)

In research with the Coalition of Essential Schools (McQuillan and Muncey, 1994; Muncey and McQuillan, 1993, 1996), my colleague and I found that size was closely connected to implementing reforms that lasted. For one thing, small schools more easily involved a sizable percentage of faculty in reform, thereby enhancing the likelihood of generating consensus for change, precisely what Deborah Meier called for. In small schools, administrators accorded faculty greater power, perhaps because they could more easily see how that power was used. Large, comprehensive high schools were already divided. They had magnet programs, AP and honors courses, multiple tracks, and numerous autonomous departments. There was no time for "deep, ongoing discussion." By definition and in practice, people saw their work differently, and this often translated into more resistance and confusion than reform.

In emphasizing the value of intimacy and personal relationships, I am not suggesting that schools should be places where the mundane and uninspired are praised to preserve a distorted sense of student self-image. They should be places where people are critical and supportive, demanding and understanding, concerned but not naive. In fundamental ways, healthy relations between adults and adolescents make it likely that academic goals are realized. A smaller school structure can promote such relations in multiple ways.

EXTEND THE SCHOOL YEAR

To help overcome the structural as well as conceptual constraints that limit the vision and possibilities of students, teachers, and administrators, it seems logical to loosen those constraints. One unquestioned school policy seems due for such loosening, the 180-day school year, an accepted practice for nearly a century that was adopted to meet the needs of an American society quite different from today's. Since urban schools face greater challenges than most suburban or rural schools, urban school systems should extend the school year to create more time to do their job. (*But not to do more of the same thing!*)

A longer school year would make it easier for teachers to experiment with active research, project-based instruction, and work that is collaborative and multidisciplinary. Students might be given more responsibility and could work with less stringent supervision. Learning could occur outside the school building. Time might be set aside for individual student-teacher conferences, an unheard of luxury in most inner-city schools. Teachers and students might come to know one another in contexts other than the traditional forty-five-minute period. And students might realize that most teachers are concerned with their well-being.

Even if schools choose not to extend the school year, the idea of summer vacation needs to be reconsidered. It makes no sense to give students two-and-a-half months to forget too much of what they just learned; and then spend the first weeks of school reviewing what was forgotten. While the academic skills of many low-income students and non-native-English-speaking students may decrease during the summer, for those with higher levels of personal capital, the opposite is likely true. Family vacations, summer schools, and camps represent investments that are likely to enhance their personal capital. Summer vacation therefore represents one more instance in which those with higher levels of personal capital gain advantage over those less fortunate. To make educational opportunity real for more students, summer school should at least be an option for interested families.

MAKE TIME FOR TEACHERS

If schools are to be systematic about change, there must be time for teachers to do their job well; time to plan and time to reflect on their work. The logic behind this proposal is compelling: improve education by directly improving the quality of classroom teaching. Students change; society changes; technology changes; our understandings about teaching and learning change. So students get the best we can offer and so teachers maintain a sense of professional efficacy, these professionals need time to learn, reflect, and grow. American society must recognize that teaching is a difficult, challenging, draining, and demanding profession, if you do it right.

The low standards that afflict many urban schools are, in part, a reflection of the demands put on teachers and the compromises so many make, out of necessity. This is not surprising. There is little room allowed for teachers' growth; as opposed to making such growth a standard part of educational practice. Too many urban schools are intellectually stagnant. Seymour Sarason put the matter bluntly: *"Teachers cannot create and sustain contexts for productive learning unless those conditions exist for them"* (1996: 367; emphasis in original; see also, Cohen, 1995; McLaughlin and Talbert, 1993). But the structure of most urban schools precludes teachers and administrators from thinking about what they are doing, from determining whether the taken-for-granted should be taken-for-granted. Once endorsed, it becomes common sense regardless of whether it still makes sense. (While I was at the school, Russell had the exact same tracking system as was adopted in 1939.)

To provide teachers with this time on a regular basis, schools could simply have them teach fewer classes. Of course, to do this, beliefs must shift. People cannot assume, "a teacher not teaching is a teacher not working" (Wilson and Daviss, 1994: 123). For instance, students could take the same number of courses but have fewer classes. What other strategy could so directly influence instruction? The present system of inundating teachers with students and responsibilities does little but exhaust some and force others to compromise in ways that are professionally and personally unsatisfying. There is a limit to the value of contact time with students. Allowing teachers greater time, either individually or collectively, to plan their work, could translate into more productive learning for students and more reasonable working conditions for teachers. In addition, this would allow schools to shift greater responsibility to students, a logical move if schools are to help create informed and responsible citizens capable of educating themselves as adults.

A second way to make time for teachers would be to simply decrease the number of credits required to graduate. As this study demonstrated, what students encountered in many courses was of dubious value. Although many policymakers and legislators may believe that the remedy for low expectations and poor achievement among urban schools is to increase the number of courses students must take, that seems pointless unless something is done to alter the nature of the courses themselves. When the standards and expectations are so low, what benefits derive from more-of-the-same? Rather, schools need to alter what goes on within classrooms. And freeing teachers to plan, reflect, and collaborate will encourage such change.

To improve urban schooling, not only do teachers need more time, they need less power. Conversely, students need more power and more responsibility. As Seymour Sarason urged: "[T]o alter the power status of teachers and parents . . . without altering power relationships in the classroom is to limit drastically the chance of improved educational outcomes" (1990: 55). Teachers need to relinquish some authority, but doing so is in their best interest.

STUDENTS, POWER, AND RESPONSIBILITY

A final proposal for urban school reform represents good and bad news for students. The good news is that they would get more power. The bad news is that they would also get more responsibility (Ericson and Ellett, 1990; Wang, et. al, 1995). In my mind, one reason urban teachers find teaching so difficult is because too many people, themselves included, hold teachers responsible for students' academic failure (Ericson and Ellett, 1990). A healthier and more realistic view is to explicitly negotiate new conditions of power and responsibility with students, with the goal being to help students gain more formal power. Make it clear, teachers are there to help, but accord students power to shape their education. Students should have input into defining the work they do in classrooms and they should serve on school advisory boards and governance committees. Students should evaluate teachers on a routine basis. They should be involved in their education, rather than passive bystanders. Such a conception of schooling implies a need to bring students into the process of not only defining what educational opportunity should mean, but clarifying for them the potential value of this opportunity (Grant, 1989; Ogbu, 1992).

To make this political shift and embrace students as more participatory partners in their education, schools cannot naively assume the political empowerment of students will be a one-way process initiated by faculty and done to students (Muncey and McQuillan, 1991); rather, they need to think about such change as a collective undertaking that will require shifts in thinking very much of a political nature. Any faculty looking to accord students a greater voice in school matters will face two questions: What power and responsibility legitimately belong to students? And, how will they obtain and enact their power?

Furthermore, students will need help developing skills appropriate to a democratic education. A structured institutional policy that delineates students' increasing rights and degrees of responsibility as they proceed through their education seems to offer a logical structure for approaching this issue (Gutman, 1987: 92–93). Yet it should always be kept in mind that most students have little, if any, experience enacting formal power in schools. When they first gain power, some will misuse it. Teachers will be insulted. Trust violated. This is likely when people are learning to develop responsibility. As with learning anything, people will, at times, fail or disappoint. This is easily accepted in algebra class or on the basketball court. It is harder when power, authority, and trust are involved. But if reform is to be systematic and include students, schools will need to help them learn how to enact responsibility. That is logical, not to suggest it will be easy.

In terms of student empowerment one critical relationship must be kept in mind—the relationship *between* students (Stanton-Salazar, 1996). I cannot help but feel that schools and students would both benefit tremendously if schools helped students learn to support and trust each other. Yet peer relations are typically a double-edged sword. In some cases peers are thoughtful and comforting. In others, they are spiteful and destructive. To some degree this relationship is so unpredictable because few schools give any thought to how they could make it healthier and more productive. Rather than allowing chance to determine so much of peer relations, there are a range of ways in which schools could help students learn to support each other. It could occur in the classroom, through having students edit one another's work or co-present projects. In advisories, students could provide moral support for one another. Schools could initiate peer counseling and peer mediation programs. The possibilities are considerable.

Further, since students generally enjoy one another's company, it makes sense that reforms consider how students could work collaboratively for their educational betterment. Students already do this routinely in theater, music, and athletic programs; and it seems revealing that students usually volunteer for these activities and experience notable growth as a result of their involvement. Promoting greater peer collaboration could allow more of the energy generated by peer relations to be used for educational ends.[3]

There is considerable research evidence to support the effectiveness of the policies just discussed. The policies themselves are simple, yet drastic enough so they would have an effect. The ideas are straightforward; making them work and teasing out their full implications will be a challenge. Hopefully, the simple-but-complex nature of the proposed reforms will be a plus. While the directions for change are clear—shrink school size, extend the school year, create time so teachers can do their job, negotiate new conditions of power and responsibility with students—the reforms are not overly prescriptive. Those embracing the overarching framework would still need to draw on their own expertise and the community's sense of appropriate schooling to determine what specific schools will look like.

From the outset, these changes should have multiple effects on schools, and these effects should suggest a sense of synergy to the restructured system. By creating smaller schools, for example, students, teachers, and administrators will know each other better. In turn, learning should improve and schools should be more orderly. A longer school year will free teachers to expose students to a wide range of activities. Students could strengthen their social networks by experiencing more intensive relations with school personnel. A longer year would provide teachers with time to think about their work and know students better. Giving students more responsibility, like service-learning projects or independent research, would free teachers to plan and organize school matters. Admittedly, this is an optimistic way to look at the proposed system. But two points are key. First, the emphasis is on improving student-teacher relations so as to enhance student achievement; and second, the means to that end are mutually supportive.

Implementing these proposals systematically could be a relatively straightforward process. For instance, a school system, or number of school systems (as Wilson and Daviss [1994] propose), would create smaller schools and provide teachers with more professional planning time and less teaching time. They then systematically study the new school and its practices. After a reasonable period, they assess what happened and determine whether the outcomes fit with what the school community had set as reasonable expectations. If there is interest in the program, create more. If there is little interest, eliminate the program.

If any urban school districts would consider implementing the proposals outlined here, and would commit to systematically assessing the development and merit of these proposals, I would be glad to work with them.

IT AIN'T JUST EASTOWN

What occurred in Eastown was not unique to this city. The beliefs, processes, and outcomes I described are generalizable to other urban schools, as is the possibility that the situation may worsen.[4] Many American cities are losing middle-income residents, while increasing numbers of low-income, non-English-speaking, persons of color move in. What occurred at Russell High parallels what I have seen in Boston, New York City, Baltimore, Fort Worth, Providence, and

Portland, Maine, as well as what other researchers have found in low-income, urban, multi-ethnic schools: (1) teaching strategies that compromise academic standards in the interest of order and control (Anyon, 1980; Haberman, 1991; McNeil, 1986; Sizer, 1984; Wilcox, 1982); (2) a comparable emphasis on control and order by administration, with less concern for academic matters (Cusick, 1983; McNeil, 1986); (3) disproportionate numbers of low-income, special education, and limited-English proficient students and disproportionately high dropout rates, suspension rates, failure rates, and rates of student turnover (Fine, 1991; Muncey and McQuillan, 1996); (4) a student subculture that valued the social more than the educational (Everhart, 1983; Powell, et al., 1985; Willis, 1977); (5) demoralized teachers (Sizer, 1984); and (6) an inability to implement reforms that altered the routines of school life (Cross, 1987; Firestone, et. al, 1989; McQuillan and Muncey, 1994; Muncey and McQuillan, 1993).

CHANGING BELIEFS, AGAIN

Although I feel Russell High could reclaim its reputation and serve students more equitably, it would be naive not to acknowledge that it would be even easier for the status quo to endure. Or as the historical analysis of the school suggested, the situation may worsen. In the state, wealth and poverty were becoming increasingly concentrated in specific cities and neighborhoods and within specific populations, often along racial lines. As a result those with political influence are unlikely to interact with and therefore understand the predicament faced by society's disadvantaged, most of whom are children. Indeed, if these persons listen to the prevailing caricatures of educational opportunity, they may believe everything is fine. The situation is therefore unlikely to improve because there is little sense that it needs improvement. What needs to improve are the individuals who comprise the system, not the system itself. Moreover, in a time of fiscal conservatism and widespread skepticism of any tax proposal, large urban schools are viewed as cost-effective, at least in the short-term. Maintaining the status quo requires no new taxes.

To change this situation, beliefs must shift. This is where the cultural intersects with the financial. To gain financial support for urban schools, people must believe it is needed. Americans funded the Civil Rights Movement because they believed it was important and worthy. Belief was key. There must be a comparable consensus created that focuses on improving educational opportunity in urban America.

To begin to initiate such a shift in American thinking, those who create small schools must document their work, and publicly acknowledge both strengths and weaknesses. They will need data to substantiate the value of what goes on within their schools. And these data should be wide-ranging: attendance and dropout rates, course failure rates, scores on achievement tests and College Boards. Advocates of urban schools also need to highlight the cost of failure. Ignorance comes with a price, but that price is not easily ascertained. Nonetheless, one can begin to piece together an estimate. For instance, the National Adult Literacy Survey estimated that nearly two-thirds of all U.S. prison inmates are school dropouts (although 17 percent have earned a GED, Graduate Equivalency Degree, most while incarcerated) (Haigler, et al., 1994). Moreover, those "states with the lowest dropout rates have fewer prisoners [per capita] than those states with the highest dropout rates" (Burrup, et al., 1996: 21). America has tripled its prison space since 1983. These are expenses that improved schooling might decrease. Furthermore, like incarceration, single-parenthood and the likelihood of receiving welfare correlate with low levels of educational attainment. They must have similar costs. This information needs to be brought into the public debate.

Finally, to change what people believe, prevailing conceptions of educational opportunity must be challenged. There needs to be a voice that highlights the collective as well as the individual, that will question the unquestioned, and that will acknowledge students. Popular images and assumptions must be challenged. Consider how Americans often draw on classic notions of rugged individualism to portray urban education. The film *Stand and Deliver* focused on an inner city Los Angeles math teacher, Jaime Escalante, whose entire class, mostly Latino, passed the advanced placement calculus test even though the testing agency accused his students of cheating and required them to re-take the exam. *Small Victories*, by Samuel Freedman (1990), celebrated the efforts of an English teacher at a New York City high school ranked among the worst ten percent in the state—which nonetheless had ninety-two percent of its graduates go on to higher education. In Patterson, New Jersey, the singular efforts of Principal Joe Clarke drew an onslaught of public attention: the cover of *TIME* magazine, a television movie, a job offer from President Reagan. With a bull horn in one hand and a Louisville slugger in the other, Clarke offered a compellingly American image: an urban John Wayne prepared to single-handedly remedy a system out-of-control.[5]

Russell High, too, had its multicultural embodiment of the American Dream: the valedictorian for the Class of 1990, a refugee from the Vietnam War. He had come to the United States five years prior and worked forty hours a week while attending school. His graduation remarks extolled individual initiative and praised America as a land of opportunity:

> Only five years ago I was in Saigon, Vietnam. I was finally able to escape from the Communists . . . and after fifteen months of struggling . . . I was welcomed to live in America. I want to tell my classmates that we must remember how lucky we are to live in America. I want to tell them that we must work hard in order to make a good future for ourselves . . . I want to tell them that suffering and struggling often bring happiness and success later.

These are optimistic stories told to people who already believe that effort should be rewarded, that educational opportunity exists. Americans are ready to believe (and remember) these stories. They fit with our expectations. But there is a less optimistic side to these tales as well, one that generally receives less attention: Jaime Escalante, the calculus teacher, transferred to another school because of alleged threats and harassment from colleagues and the local teachers' union. The English teacher featured in *Small Victories* resigned the year after her classroom efforts were documented, a victim of professional exhaustion. As in most John Wayne movies, Joe Clarke, too, eventually left town. And despite intervention by the governor, Russell's valedictorian was denied admission to the state university because his score on an English-proficiency exam fell below the university minimum. Rugged individualism is more complex than many Americans realize.

A recent educational controversy in Boston offers another compelling example of how the lens through which we view such stories needs to change. A white student who had been denied entrance to the city's most prestigious "exam" school, Boston Latin, challenged the school system's quota policy that set aside thirty-five percent of all school placements for students of color. In looking at this incident, as Americans, we have a built-in bias. We tend to see such controversies from an individual point of view, and to interpret equity and justice in those terms. Throughout media coverage of the ruling attention focused on whether the student's individual rights had been violated. Should this flagship of the Boston public school system be allowed to guarantee that thirty-five percent of its students would be students of color? Was this fair to those with higher exam scores?

The irony of this ruling is exasperating. Here is a student saying she wants to enroll in the city's most desirable high school, and the court ruled that it is discriminatory to exclude her from the school since her exam scores were higher than a number of African American and Hispanic students. Indeed, this very same judge issued the original busing order for Boston schools in 1973. Now he had come to understand the situation differently. In many respects, the incident had shifted from a concern with the rights of groups historically disadvantaged by the status quo, to the rights of individuals disadvantaged by the rights of groups. In essence, the judge was saying that guaranteeing opportunity now was no longer as problematic. There is equal opportunity—or at least there is greater opportunity than there was in 1973—so there is less need to provide anyone with preferential treatment. In fact, doing so is likely unconstitutional. But why then would this young woman want to enroll in Boston Latin? If the system were truly equitable, it wouldn't make any difference. Isn't this student simply asking that she receive preferential treatment, based on her academic performance, in an unequal system? Why doesn't anyone say that the entire system needs to be made equal, that all schools should be places students want to go? Why isn't this issue part of the dialogue? If the school system were equitable, no one would be concerned with this matter.

A NEW MYTH

Throughout this work I characterized educational opportunity as a myth, an illusion for many Eastown students. But I'm not saying get rid of myths. Society needs myths. Who cares if George Washington actually chopped down that cherry tree? It is a lesson in honesty. Who cares if, on his death bed, George Gipp really told Knute Rockne that, some day when all looked lost, to "win one for the Gipper." It is a tale of compassion and hope. Myths hold societies together. They create common ground. People will always create myths. It's one way we make sense of our lives. But the message needs to shift. It is time for a new direction, new symbols, and new myths: students as advocates for one another; teachers as respected intellectuals; schools as places that honor the collective and cooperative, as well as the individual and competitive.

The symbol of the lone American cowboy braving the frontier has lost its practical integrity. It is simplistic and inappropriate. To continue to see life as a largely individual experience is to delude ourselves about educational opportunity and to mask grave inequities in American society.

APPENDIX

Methodological Reflections

> Ethnographers are more and more like the Cree
> hunter who (the story goes) came to Montreal to
> testify in court concerning the fate of his hunting
> lands in the new James Bay hydroelectric
> scheme. . . . [W]hen administered the oath he
> hesitated: "I'm not sure I can tell the truth. . . . I
> can only tell what I know."
> —James Clifford, *Writing Culture:*
> *The Poetics and Politics of Ethnography*

This ethnography offered a cultural analysis of educational opportunity that centered on the beliefs and values of students, teachers,
administrators, and others associated with the Eastown School
System. It looked at the issue of educational opportunity from various
points of view: from inside classrooms, in the context of the larger
school system, through the work of a school reform committee, from
an historical point of view, and in a school assembly and TV news
program. Drawing on the understandings created by considering
these multiple perspectives on educational opportunity, I identified
a series of interrelated beliefs, all of which had implications for
students' education:

1. People saw educational opportunity as largely an individual
    phenomenon and thereby overlooked its collective and systemic
    nature.

2. For many, educational opportunity was an unquestioned assump-
    tion. Students were being offered an education. It was their
    responsibility to take advantage of the opportunity.

3. Educational opportunity was understood as something defined for, not by, students; their role in the educational process was a passive, subordinate one.

Ultimately, I argued that educational opportunity for Russell High students was flawed, and that these unquestioned beliefs contributed to this injustice.

In making this argument, I relied on an interpretivist approach (Geertz, 1973; Peshkin, 1978; Varenne, 1977; Willis, 1977), seeking to understand what happened at Russell High from the perspective of those intimately involved in that experience—students, teachers, and administrators. Initially, my research focused on a reform initiative undertaken by the school in conjunction with the Coalition of Essential Schools (Muncey and McQuillan, 1996). That is how I came to be at the school. Over time, I realized that many people involved with Russell High were victimized and disadvantaged through their association with the school. Therefore, I also adopted a critical ethnographic stance. Although I continued studying the reform effort, I also began to look at the school in a broader context and to consider what happened at Russell High in terms of equity and opportunity. Ultimately, I hoped to reveal how many unquestioned practices and beliefs promoted systemic inequities—and thereby to change how people understood educational opportunity.

QUALITATIVE RESEARCH AND VALIDITY

As this study argues for a particular point of view and suggests ways to improve urban schooling, issues of research validity are critical. To evaluate any research findings people need a means to judge what is described. As a general guideline I embrace Clifford Geertz's metaphorical assertion: "A good interpretation of anything . . . takes us into the heart of that of which it is the interpretation" (Geertz, 1973: 18). Attending to "realist" conceptions of validity (e.g., House, 1991), Joseph Maxwell wrote: "[N]ot all possible accounts of some individual, situation, phenomenon, activity, text, institution, or program are equally useful, credible, or legitimate. . . . Validity, in a broad sense, pertains to this relationship between an account and something outside of that account . . . the phenomena the account is *about* . . . whether this something is construed as objective reality, the constructions of actors, or a variety of other possible interpretations" (1992: 282–83).

In this study validity centered on how cultural values influenced conceptions of educational opportunity, and consequently the educational experience of Russell High students. That is what the ethnography was *about*. A desire to illuminate the relationship between culture and educational opportunity informed my decisions regarding whose voice to represent, what events to look at, and what questions to explore. To avoid distorting the topics addressed, I sought to provide a representative sampling of the persons and points of view relevant to the topics addressed, and to situate these perspectives in a context that considered "a number of interacting causes that joined together to produce the event . . ." (House, 1991: 6; see also, Erickson, 1984; Hansen, 1979; Ogbu, 1974, 1981). What follows draws on a "checklist" of threats to validity that considers issues of descriptive, interpretive, theoretical, and evaluative validity (Maxwell, 1992). I also discuss how my five-year research design strengthened the validity of this research.

Descriptive Validity

Descriptive validity is concerned primarily with "factual accuracy" (Maxwell, 1992: 285). Phrased as a question: are data truly representative of what they purport to describe? This foundational category involves issues and questions upon which people could ultimately agree, given adequate information. For instance, this teacher taught a lesson on this topic on this day; or, this student offered this particular comment during this class. Description is a low level of abstraction but it is essential to one's overall analysis because all other categories of validity are built on descriptive accuracy.

I dealt with issues of descriptive validity in various ways. First, having conducted research at Russell High for five years, I have what has been termed "ethnographic authority." Put simply, I spent a great deal of time at Russell High. I attended classes, sat in on meetings, and went to softball, basketball, and football games. I talked with students, teachers, administrators, guidance counselors, and parents. I can create a true-to-life picture of the school based on "having, one way or another, truly 'been there'" (Geertz, 1988: 4–5). Further, I attended every event for which I offer first-hand descriptions (including interviews as well as classroom observations). I either took notes during the event itself or, less often, taped the event as well and combined field notes with transcriptions to recreate the experience. In a related vein, so the behaviors and words of those involved with this research might speak for themselves to some extent, my writing relies extensively on the voices of those studied and descriptions of their actions, although I, of course, edited these data.

Interpretive Validity

Threats to validity also emerge at the second level of abstraction from real life, the interpretive level, where one seeks "to comprehend phenomena not on the basis of the researcher's perspective and categories, but from those of the participants in the situations studied" (Maxwell, 1992: 289). These data are inevitably emic, as they include "intention, cognition, affect, belief, evaluation, and anything else that could be encompassed by what is broadly termed the 'participants' perspective'" (Maxwell, 1992: 288). While meaning is based largely on the accounts of one's informants, ultimately, all accounts are constructed by the researcher. Consequently, the interpretive level is more complex and more open to disagreement than the descriptive.

To address issues of interpretive validity and to honor the views of those with whom I worked, I had these persons read and respond to what I wrote. In my initial agreement with Russell High, as well as in the ensuing arrangements made with those who contributed directly to my research, it was understood that these persons could read and respond to relevant sections of the manuscript. For instance, when I shared drafts of Chapter 2 with the teachers who taught the history course, their reactions led me to alter my interpretations. When I first reviewed my data, what caught my attention was how the teachers seemed to hold students responsible for their inability to complete course work. After sharing my initial drafts with the teachers, they offered alternative and complementary interpretations. For one, their "reactions" to the students' inability and unwillingness to complete coursework were not uniform; the degree to which they saw individual students as responsible for failing to complete course work varied. Reviewing my field notes, this became apparent. The teachers also described problems they encountered trying to design and teach this course and said they were "groping" as much as students. One teacher wrote in response to an early draft: "I don't think the dynamics between the three of us is central to your thesis but it did complicate implementing an experimental curriculum. My own perception is that it made it more challenging to establish a positive and trusting classroom climate." Another team member responded:

> You note the experimental nature of our work in one footnote. I'd like to see you emphasize more strongly that the teachers were learning also. . . . I think it changes the use you can legitimately make of the class in this chapter. . . . [R]eaders need to see the larger context in order to evaluate the teachers' work.

Again, in reviewing my field notes I realized I had focused on what the teachers were doing in the classroom—curricular and pedagogical decisions they made—and paid little attention to intra-team dynamics and the student subculture. The final draft then reflected a different view of the teachers' work, one which, I feel, offers a more complete understanding of the class.

Moreover, when the persons with whom I worked read what I wrote, or otherwise came to understand the nature of my research (often by participating in an interview and asking questions about my research), many volunteered perspectives that might not have been accessible to me personally, and suggested related areas for research. Faculty put me in touch with Russell graduates and retired faculty who helped me write the "history" chapter. I was told when the television special on Russell High would be aired and when important school committee meetings were held. If I missed a school meeting, people always filled me in on what happened. This assistance enriched my understandings of life at Russell High, precisely what interpretive validity is founded upon. In effect, honoring the tenets of critical ethnography helped me create a more complete under-standing of the school and educational opportunity.[1]

Theoretical Validity

All theories are made up of two components: concepts and constructs and the relationships between those concepts and constructs (LeCompte and Preissle, 1993). In this sense, theoretical under-standing refers to "an account's function as an *explanation*, as well as a description or interpretation, of the phenomena" (Maxwell, 1992: 291). Two concepts central to this study are educational opportunity and individualism. A relationship would be that by focusing so extensively on individual performance, society often understands educational success and failure as individual phenomena, thereby overlooking systemic influences. In contrast to description and interpretation, theoretical understandings represent a greater level of abstraction from one's data, although theoretical understandings are based on description and interpretation. People may agree on the "facts" (description and interpretation), while the theoretical under-standings derived from these understandings may differ considerably.

In assessing theoretical validity another point should be kept in mind: while theory derives from description and interpretation, it cannot explain everything about what was described and interpreted. Theory is necessarily selective, a synthesis of one's data, research goals, and philosophical orientation (among other factors). In turn, these understandings are used to delineate concepts and constructs as well as their interrelationship(s). The critical question then becomes: how were data selected to illuminate your point of view? As I sought to blend a realist perspective with a critical stance in this work, my selection of data was not random. I provided examples that exemplified both the theoretical and critical positions I sought to address. Still, I didn't want to create a caricature of Russell High or Eastown. I therefore sought a balance in my writing: to provide a rich contextual understanding of Russell High and within that framework to highlight issues central to my research, without distorting the nature of life at the school, in particular, educational opportunity. A brief recounting of why I presented what I did and how these presentations fit with the overall focus of this ethnography should assist the reader in assessing theoretical validity.

Chapter 1 established a philosophical overview to this study: outlining how educational opportunity was commonly understood in individual, and therefore largely unproblematic, and non-systemic ways; and how students had little formal input into determining the education they received. To balance the prevailing tendency of emphasizing the individual nature of educational opportunity, Chapters 2 and 3 emphasized the collective influence of the student population. Chapter 2, the history course, offered insight into how the student subculture helped preserve the status quo; specifically, why it was difficult to maintain classroom standards and how students were active participants in disadvantaging themselves. Chapter 3 outlined how various Russell High policies and practices were tied to the limited social and cultural capital Russell students possessed, their collective nature.

I used a day-in-the-life of a Russell High senior as the focus for Chapter 4 because, if students were not attending classes, for whatever reasons, their actions had implications for educational opportunity. Further, it was clear that skipping class at Russell High was rampant. The assistant principals, those who attended to these institutional violations, admitted they were often unable to deal with the paperwork and disciplinary follow-up required by the large number of students who skipped class. Cutting class was a frequent topic of conversation in 1992 Committee Meetings and other teacher meetings. Throughout most days streams of Russell students came and went from the school—some leaving to hang out on The Avenue while others returned.

Moreover, in following a particular student I described a number of unflattering classes. The question then arises: were these classes routine? To address this concern, it helps to recall that the "routine" at Russell High was neither effective nor pleasant to describe. By many measures, Russell students were learning little and the school was unsuccessful. Over the five years of my research I calculated a fifty-seven percent dropout rate; the number of suspensions was said by the principal to have increased 450 percent in "recent years" (a study of all Eastown secondary schools found that suspensions increased three-fold from 1983 to 1993); a report from the coordinator of the Essential School noted that students failed forty percent of all courses they took. In both 1987 and 1989 Russell had the lowest Metropolitan Achievement Test scores of any school in the state. In light of the school's collective performance and my understandings of classroom learning, these classes seemed reasonably representative of the range in quality at Russell High.

Chapter 5 revealed how difficult it can be for teachers to collectively break from institutional constraints, as so many forces work against such change. The school's schedule did not provide time for all teachers to meet; the teachers defined "reform" as intensifying strategies and policies they had already embraced, not rethinking the nature of the work they did; and students had no voice in this process. Chapter 6 offered an historical perspective on Russell High, focusing on the "riot" of 1969 to provide a sense for how the school's present-day reputation had evolved—a critical development since the "riot" ostensibly occurred because of African American students' concerns with educational opportunity. Chapter 7 offered insight into how an uncritical faith in individualism was promoted at both the school site and in local media. And Chapter 8 set Russell High in a community context and suggested that the existing socioeconomic, neighborhood, and political divisions would make it difficult to resolve the issues raised by this study. Moreover, the concepts and proposed inter-relationships presented throughout this ethnography are consistently linked with comparable concepts and interrelations from the research literature. What I described at Russell High was far from unique.

Evaluative Validity

In great part, evaluative validity "depend[s] on the particular description, interpretation, or theory one constructs" (Maxwell, 1992: 295), thereby raising the following questions: On what do you base your evaluation? Were descriptions accurate? Do the theoretical categories derive from sound description and interpretation? Has your theory proven accurate and illuminating? Does your evaluation logically derive from your theory? The credibility of one's evaluative framework rests largely on these building blocks.

Without question, my theoretical stance influenced my evaluative comments on Russell High and the Eastown School System. Russell teachers, for instance, regularly said they could improve student performance if they could enforce more stringent punitive sanctions. And clearly at times, teachers faced difficult predicaments, occasionally involving violence and threats of violence. I understood and witnessed the problems they regularly discussed, but I felt their perceptions had been so reinforced by multiple systemic influences, perhaps the most powerful being the teachers' own shared belief in the effectiveness of behaviorist practices, that their view was distorted, serving to "perpetuate, as much as to explain, social phenomena" (Anderson, 1989: 253).

In my opinion the teachers saw the trees; to me, the forest looked very different. In suggesting future directions for urban schools I therefore said nothing about finding more effective ways to implement institutional sanctions. Rather, a more fundamental question needed to be addressed, one which Russell teachers seldom raised: what educational opportunities are in the students' best interest? The dropout rate, the number of course failures, and the prevalence of students skipping class, among other factors, made this question more critical. Further, a central idea derived from my work is that, to improve educational opportunity, teachers, administrators, and students need to change their beliefs about education; but this will not occur unless these persons change their experiences in significant ways. Both of these evaluative positions were closely linked with my theoretical understandings.

The Role of Time

In terms of enhancing the validity of qualitative research, the long-term nature of ethnographic studies offers some clear advantages. In a straightforward sense, such a research design provides increased opportunities to triangulate data. You simply hear more points of view and experience more of what you study from which to construct an understanding (Denzin, 1978). You also gain a longitudinal perspective on your topic, a sense for the flow of life, which allows you to assess whether what you observe is a unique phenomenon, a normal part of routine, or something in-between.

In addition, an extended time frame provides opportunities to develop rapport with those involved with your research. Since one's representations of social life are only as rich as "our informants can lead us into understanding" (Geertz, 1973: 20), this point is critical. When I began my research certain faculty seemed skeptical of my presence. In one instance a teacher who said I could observe her class later was clearly upset, to the point of telling me, "I'm sick of having people from [a local university] visit my class." I opted not to observe her class and assumed she was either having a bad day or that I had said or done something to upset her. The key point was: I did not understand why this occurred. On that day, I could only guess. Over time, I learned of considerable resentment toward the university because of what some saw as its heavy-handed and self-centered involvement at the school.

For a few Russell teachers these power dynamics were epitomized by a study of Eastown schools conducted by university researchers that criticized the curricula and teaching styles in many classrooms. The study was initiated with no prior agreement or understanding of the research goals by those classroom teachers involved, and the researchers never provided opportunities for teachers to respond to what they wrote. The teacher who was upset that day had been involved with that study. As I learned of such concerns, my understanding of the incident became richer. I now saw the teacher's reaction as potentially reflecting a range of interrelated motivations: an act of professional pride, someone exerting power, resentment toward the university. (The teacher may also have been having a bad day.) In addition, it was clear I would have to be especially sensitive to issues of professional respect in my dealings with Russell faculty. Fortunately, my extended research design provided me with time and opportunities to do so.

In a related sense, having time to get to know those with whom I worked allowed me and these persons to openly debate what I wrote as well as my understandings of the school. As previously mentioned, the first drafts of Chapter 2, the history class, were critical of the teachers. I largely endorsed the student point of view and felt the teachers blamed students when students lacked the requisite skills to complete many course assignments. When I shared early drafts with the teachers, they voiced perspectives I had not considered. And their feedback shaped the final product. Because we had developed mutual respect, I was comfortable asking hard questions and saying and writing some critical things. I felt I could confront these persons with questions and hypotheses one might not want to raise for fear of undermining a relationship. Moreover, doing so did not close off our dialogue; rather, it was in many ways enriched. Undoubtedly, it would have been easier and more satisfying not to suggest controversial and potentially insulting interpretations of life at Russell High to those with whom I worked. Yet, I feel researchers may in some cases effectively silence those with whom they work precisely because they find it easier to overlook difficult tensions. If researchers don't know those being researched well enough to ask hard questions, they may ignore issues that are critical to creating a rich ethnographic understanding.

SOME FINAL THOUGHTS ON THE "C" WORD

Culture is a concept that is integral to this study. It is also a theoretical construct that, of late, has come increasingly under attack (see, for instance, Abu-Lughod, 1991; Bourdieu, 1990a, 1990b; Clifford, 1988). In these closing remarks, I want to address two inter-related concerns critics of the culture concept have raised: first, that researchers present culture as though it were a *fait accompli*, an influence so powerful people mindlessly adhere to its guidelines; and second, that culture is a static, unchanging phenomenon. In my view, these are naive conceptions of culture; criticism is warranted. Unquestionably, culture is a "contested" phenomenon (Clifford, 1986) that individuals can use to their strategic betterment, not an unwavering prescription for behavior. This ethnography presented numerous instances where traditional conceptions of educational opportunity were challenged. The "riot" of 1969 was linked to students questioning prominent cultural assumptions. In 1992 Committee meetings, many different conceptions of educational opportunity surfaced. So, too, teachers and a university professor discussed a range of views on educational opportunity during a planning period meeting (described in Chapter 7). Yet in all these contexts people's beliefs and values, their culture, endured. The "riot" didn't change Russell High for long. The 1992 Committee had little effect on the school. And many ideas presented during the planning period went no further than that meeting.

Clearly, culture is a contested phenomenon; but just as clearly, culture usually wins these contests. That's why it's culture. These are beliefs that have been sustained through time, that are affirmed by the status quo, that are expected. Indeed, even when people's actions at Russell High deviated from the norm, in an ironic twist of cultural fate, doing so often bolstered the status quo by highlighting the norm itself, and its importance, through its violation. In my five years at the school, cultural values weren't transformed, they endured, despite efforts at reform. While it is naive to assume that culture is a static phenomenon, it is equally naive to assume every ethnography will document appreciable change. Genuine culture is resilient.

NOTES

1. Educational Opportunity Through the Lens of American Culture

1. Eastown, the names of all high schools, and all persons' names, except one, are pseudonyms. The Coalition of Essential Schools, discussed later this chapter, is the name of an actual reform initiative and its Chairperson, Theodore Sizer, is referred to by his true name (in Chapter 7).

2. For an insightful and amusing look at how culture can influence perception, see Laura Bohannon's (1977), "Shakespeare in the Bush." To appreciate how culture can operate in the classroom and in the research process itself, see George and Louise Spindler's (1988) comparative look at American and German classrooms.

3. See Brightman (1995) for a comprehensive assessment of how the concept of "culture" has been recently subjected to scrutiny and criticism.

4. Capital letters signal increased volume in the speaker's voice.

5. However, when disaggregated by race, a different picture emerged:

Whites [83 percent of survey respondents] in America seem convinced that, on the whole, blacks and other minority children have the same educational opportunities as whites. This conviction has not changed since 1975, when the question was first asked in these surveys. But nonwhites (who make up 14 percent of the sample in the [1990] poll) have a considerably different view. A disturbing 38 percent see inequality of opportunity in education. (Elam, 1990: 4)

Clearly, one's race/ethnicity can influence perceptions of educational opportunity. I maintain, however, that our cultural values often cross racial and ethnic lines.

6. Summarizing the research of Murphy and Beck (1995), Dick Corbett and Bruce Wilson concluded: "[T]he rationale for most forms of site-based management . . . is improved student performance, yet students are mostly absent in any capacity in the models covered in the review" (1995: 13). Corbett and Wilson also found that school reform literature reflected a comparable lack of attention to students: "Despite . . . repeated calls for reform aimed at students, young people themselves occupy, at best, a minuscule part of the literature on the process of changing and reforming education" (1995: 12).

215

7. Other researchers offer more comprehensive analyses of race/ethnicity and educational opportunity (e.g., Delpit, 1988; Foley, 1990, 1991; Fordham, 1988, 1996; Gibson, 1988; Gibson and Ogbu, 1991; Hacker, 1992; Heath, 1983; Lucas, et al., 1990; McCarthy, 1990; McDermott, 1987; Ogbu, 1974, 1987; Phillips, 1983; Solomon, 1992; Spindler and Spindler, 1988; Trueba, 1988, 1989), and socioeconomic status and educational opportunity (Anyon, 1980; Bowles and Gintis, 1976; Hanson, 1994; Katz, 1971; Wells and Crain, 1994; Wilcox, 1982; Willis, 1977).

8. Certainly, the collective nature of a student population has a pronounced effect on educational achievement. As James Coleman wrote:

[T]he apparent beneficial effect of a student body with a high proportion of white students comes not from racial composition per se, but from the better educational background and higher educational aspirations that are, on average, found among white students. *The effects of the student body environment upon a student's achievement appear to lie in the educational proficiency possessed by that student body, whatever its racial or ethnic composition.* (Coleman, 1990: 92–93; excerpted from Coleman et al., 1966; emphasis added)

9. During the eighties race/ethnicity correlated closely with income and education: whites were disproportionately more likely than persons of color to earn a higher income and to have a higher level of educational attainment. According to the 1990 census, median household income in the United States was $28,906. Yet the median household income for whites was $30,406; for Hispanics it was $21,921; and for African Americans it was $18,083. Further, 12.8 percent of the country lived below the poverty level. When disaggregated according to race/ethnicity, only 10.0 percent of whites lived below the poverty level while 26.2 percent of Hispanics and 30.7 percent of African Americans did (U.S. Bureau of the Census, 1990).

In terms of formal education, on the secondary level, a "report card" issued by the Department of Education through the National Assessment of Educational Progress, using 1988 data, found that "the achievement of minority students has improved over the years," but added, "Sadly, the gaps between minority and white students are still large [even though] the performance of white students has remained stagnant over nearly two decades" (*Los Angeles Times*, 1990). Moreover, enrollments in higher education during the eighties suggest that the disadvantages experienced by many in high school affected college attendance as well. Although the number of African American and Hispanic students (the two largest groups of persons of color in the United States) attending American colleges increased by 10.5 and 61.0 percent respectively during the eighties, the college-going rates of 18-to-24-year-old African American and Hispanic high school graduates remained unchanged. In effect, increases in the number of these persons going to college paralleled increases in their numbers in the larger population. In contrast, the college-going rate for Whites increased from 33 percent in 1981 to 40 percent in 1989 (U.S. Department of Education, 1992).

10. As the Harvard Education Letter noted: "In part because of the recent and continuing influx of new immigrants, minority students today

outnumber white students in twenty-five of the nation's twenty-six largest urban school systems" (1988: 1).

11. Five years is certainly longer than most ethnographies. I was afforded this opportunity because of my affiliation with the Coalition of Essential Schools.

12. Unquestionably, there is more to ethnography than these three features. For a more complete discussion, see, for example, Agar (1980), Erickson (1984), Hammersly (1992), Maanen (1988), and Stocking (1983).

13. The press and community termed this event a "riot" but many participants said it was a protest to highlight inequities perpetrated by the school system. Nonetheless, those involved with whom I spoke readily admitted that "it got out of hand" and that substantial damage was done. To signal the term's contested nature, it is framed with quotation marks.

2. WINNING THE BATTLE AND LOSING THE WAR

1. Portions of the material presented in this chapter are included in a work published by Yale University Press, *Reform and Resistance in Schools and Classrooms: An Ethnographic View of the Coalition of Essential Schools* (Muncey and McQuillan, 1996).

2. I determined the dropout rate by tracking the number of students in five graduating classes—1986 through 1990—from their freshman year through graduation and dividing the number of graduates by the number of students enrolled as freshmen. This assumes that the number of students who transferred into and out of Russell High during those five years was relatively balanced.

3. Due to concerns with confidentiality, I offer no citations for the teachers' writing.

4. Three students made this transition.

5. This development suggests something of the difficulty of school change. After two years of restructuring, the school was still uncertain how to represent a grading change that was fundamental to the reform.

6. As noted in Chapter 1, Elena was an exceptional student. She had been in the other Essential School history class but asked to be transferred half-way through the year because she felt the class went too slowly. Unlike many of her classmates, she came from a family of highly educated persons: her father was a lawyer and her mother was working toward a Ph.D.

7. Throughout this study, students' work is presented exactly as they produced it.

8. The class alluded to by the student teacher occurred midway through the course. By June, the student teacher had considerable rapport with students. Still, her reaction is revealing.

9. That job demands can lead teachers to "compromise" (Sizer, 1984) is well documented (Cusick, 1983; McNeil, 1986; Woods, 1983). Moreover, while the teachers adjusted their expectations to accord more closely with student abilities, as is discussed later, many of their actions reflect lower expectations and the quality of much student work appeared poor for 10th grade.

10. In fact, there were four other public high schools in Eastown. Since the "alternative" school enrolled less than five percent of public high school students, I excluded it from the ensuing discussion.

11. Much of Russell's student population, for instance, was low-income, more so than any other Eastown high school. According to a self-study conducted as part of an accreditation process in April 1990, 62.3 percent of the student body were approved for free or reduced-price lunches. The same year, 40.1, 33.9, and 9.2 percent of the students at Travis, Archibald, and Latin High, respectively, (Eastown's three other public high schools) received this benefit.

The educational backgrounds and occupations of Russell parents also suggested a lack of personal capital. A survey administered in the spring of 1990 to roughly one-third of all Russell students found that 25.0 percent of their fathers and 30.3 percent of their mothers had not graduated from high school. For 40.3 percent of the fathers and 24.8 percent of the mothers, students were either "uncertain" of their highest level of educational attainment or they left the question blank. Students also reported that 11.9 percent of the fathers and 10.9 percent of the mothers had earned college degrees. In the same survey, students reported that the three largest occupational categories for their fathers were unskilled worker (e.g., laborer, jewelry worker), semi-skilled worker (e.g., machine operator, nurse's aid) and skilled worker (e.g., mechanic, baker)—which combined, made up 23.4 percent of the sample. The three largest categories for their mothers were unskilled worker, semi-skilled worker, and homemaker—which combined, comprised 28.4 percent of the sample. Again, 42.1 and 43.0 percent, respectively, of the sample offered no information or were "uncertain" about their father's or mother's occupation—by far, the largest response categories for this section of the survey. Students also reported that 7.3 percent of their fathers and 6.6 percent of their mothers worked in "professional" occupations, those requiring post-secondary schooling (e.g., clergy, dentist, professor).

12. This is not to suggest that counter-school values arise only in schools with sizable numbers of students with low personal capital. In spring 1995, students at Greenwich (Conn.) High School, one of America's more affluent communities, included blatantly racist remarks in the yearbook. While conducting research on the Coalition of Essential Schools (Muncey and McQuillan, 1996) some upper-income schools in our study encountered problems with cheating, anti-Semitism, vandalism, and robberies.

13. In line with this concern, the university professor noted:

As long as the three of us were taking turns teaching, no one teacher was able to establish and maintain the positive working relationship with the kids that they clearly needed in order to take the significant risks—and to put in the necessary effort—to complete the assignments. From our experience, I'd suggest starting slowly and devoting considerable time and effort to establishing a positive classroom climate.

3. Low Cultural and Social Capital, Continued

1. Although not in as detailed or comprehensive a fashion, other researchers have identified much the same (e.g., Dollard, 1957; Havighurst, et al., 1962; Hollingshead, 1949; Lynd and Lynd, 1929; Warner, 1949).

2. The alternative school was relatively new and was not part of the desegregation plan. As the school enrolled less than five percent of the public high school population, it is not part of the ensuing analyses of the school system's structure and the outcomes it promoted.

3. Although nearly sixty-five percent of those in Eastown were white (U. S. Bureau of the Census, 1990), the school system was so diverse because roughly twenty percent of all students, mostly white and upper income, attended private or parochial schools.

4. Initially, many students expressed similar reservations. Over time, most said their original expectations, especially regarding violence and racial tension, were unfounded.

5. Based on freshman class enrollment during my research, 500 suspensions would translate into an average of about one-and-a-half suspensions per student.

6. While these comments may seem harsh, all three administrators had good rapport with students. Most students expressed respect for them and felt they treated students fairly.

7. In doing an informal "climate study" of Russell High in April 1988, a teacher administered a survey to his classes. By far, students cited "the most serious problem at Russell" as being "a lack of discipline."

8. This lack of community may have been heightened by two factors: students' residential mobility and the number of ESL students. Russell had the highest rate of student turnover among Eastown's high schools. A look at the class of 1989 is revealing. In October 1985, 343 students enrolled as freshmen. By senior year the class graduated 130 students—sixty-nine of whom spent all four years at Russell, twenty percent of the original class. Further, roughly one-quarter of Russell students were limited-English-proficient. Since these students took many ESL classes and had limited fluency, they were segregated within the school.

9. Guidance counselors estimated the actual number was higher since some students who enrolled briefly were never recorded by the central office as either enrolling or leaving Russell.

10. This formula (the number of students enrolled at a school divided by the number of transactions by guidance) provides a standardized measure to compare the mobility of student populations. I am not suggesting that Russell High had nearly its entire student population change in the course of a school year.

11. Russell students who used public transportation to get to and from school, between fifty-five and sixty-five percent of the school, did not pay for the service, but they had to pick up bus tokens during lunch.

12. Moreover, relative to those more affluent, Russell students were less able to improve their academic standing by taking summer enrichment courses or SAT-prep classes. As Patricia McDonough (1991) found in a study of four guidance departments, more affluent students were more able to influence their academic status.

13. Some of the teachers' analyses drew on unsubstantiated notions of deficit theory—e.g., "This is a population . . . in need of being re-educated in terms of their morals and values"; "They're not nurtured to read or do enlightening activities," etc. Since the school never made time to assess such assumptions, it is not surprising that teachers who truly seemed to care about students still held these views.

14. Footnote 1 in Chapter 2 explains how I determined the drop-out rate.

15. To some degree, these scores reflected the high number of LEP students Russell served. Since the ESL program was often over enrolled, to accommodate students with very limited English fluency, students with better but still limited proficiency were mainstreamed. These students took the MAT exam.

16. Some related factors are further revealing of differences among the schools and how personal capital could influence academic achievement. At Russell, student SAT scores closely correlated with "level of parental education." Those whose parents had not graduated from high school had the lowest average; those whose parents earned high school diplomas came next; those whose parents earned bachelors degrees were next; and students whose parents earned a graduate degree had the highest average. The same held true at Travis, Archibald, and Latin, with minor inconsistencies. SAT performance also correlated with reported family income for Russell, Travis, and Archibald students. As family income rose, so did the mean verbal and math scores. This relationship did not hold for Latin students since Latin offered some low-income students access to a school other than their zoned, feeder school. (In line with Coleman's [1990] thesis, this development suggests that a student body's composition can offset deficits in personal capital.) Finally, at all four schools students' scores corresponded to their academic aspirations, with minor inconsistencies at Travis and Archibald. Those who planned to earn a bachelor's degree had the lowest average score; those who wanted to earn a master's degree had a higher average; and the

highest average was among students who planned to earn a "doctoral or related degree."

4. One Student's World at Russell High

1. Individualism is a topic that has been debated within the arenas of developmental and cognitive psychology as well. Work by developmental psychologists has been criticized for focusing on the construction of knowledge within individual minds as produced by cognitive processes (see Bruner, 1986; Walkerdine, 1988). In a similar vein, cognitive psychologists have been criticized for looking at the individual mind in isolation, exclusive of the social and collective (see Lave, 1988).

2. Drawing on popular culture to support this argument, I feel it is no coincidence that Bart Simpson's school is directed by Principal Skinner.

3. The pervasiveness of this assumption may be most apparent when one transgresses this belief. As both a student and teacher, I found that students consistently resisted attempts at enacting collective punishments, often aggressively, suggesting that cultural norms were violated and that such reactions were justified.

4. Again, *The Simpsons* offers insight into this issue. In one episode Lisa Simpson, very much a model student, comes to identify with a group of "bad girls." She then welcomes detentions, bad grades, and other punitive sanctions imposed by the school because they earn her the respect of her new-found friends.

5. Given the "secondary socialization" characteristic of formal schooling, strategy seems especially useful for illuminating student behavior. As secondary socialization involves a more distanced sense of self than primary socialization, the role "student" is often seen as a strategy to be manipulated and less of a fixed identity. Peter Berger and Thomas Luckmann discussed the logic of this perspective:

> [The student] apprehends his school teacher as an institutional functionary in a way he never did his parents, and he understands the teacher's role as . . . [an] institutional functionary with the formal assignment of transmitting specific knowledge. The roles of secondary socialization . . . are readily detached from their individual performers . . . the consequence is to bestow on the contents of what is learned in secondary socialization much less subjective inevitability than the contents of primary socialization possess. (1966: 161)

6. Lacking credits needed to graduate, Rafael had to take two English courses as a senior.

7. Further, given their family backgrounds and low levels of personal capital, many Russell students had a limited sense of the opportunities

offered by formal education. The value of a high school education may therefore have been even that much more dubious for them. This day in the life of Rafael Jackson certainly suggests why this may be so.

8. Most of Rafael's classes had fewer than twenty students in them, some as few as ten. This was typical at Russell. Although union guidelines set the maximum number of students in any single class at twenty-six, because students were absent so often, most teachers regularly dealt with a dozen or fifteen students in their classes.

9. Although I focus on the degree to which work was kept simple as a way to maintain order in the classroom and school, a complementary influence was also at work. That is, many faculty saw students as incapable of doing advanced work. Basic skills were a necessary prerequisite to students undertaking more challenging work (Page, 1987b: 451).

5. REFORM THAT REPRODUCED

1. Suggesting that a commitment to behaviorist practices permeated the school system, the same study found that middle school suspensions increased 400 percent and the elementary school rate increased 700 percent. During this time the student population increased nineteen percent.

2. For this chapter, culture and paradigm are essentially interchangeable. Both represent value systems that encourage people to see the world in a particular way, and therefore not to see it in alternative ways.

3. During the 1989–90 school year faculty visited several "exemplary" secondary schools. Students were included in a few of these visits and their reactions were included as part of a report published in one edition of *The 1992 Newsletter*.

4. In this meeting the Essential School was cited as a model of what Russell could be. The coordinator noted, for example, that students who might otherwise be "hard-core failures" were carrying books home, that the program had advisories which provided students with adult advocates, and that a leadership committee had been created. A teacher in the program said turnout for parents' night was the best she ever experienced. While these statements were accurate, the Essential School experienced resistance to its reforms and some innovations were abandoned. By the end of the program's first semester, the leadership committee was dissolved, as were town meetings, a forum intended to promote student input into the program. Although the coordinator said the Essential School allowed students to take exams "until they pass," by the end of the first year, the minimum acceptable grade was lowered from B to C. A year later, the Essential School reinstituted the F. By the program's third year, advisories were optional: teachers who wanted to could be an advisor; those who didn't, were not required to do so. This is not to denigrate the efforts of the Essential School, but to highlight the difficulty of enacting lasting change.

5. The "exhibition" has been promoted by the Coalition of Essential Schools (Sizer, 1992; Wiggins, 1987, 1989).

6. RESPECTABILITY LOST

1. The press and many in the community termed this event a "riot," but many participants said it was a protest aimed at highlighting inequities perpetrated by the school system. Nonetheless, those involved readily admit "it got out of hand," that substantial damage was done. To signal the term's contested nature, it is framed with quotation marks.

2. In terms of being prepared for challenges to the status quo initiated by students, Robert Hampel found:

> The turmoil in high schools in the late 1960s began suddenly, without much warning. Previously, cautious experimentation was the limit of reform. Modest changes usually enlarged the course catalog without modifying the traditional school atmosphere. The tinkerings made no room for political protest, black pride, or student rights, all issues of great importance to college activists several years before high school unrest flared. Despite the college protests, few public school administrators foresaw the school ferment of the late 1960s. In 1968, approximately three quarters of the principals lacked contingency plans for responding to student demonstrations. (1986: 104)

3. This section of Russell's history draws extensively on a report written by a teacher/historian, "A Factual History of Russell High School." The author relied mainly on yearbooks and school newspapers to research her report.

4. This citation comes from a study of the city's integration efforts entitled, Desegregation in Eastown.

5. African American students and school administrators differed on this incident: Administrators claimed African American students attempted to sexually assault a white girl. They wanted to punish those who did this, although no assault charges were ever filed. African American students said the principal fabricated the incident to try and intimidate them. In their view, the "riot," which occurred on the day the principal made this allegation, began in part as outrage to the allegation.

6. These descriptions come from the respective course syllabi.

7. The following year, many repairs were made after voters passed a bond that provided funds to improve the condition of city schools.

8. Although I juxtapose African American perceptions with those of whites, the African American response was not uniform. Some African American students who were to perform in a play the weekend following the "riot" cleaned the school to prepare for the play, even though most boycotted school-related activities. In similar fashion, some whites supported the students' actions.

9. Being "in violation" meant that a school's population deviated more than fifteen percent from the overall percentage of persons of color in the school system.

7. AFFIRMING THE MYTH OF EDUCATIONAL OPPORTUNITY

1. Although I rely on but one assembly and one media presentation to make my argument, these findings are substantiated by more extensive analyses: a comparative look at three Russell High assemblies (McQuillan, 1994) and an analysis of the news program and a newspaper special on Russell, the two most extensive media examinations of the school during my research (McQuillan, 1996).

2. This "formula for success" was featured in Jones' autobiography.

3. To convey something of Jones' speaking style, I employ capital letters, italics, and bolding. Normal text signifies a normal tone of voice. Italics denote a shift in pronunciation, an inflection intended to emphasize. Capital letters signal that Jones was shouting. Boldened capitals signal that he shouted even louder. Capitals and italics are combined when Jones shouted and put inflection into his voice.

4. Because Jones' presentation in March 1989 was received so positively, the school department hired him to address all Eastown juniors and seniors the following fall. The event was held in the local civic center and nearly 12,000 students from throughout the state attended. This talk closely paralleled the first. Many quotes cited in these *Gazette* articles were exactly what Jones said in his March appearance. The use of student reactions included in these articles, therefore, seems appropriate.

5. These letters seem especially relevant since this middle school enrolled over seventy percent students of color and was a feeder school for Russell.

6. Some Essential School students had faculty advisors who met with them to solicit feedback on program developments, to discuss social issues (e.g., violence and teen pregnancy), and to help students make decisions about their education.

7. During his talk Jones discussed the "common sense computer," a source of insight he said everyone had. This computer helped people determine an appropriate course(s) in life. For instance, when he entered into his computer that he wanted to make a lot of money and not work hard, it told him he had two options, sell drugs or be an airline pilot. Since it also informed him he might go to jail for dealing drugs, he chose Navy flight school.

8. Sizer's remarks offer one way to understand the actions of Rafael Jackson, the student featured in Chapter 4.

9. As Teun Van Dijk wrote, "balancing" news presentations in this ostensibly objective fashion bolsters their credibility: "The truthfulness of

events is enhanced when opinions of different backgrounds or ideologies are quoted about such events, but in general those who are ideologically close will be given primary attention" (1988: 85). Further, this presentation gave little attention to understanding the causes behind many problems presented (Apple, 1993).

10. Throughout my research at Russell, the principal and others lobbied for new lockers. During the 1989–90 school year, new lockers were installed.

11. The Charles Stuart murder occurred in Boston. Although details remain unclear, it appears the murdered woman was killed by her husband for insurance money. He then blamed an African American for the slaying.

8. EASTOWN: A CITY DIVIDED

1. The "foreign born," mostly Hispanics, Portuguese, and Asians, comprised over 19.6 percent of the city's population in 1990 (31,503 persons), an increase of forty-nine percent from 1980 (U.S. Bureau of the Census, 1990).

2. Throughout this chapter "persons of color" include African Americans, American Indians, Eskimos, Aleuts, Asians, Pacific Islanders, and Hispanics.

3. In these two instances (i.e., for median-income distribution and median income of persons of color), I used household as the relevant unit rather than families because these data were not available for families. Nonetheless, while the income figures would be different for families, the relative distribution and differences would be much the same.

4. There are thirty-seven census tracts in Eastown.

5. This development paralleled a national trend. In 1986, 27.5 percent of all African American schoolchildren and 30.0 percent of all Hispanics were enrolled in the twenty-five largest central-city school districts, while only 3.3 percent of all white students were in these same twenty-five districts (Edsall and Edsall, 1991a: 85).

6. Massey and Denton (1989) offer a thorough and disturbing analysis of "hypersegregation" in U.S. cities.

9. SO WHAT?

1. Two other prominent dimensions to the school reform process would be the technical and political (House and McQuillan, 1997).

2. Changing belief is difficult, even if research documents that one approach is more effective than another. This is not only true for educators. As Sarason (1990) found in his study of innovation, or lack thereof, in the field of medicine:

The passage of time and the dissemination of findings are insufficient as explanations of a change in practice, either its acceptance or pace. No less important are the nature and strength of belief systems of people embedded in organizations whose culture, structure and traditions vary considerably in regard to change. . . . [Too many people] assume that change is achieved through learning and applying new or good ideas. They seem unable to understand what is involved in unlearning what custom, tradition, and even research have told [them] is right, natural, and proper. (1990: 101)

Thomas Kuhn (1962) found attitudes toward change among scientists to be similar: people did not simply abandon paradigms even when they were refuted by "scientific" proof.

3. As this ethnography examined those contexts in which educational opportunity was problematic at Russell High, I included no examples of exemplary classrooms or programs. Yet while I was there, pockets of the school displayed excellence. The theater program had a history of outstanding performances and that tradition held true during my research. The track and wrestling teams were consistently competitive on a statewide and even national basis. Although the Essential School encountered controversy and resistance, many students and teachers greatly appreciated the opportunities this program created. For those interested in change, it seems suggestive that these programs—theater, athletics, and the Essential School—to varying extents, embodied many of the same ideas as what was outlined in the previous proposals:

- All promoted extended relations between students and adults. Theater classes lasted two periods. To prepare for plays, students rehearsed outside normal school hours. Many students were involved with theater for multiple years. Track and wrestling practices usually lasted a couple hours and athletes worked with their coaches for a number of seasons. The track team even worked together in the off-season. The Essential School also offered double-period classes and students took many classes as a cohort and commonly stayed with some of the same teachers for consecutive years.
- Students had power and responsibility. The older theater students and athletes were looked to for leadership by adults and younger students. Theater students and athletes could choose not to come to practice, but they were part of a team and were depended upon by others. Essential School students had a choice about doing work. They could take "incomplete" grades if they wanted to. Teachers often allowed Essential School students a say in assignments they did.
- There was active cooperation among students and between students and adults. These people expressed a sense of "being in it together." In theater and sports, the interdependence was self-evident. Everyone, adults and adolescents alike, was working toward common goals. In the Essential School teachers incorporated a considerable degree of collaborative work into their classes, two of the more popular being cooperative learning and peer editing.
- What students were asked to do seemed authentic; it had meaning to them, both on an individual and group basis. For drama students and

athletes, public performances always served as motivation for their work. To a lesser degree, Essential School teachers tried to incorporate a "real world" relevance into their lessons and to make their lessons responsive to student interests.

- Through these various activities, students and adults created a sense of community, of mutual support and caring. To varying degrees, participants shared a common identity.

4. In this sense, my study of Russell High represents an instance of "studying the typical," that is, "choosing sites on the basis of their fit with a typical situation" (Schofield, 1990: 210). If one hopes others will appreciate the value of insights gained in one context and consider their applicability for comparable settings, the issue of generalizability, "the extent to which one can extend the account of a particular situation or population to other persons, times, or settings than those directly studied" (Maxwell, 1992: 293), becomes salient. Addressing the issue of generalizability in qualitative research, Ernest House wrote: "although patterns of events do not repeat themselves exactly, there are transfactual causal structures that influence events and that operate in different settings even though their interactions with other causal mechanisms may not produce the same events from site to site" (1991: 8).

5. After alluding to America's propensity to embrace "machismo" leadership as a solution to social concerns, including school reform, Deborah Meier observed:

[T]he most popular image/model of a reformist principal is not of a great teacher bringing teacherly insights to bear on governance, but of the bold, iron-fisted, charismatic leader who brings change by force of personality. We see the latter in the media, often achieving dramatic success in adverse circumstances. . . . But it's important to remember that even at best these heroes are usually charismatic bullies (it's not surprising that they're rarely women), and that they sometimes confuse "law and order" with a disrespect for any law besides themselves. . . . The violence of the young is quelled by counter-violence. The problem is . . . that these are not images of adulthood that encourage youngsters or teachers to use their minds well, to work collaboratively, or to respect the views of others. . . . Their latent political consequences for a democratic society are dangerous. They are a product of both despair and loss of direction; democratic ideals adrift. (1995: 127–28)

APPENDIX

1. The point here is that attending to ethical concerns can enhance one's understanding. It is not to suggest that one should attend to ethical issues only when they accord with methodological concerns.

REFERENCES

Abu-Lughod, Lila. 1991. "Writing Against Culture." In R. Fox (ed.), *Recapturing Anthropology*. Santa Fe, N.Mex.: School of American Research Press, pp. 137–62.

Agar, Michael. 1980. *The Professional Stranger: An Informal Introduction to Ethnography*. New York: Academic Press.

Alexander, K., and R. Salmon. 1995. *American School Finance*. Boston: Allyn and Bacon.

Anderson, Gary. 1989. "Critical Ethnography in Education: Origins, Current Status, and New Directions." *Review of Educational Research* 59 (3): 249–70.

Anyon, Jean. 1980. "Social Class and the Hidden Curriculum of Work." *Journal of Education* 162 (1): 67–92.

Apple, Michael. 1993. *Official Knowledge, Democratic Education in a Conservative Age*. New York: Routledge.

Ball, Stephen. 1980. "Initial Encounters in the Classroom and the Process of Establishment." In Peter Woods (ed.), *Pupil Strategies*. London: Croom Helm, pp. 144–62.

Becker, Adeline. 1990. "The Role of the School in the Maintenance and Change of Ethnic Group Affiliation." *Human Organization* 49 (1): 48–55.

Bellah, Robert, Richard Madsen, William Sullivan, Ann Swidler, and Steven Tipton. 1985. *Habits of the Heart*. New York: Harper and Row.

Benedict, Ruth. 1946. *The Chrysanthemum and the Sword*. Boston: Houghton Mifflin.

Berger, Peter, and Thomas Luckmann. 1966. *The Social Construction of Reality*. Garden City, N.Y.: Doubleday.

Bidwell, Charles and Thomas Hoffer. 1996. "Social Capital and Social Control: Interaction and Attainment in the American High School." Paper presented at the American Educational Research Association meetings, New York.

Blumer, Herbert. 1962. "Society as Symbolic Interaction." In A. Rose (ed.), *Human Behavior and Social Processes*. New York: Houghton Mifflin, pp. 78–93.

———. 1969. *Symbolic Interactionism*. Englewood Cliffs, N.J.: Prentice-Hall.

Bohannon, Laura. 1977. "Shakespeare in the Bush." In J. P. Spradley (ed.), *Conformity and Conflict*, 3rd edition. Boston: Little, Brown, and Co., pp. 13–23.

Bourdieu, Pierce. 1985. "The Genesis of the Concepts 'Habitus' and 'Field'." *Sociocriticism* 2 (2): 11–24.

———. 1990a. *The Logic of Practice*. Stanford, Calif.: Stanford University Press.

———. 1990b. *In Other Words: Towards a Reflexive Sociology*. Stanford, Calif.: Stanford University Press.

Bowles, Samuel, and Herbert Gintis. 1976. *Schooling in Capitalist America*. New York: Basic Books.

Brightman, Robert. 1995. "Forget Culture: Replacement, Transcendence, Relexification." *Cultural Anthropology* 19 (4): 509–46.

Brodkey, Linda. 1987. "Writing Critical Ethnographic Narratives." *Anthropology and Education Quarterly* 18 (2): 67–76.

Brophy, Jere, and Carolyn Evertson. 1981. *Student Characteristics and Teaching*. New York: Longman.

Bruner, Jerome. 1986. *Actual Minds, Possible Worlds*. Cambridge, Mass.: Harvard University Press.

Burrup, Percy, Vern Brimley, Jr., and Rulon Garfield. 1996. *Financing Education in a Climate of Change*. New York: Simon and Schuster.

Carlson, Dennis. 1992. *Teachers and Crisis*. New York: Routledge.

Chandler, Susanne. 1992. "Learning for What Purpose? Questions When Viewing Classroom Learning from a Sociocultural Curriculum." In H. Marshall (ed.), *Redefining Student Learning: Roots of Educational Change*. Norwood, N.J.: Ablex, pp. 33–38.

Clifford, James. 1986. "Introduction: Partial Truths." In J. Clifford and G. Marcus (eds.), *Writing Culture: The Poetics and Politics of Ethnography*. Berkeley: University of California Press, pp. 1–26.

———. 1988. *The Predicament of Culture*. Cambridge, Mass.: Harvard University Press.

Clune, William. 1995. "Accelerated Education as a Remedy for High-Poverty Schools." *University of Michigan Journal of Law Reform* 28 (3): 665–80.

Cohen, David. 1995. "What Is the System in Systemic Reform?" *Educational Researcher* 24 (9): 11–17, 31.

Cohen, Stanley, and Jock Young. 1981. *The Manufacture of News: Deviance, Social Problems, and the Mass Media*. Beverly Hills, Calif.: SAGE.

Coleman, James S. 1961. *The Adolescent Society*. New York: The Free Press.

———. 1990. *Equality and Achievement in Education*. Boulder, Colo.: Westview Press.

Coleman, James S., Ernest Campbell, Carol Hobson, James McPartland, Alexander Mood, Frederic Weinfeld, and Robert York. 1966. *Equality of*

Educational Opportunity. Washington, D.C.: U.S. Government Printing Office.

Connell, Robert. 1993. *Schools and Social Justice*. Philadelphia: Temple University Press.

Corbett, Dick, and Bruce Wilson. 1995. "Make a Difference With, Not For, Students: A Plea to Researchers and Reformers." *Educational Researcher* 24 (5): 12–17.

Cotton, Kathleen. 1996. "School Size, School Climate, and Student Performance." Close-Up Series No. 20, School Improvement Research Series. Portland, Ore.: Northwest Regional Lab.

Cross, K. Patricia. 1987. "The Rising Tide of School Reform Reports." *Phi Delta Kappan* 66 (3): 167–72.

Cummins, James. 1986. "Empowering Minority Students: A Framework for Intervention." *Harvard Educational Review* 56 (1): 18–36.

Cusick, Philip. 1973. *Inside High School: The Students' World*. New York: Holt, Rinehart and Winston.

———. 1983. *The Egalitarian Ideal and the American High School*. New York: Longman.

Delpit, Lisa. 1988. "The Silenced Dialogue: Power and Pedagogy in Educating Other People's Children." *Harvard Educational Review* 58 (3): 280–98.

Denzin, Norman. 1978. *The Research Act: A Theoretical Introduction to Sociological Methods*. New York: McGraw-Hill.

Dewey, John. 1902. *The School and Society*. Chicago: University of Chicago Press.

Dijk, Teun van. 1988. *News As Discourse*. Hillsdale, N.J.: Erlbaum.

Dollard, John. 1957. *Caste and Class in a Southern Town*. Garden City, N.Y.: Doubleday.

Edsall, Thomas, and Mary Edsall. 1991a. "Race." *The Atlantic Monthly* 267 (5): 53–86.

———. 1991b. *Chain Reaction: The Impact of Race, Rights, and Taxes on American Politics*. New York: Norton.

Elam, Stanley. 1990. "The 22nd Annual Gallup Poll of the Public's Attitudes Toward the Public Schools." *Phi Delta Kappan* 72 (1): 41–55.

Erickson, Frederick. 1984. "What Makes School Ethnography 'Ethnographic'?" *Anthropology and Education Quarterly* 15 (1): 51–66.

Ericson, David, and Frederick Ellet, Jr. 1990. "Taking Student Responsibility Seriously." *Educational Researcher* 19 (9): 3–10.

Evangelauf, Jean. 1992, January. "Minority-Group Enrollment at Colleges Rose 10% from 1980 to 1990, Reaching Record Levels." *The Chronicle of Higher Education*.

Everhart, Robert. 1983. *Reading, Writing, and Resistance*. Boston: Routledge and Kegan Paul.

Fine, Michelle. 1991. *Framing Dropouts: Notes on the Politics of an Urban Public High School.* Albany: State University of New York Press.

Fine, Michelle, and Pearl Rosenberg. 1983. "Dropping Out of High School: The Ideology of School and Work." *Journal of Education* 165: 257–72.

Firestone, William, Susan Fuhrman, and Michael Kirst. 1989. "The Progress of Reform: An Appraisal of State Educational Initiatives." Center for Policy Research. New Brunswick, N.J.: Rutgers University.

Foley, Douglas. 1990. *Learning Capitalist Culture: Deep in the Heart of Tejas.* Philadelphia: University of Pennsylvania Press.

———. 1991. "Reconsidering Anthropological Explanations of Ethnic School Failure." *Anthropology and Education Quarterly* 22 (1): 60–86.

Fordham, Signithia. 1988. "Racelessness as a Factor in Black Students' School Success: Pragmatic Strategy or Pyrrhic Victory?" *Harvard Educational Review* 59 (1): 54–84.

———. 1996. *Blacked Out: Dilemmas of Race, Ideology, and Success at Capitol High.* Chicago: University of Chicago Press.

Fordham, Signithia, and John Ogbu. 1986. "Black Students' School Success: Coping with the Burden of 'Acting White'." *Urban Review* 18 (2): 176–206.

Freedman, Samuel. 1990. *Small Victories: The Real World of a Teacher, Her Students, and Their High School.* New York: Harper and Row.

Fullan, Michael, and Susan Stiegelbauer. 1991. *The New Meaning of Educational Change.* New York: Teachers College Press.

Gee, James. 1990. *Social Linguistics and Literacies: Ideology and Discourses.* New York: Falmer Press.

Geertz, Clifford. 1973. *The Interpretation of Cultures.* New York: Basic Books.

———. 1983. *Local Knowledge: Further Essays in Interpretive Anthropology.* New York: Basic Books.

———. 1988. *Works and Lives: The Anthropologist as Author.* Stanford, Calif.: Stanford University Press.

Gibson, Margaret. 1988. *Accommodation Without Assimilation: Sikh Immigrants in an American High School.* Ithaca, N.Y.: Cornell University Press.

Gibson, Margaret, and John Ogbu. 1991. *Minority Status and Schooling: A Comparative Study of Immigrant and Involuntary Minorities.* New York: Garland.

Giroux, Henry. 1996. "Hollywood, Race, and the Demonization of Youth: The 'Kids' Are Not 'Alright'." *Educational Researcher* 25 (2): 31–35.

Good, Thomas, and Jere Brophy. 1987. *Looking in Classrooms.* New York: Harper and Row.

Grant, Carl. 1989. "Urban Teachers: Their New Colleagues and Curriculum." *Phi Delta Kappan* 70: 764–70.

Gutman, Amy. 1987. *Democratic Education.* Princeton, N.J.: Princeton University Press.

Haberman, Martin. 1991. "The Pedagogy of Poverty Versus Good Teaching." *Phi Delta Kappan* (December): 290–94.

Hacker, Andrew. 1992. *Two Nations, Black and White: Separate, Hostile, Unequal.* New York: Charles Scribner's Sons.

Haigler, Karl, Caroline Harlow, Patricia O'Connor, and Anne Campbell. 1994. *Literacy Behind Prison Walls.* Washington, D.C.: U.S. Government Printing Office.

Hammersly, Martyn. 1992. *What's Wrong With Ethnography?* London: Routledge.

Hampel, Robert. 1986. *The Last Little Citadel.* Boston: Houghton Mifflin.

Hansen, Judith Friedman. 1979. *Sociocultural Perspectives on Human Learning: Foundations of Educational Anthropology.* Prospect Heights, Ill.: Waveland Press.

Hanson, Sandra L. 1994. "Lost Talent: Unrealized Educational Aspirations and Expectations Among U.S. Youths." *Sociology of Education* 67 (3): 159–83.

Hargreaves, Andy. 1996. "Revisiting Voice." *Educational Researcher* 25 (1): 9–21.

Hartman, Paul. 1981. "News and Public Perceptions of Industrial Relations." In S. Cohen and J. Young (eds.), *The Manufacture of News.* Beverly Hills, Calif.: SAGE, pp. 459–79.

Harvard Education Letter. 1988. "Cultural Differences in the Classroom." *The Harvard Education Letter* 4 (2): 1–3.

Hatton, Elizabeth. 1989. "Levi-Strauss's *Bricolage* and Theorizing Teachers' Work." *Anthropology and Education Quarterly* 20 (2): 74–96.

Havighurst, Robert, Paul Bowman, Gordon Liddle, Charles Matthews, and James Pierce. 1962. *Growing Up in River City.* New York: John Wiley and Sons.

Heath, Shirley Brice. 1983. *Ways with Words: Language, Life, and Working in Communities and Classrooms.* New York: Cambridge University Press.

Henry, Jules. 1963. *Culture Against Man.* New York: Vintage.

Hill-Burnett, Jaquetta. 1969. "Ceremony, Rites, and Economy in the Student System of an American High School." *Human Organization* 21 (1): 1–10.

Holland, Dorothy, and Margaret Eisenhart. 1990. *Educated in Romance: Women, Achievement, and College Culture.* Chicago: University of Chicago Press.

Hollingshead, August. 1949. *Elmtown's Youth.* New York: John Wiley and Sons.

House, Ernest. 1991. "Realism in Research." *Educational Researcher* 20 (6): 2–9, 25.

House, Ernest, and Patrick McQuillan. 1997. "Three Perspectives on School Reform." In A. Lieberman (ed.), *International Handbook of Educational Change: Roots of Educational Change*. Dordrecht, The Netherlands: Kluwer Academic.

Howe, Kenneth. 1993. "Equality of Educational Opportunity and the Criterion of Equal Educational Worth." *Studies in Philosophy and Education* 11: 329–37.

———. 1997. *Understanding Equal Educational Opportunity*. New York: Teachers College Press.

Hsu, Francis. 1983. *Rugged Individualism Reconsidered: Essays in Psychological Anthropology*. Knoxville: University of Tennessee Press.

Jackson, Philip. 1968. *Inside Classrooms*. Chicago: University of Chicago Press.

Katz, Michael. 1971. *Class, Bureaucracy, and Schools: The Illusion of Educational Change in America*. New York: Praeger.

Keedy, John. 1995. "Teacher Practical Knowledge in Restructured High Schools." *The Journal of Educational Research* 89 (2): 76–89.

Keesing, Roger. 1981. "Theories of Culture." In R. W. Casson (ed.), *Language, Culture, and Cognition*. New York: Macmillan, pp. 42–66.

Kertzer, David. 1988. *Ritual, Politics, and Power*. New Haven, Conn.: Yale University Press.

Klein, Edward. 1991. "We're Talking About a Revolution." *Boston Globe Parade Magazine* (August 25).

Kohn, Alfie. 1992. *No Contest: The Case Against Competition*. Boston: Houghton Mifflin.

Kozol, Jonathan. 1991. *Savage Inequalities*. New York: Crown.

Kuhn, Thomas. 1962. *The Structure of Scientific Revolutions*. Chicago: University of Chicago Press.

Lather, Patti. 1986. "Research as Praxis." *Harvard Educational Review* 46 (3): 257–77.

Lave, Jean. 1988. *Cognition in Practice: Mind, Mathematics and Culture in Everyday Life*. New York: Cambridge University Press.

Leach, Edmund. 1954. *Political Systems of Highland Burma*. Boston: Beacon Press.

———. 1969. *Genesis as Myth and Other Essays*. London: Jonathan Cape.

Leacock, Eleanor. 1969. *Teaching and Learning in City Schools: A Comparative Study*. New York: Basic Books.

LeCompte, Margaret, and Judith Preissle. 1993. *Ethnography and Qualitative Design in Education Research*. Orlando, Fla.: Academic Press.

Lee, Valerie, Julia Smith, and Robert Croninger. 1995. "Another Look at High School Restructuring." In *Issues in Restructuring Schools*. Center on Organization and Restructuring of Schools, Wisconsin Center for Education Research. Madison: University of Wisconsin.

Lefrancois, Guy. 1983. *Psychology*. Belmont, Calif.: Wadsworth.

Lesko, Nancy. 1986. "Individualism and Community: Ritual Discourse in a Parochial High School." *Anthropology and Education Quarterly* 17 (1): 25–39.

———. 1991. "Implausible Endings: Teenage Mothers and Fictions of School Success." In N. B. Wagner (ed.), *Current Perspectives on the Culture of Schools*. Cambridge, Mass.: Brookline, pp. 45–64.

Lippman, Laura, Shelley Burns, and Edith McArthur. 1996. *Urban Schools: The Challenge of Location and Poverty*. Washington, D.C.: U.S. Department of Education.

Lucas, Tamara, Rosemary Henze, and Ruben Donato. 1990. "Promoting the Success of Latino Language-Minority Students: An Exploratory Study of Six High Schools." *Harvard Educational Review* 60 (3): 315–40.

Lynd, Robert S., and Helen Merrel Lynd. [1929] 1956. *Middletown*. New York: Harcourt, Brace, Jovanovich.

MacLeod, Jay. 1987. *Ain't No Makin' It: Leveled Aspirations in a Low-Income Neighborhood*. Boulder, Colo.: Westview Press.

Mannen, John Van. 1988. *Tales of the Field: On Writing Ethnography*. Chicago: University of Chicago Press.

Massey, Douglas, and Nancy Denton. 1989. "Hypersegregation in U.S. Metropolitan Areas: Black and Hispanic Segregation Along Five Dimensions." *Demography* 26 (3): 373–92.

Maxwell, Joseph. 1992. "Understanding and Validity in Qualitative Research." *Harvard Educational Review* 62 (3): 279–300.

McCarthy, Cameron. 1990. *Race and Curriculum: Social Inequality and the Theories and Politics of Difference in Contemporary Research on Schooling*. New York: Falmer Press.

McDermott, Ray. 1987. "Achieving School Failure: An Anthropological Approach to Illiteracy and Social Stratification." In G. D. Spindler (ed.), *Education and Cultural Process*. Prospect Heights, Ill.: Waveland Press, pp. 132–54.

McDermott, Ray, and Hervé Varenne. 1995. "Culture *as* Disability." *Anthropology and Education Quarterly* 26 (3): 324–48.

McDonough, Patricia. 1991. "Who Goes Where to College: Social Class and Organizational and Context Effects." Paper presented at the annual meeting of the American Educational Research Association, Chicago.

McLaughlin, Milbrey. 1993. "Embedded Identities: Enabling Balance in Urban Contexts." In S. Heath and M. McLaughlin (eds.), *Identity and Inner-City Youth*. New York: Teachers College Press, pp. 36–68.

McLaughlin, Milbrey, and Joan Talbert. 1993. *Contexts that Matter for Teaching*. Stanford, Calif.: Center for Research on the Context of Secondary School Teaching.

McNeil, Linda. 1986. *Contradictions of Control*. New York: Routledge.

McQuillan, Patrick. 1994. "Ritual Reaffirmation of Individualism in High School Assemblies." Paper presented at the American Educational Research Association meeting, New Orleans, La.

――――. 1996. "Media Representations of Educational Opportunity in an Urban American High School: A Cultural Analysis." Paper presented at the American Anthropological Association meeting, San Francisco.

McQuillan, Patrick, and Donna Muncey. 1994. "Change Takes Time: A Look at the Growth and Development of the Coalition of Essential Schools." *Journal of Curriculum Studies* 26 (3): 265–79.

Meier, Deborah. 1995. *The Power of Their Ideas: Lessons for America from a Small School in Harlem*. Boston: Beacon Press.

Metz, Mary. 1990. "Real School: A Universal Drama Amid Disparate Experience." In D. Mitchell and M. E. Goetz (eds.), *Educational Politics for the New Century: The Twentieth Anniversary Yearbook of the Politics of Education Association*. Philadelphia: Falmer Press, pp. 53–78.

Moll, Luis, and Stephen Diaz. 1987. "Change as the Goal of Educational Research." *Anthropology and Education Quarterly* 18 (4): 300–11.

Muncey, Donna, and Patrick McQuillan. 1993. "Preliminary Findings from a Five-Year Study of the Coalition of Essential Schools." *Phi Delta Kappan* 74 (6): 486–89.

――――. 1991. "Empowering Nonentities: Students in Educational Reform." Working Paper No. 5. The School Ethnography Project. Providence, R.I.: Brown University.

――――. 1996. *Reform and Resistance in Schools and Classrooms: An Ethnographic View of the Coalition of Essential Schools*. New Haven, Conn.: Yale University Press.

Murphy, Jere, and Lynn Beck. 1995. *School-Based Management as School Reform: Taking Stock*. Thousand Oaks, Calif.: Corwin Press.

National Commission on Excellence in Education. 1983. *A Nation at Risk: An Imperative for Educational Reform*. Washington, D.C.: U. S. Department of Education.

Newmann, Fred, and William Clune. 1992. "Brief to Policymakers." Center on the Organization and Restructuring of Schools. Madison: University of Wisconsin.

Noddings, Nel. 1992. *The Challenge to Care in Schools: An Alternative Approach to Education*. New York: Teachers College Press.

Oakes, Jeannie. 1985. *Keeping Track: How Schools Structure Inequality*. New Haven, Conn.: Yale University Press.

――――. 1986. "Tracking, Inequality, and the Rhetoric of Reform: Why Schools Don't Change." *Journal of Education* 168 (1): 60–80.

Ogbu, John. 1974. *The Next Generation*. New York: Academic Press.

———. 1981. "School Ethnography: A Multi-Level Approach." *Anthropology and Education Quarterly* 12 (1): 3–29.

———. 1987. "Variability in Minority School Performance: A Problem in Search of an Explanation." *Anthropology and Education Quarterly* 18 (4): 312–34.

———. 1992. "Understanding Cultural Diversity and Learning." *Educational Researcher* 21 (1): 5–14.

Olson, Scott. 1989. "Mass Media: A Bricolage of Paradigms." In S. King (ed.), *Human Communication as a Field of Study*. Albany: State University of New York Press, pp. 60–84.

"An Open Letter to the Students Who Walked." 1994. *Rocky Mountain News* (December 6), p. 37A.

Page, Reba. 1987a. "Teachers' Perceptions of Students: A Link Between Classrooms, School Cultures, and the Social Order." *Anthropology and Education Quarterly* 18 (2): 77–99.

———. 1987b "Lower-Track Classes at a College-Preparatory High School: A Caricature of Educational Encounters." In G. Spindler and L. Spindler (eds.), *Interpretive Ethnography of Education at Home and Abroad*. London: Erlbaum Associates, pp. 178–202.

Peshkin, Alan. 1978. *Growing Up American*. Chicago: University of Chicago Press.

Phillips, Susan. 1983. *The Invisible Culture*. New York: Longman.

Powell, Arthur, Eleanor Farrar, and David Cohen. 1985. *The Shopping Mall High School: Winners and Losers in the Educational Marketplace*. Boston: Houghton Mifflin.

Ravitch, Diane. 1985. *The Schools We Deserve: Reflections on the Educational Crisis of Our Times*. New York: Basic Books.

Raywid, Mary Anne. 1995. "Alternatives and Marginal Students." In M. C. Wang and M. C. Reynolds (eds.), *Making a Difference for Students at Risk*. Thousand Oaks, Calif.: Corwin Press, pp. 119–55.

Rivkin, Steven. 1994. "Residential Segregation and School Integration." *Sociology of Education* 67 (4): 279–93.

Roberts, Joan I. 1971. *The Scene of the Battle: Group Behavior in Urban Classrooms*. Garden City, N.Y.: Doubleday.

Rosenfeld, Gerald. 1971. *Shut Those Thick Lips: A Study of Slum School Failure*. New York: Holt, Rinehart, and Winston.

Sarason, Seymour. 1971. *The Culture of the School and the Problem of Change*. Boston: Allyn and Bacon.

———. 1990. *The Predictable Failure of School Reform*. San Francisco: Jossey-Bass.

———. 1996. *Revisiting "The Culture of the School and the Problem of Change."* New York: Teachers College Press.

Schofield, Janet. 1990. "Increasing the Generalizability of Qualitative Research." In E. Eisner and A. Peshkin (eds.), *Qualitative Inquiry in Education: The Continuing Debate.* New York: Teachers College Press, pp. 201–32.

Simon, Roger, and Donald Dippo. 1986. "On Critical Ethnographic Work." *Anthropology and Education Quarterly* 17 (4): 195–202.

Sizer, Theodore. 1984. *Horace's Compromise.* Boston: Houghton Mifflin.

————. 1992. *Horace's School.* Boston: Houghton Mifflin.

Solomon, R. Patrick. 1992. *Black Resistance in High School: Forging a Separatist Culture.* Albany: State University of New York Press.

Spindler, George, and Louise Spindler. 1987. "Cultural Dialogue and Schooling in Schoenhausen and Roseville: A Comparative Analysis." *Anthropology and Education Quarterly* 18 (1): 3–16.

————. 1988. "Roger Harkin and Schoenhausen: From Familiar to Strange and Back Again." In G. Spindler (ed.), *Doing the Ethnography of Schooling,* Prospect Heights, Ill.: Waveland Press, pp. 20–47.

Stanton-Salazar, Ricardo. 1996. "A Social Capital Framework for Understanding the Socialization of Ethnic Minority Children and Youths." Paper presented at the annual meeting of the American Educational Research Association, New York.

Stanton-Salazar, Ricardo, and Sanford Dornbusch. 1995. "Social Capital and the Social Reproduction of Inequality: The Formation of Informational Networks Among Mexican-Origin Students." *Sociology of Education* 68 (2): 103–24.

Steinberg, Laurence, Sanford Dornbusch, and Bradford Brown. 1996. *Beyond the Classroom: Why School Reform Has Failed and What Parents Can Do.* New York: Simon and Schuster.

Stocking, George (ed.). 1983. *Observers Observed: Essays in Ethnographic Fieldwork.* Madison: University of Wisconsin Press.

Trueba, Henry. 1988. "Culturally Based Explanations of Minority Students' Academic Achievement." *Anthropology and Education Quarterly* 19 (3): 270–87.

————. 1989. *Raising Silent Voices: Educating Linguistic Minorities for the 21st Century.* Cambridge, Mass.: Newbury House.

Tyack, David, and Larry Cuban. 1995. *Tinkering Toward Utopia: A Century of School Reform.* Cambridge, Mass.: Harvard University Press.

"U.S. Students' Performance: Low and Stagnant." 1990. *Los Angeles Times* (September 27).

United States Bureau of the Census. 1990. "Census Code Book."

United States Department of Education. 1988. *Research in Brief.* Washington, D.C. (June).

————. 1992. "Trends in Racial/Ethnic Enrollment in Higher Education: Fall 1980 through Fall 1990." Office of Educational Research and Improvement, Washington, D.C.

Varenne, Hervé. 1977. *Americans Together*. New York: Teachers College Press.

Walkerdine, Valerie. 1988. *The Mastery of Reason: Cognitive Development and the Product of Rationality*. London: Routledge.

Waller, Willard. 1932. *The Sociology of Teaching*. New York: Russell and Russell.

Wang, Margaret, Maynard Reynolds, and Herbert Walberg. 1995. "Introduction: Inner-City Students at the Margins." In M. C. Wang and M. C. Reynolds (eds.), *Making a Difference for Students at Risk*. Thousand Oaks, Calif.: Corwin Press, pp. 1–25.

Warner, W. Lloyd. 1949. *Democracy in Jonesville: A Study in Quality and Inequality*. New York: Harper and Row.

Warner, W. Lloyd, Paul Lunt, J. O. Low, and Leo Srole. [1941] 1963. *Yankee City*. New Haven, Conn.: Yale University Press.

Weinstein, Rhona, Sybil Madison, and Margaret Kuklinski. 1995. "Raising Expectations in Schooling: Obstacles and Opportunities for Change." *American Educational Research Journal* 32 (1): 121–59.

Wells, Amy S., and Robert Crain. 1994. "Perpetuation Theory and the Long-Term Effects of School Desegregation." *Review of Educational Research* 64 (4): 531–55.

Wiggins, Grant. 1987. "Creating a Thought-Provoking Curriculum: Lessons from Whodunits and Others." *American Educator* 11 (4): 10–17.

———. 1989. "Teaching to the (Authentic) Test." *Educational Leadership* 46 (7): 41–47.

Wilcox, Kathleen. 1982. "Differential Socialization in the Classroom: Implications for Equal Opportunity." In G. D. Spindler (ed.), *Doing the Ethnography of Schooling: Educational Anthropology in Action*. New York: Holt, Rinehart, and Winston.

Willis, Paul. 1977. *Learning to Labour*. Westmead, England: Saxon House.

Wilson, Kenneth, and Bennett Daviss. 1994. *Redesigning Education*. New York: Henry Holt and Company.

Woods, Peter. 1978. "Negotiating the Demands of Schoolwork." *Journal of Curriculum Studies* 10 (4): 301–27.

———. 1980. "The Development of Pupil Strategies." In P. Woods (ed.), *Pupil Strategies*. London: Croom Helm, pp. 11–30.

———. 1983. *Sociology and the School: An Interactionist Viewpoint*. London: Routledge and Kegan Paul.

INDEX

241

= justice

ity= one that is equal

ality= essential character